The Be...
British Country...
and Resta...

Katharine Wood- de Winne ....
Belgian and English parents. She was educated there,
reading Communications, then English Language and
Literature at Edinburgh University. Following a short
period as a freelance public relations consultant she
entered the world of travel journalism. An eighteen-
month spell touring Europe and North Africa resulted in
the book *Europe by Train* (published by Fontana), which
is one of the UK's top-selling guidebooks. As well as
working full time as Editor of a series of guidebooks for
the package market, the Fontana Holiday Guides, she is
currently involved in several projects encompassing
every aspect of the travel industry – from backpacking
students to round-the-world first-class tours. In the
course of her work she has travelled to forty-six countries, with major emphasis on Europe, North America,
the Far East and the Pacific. She is married and lives in
Perth, Scotland, with her husband and young sons,
Andrew and Euan, who frequently accompany her on
her globetrots.

This latest book on country house hotels is the culmi-
nation of several years research. Having visited many of
the country's best as a form of recreation she decided to
turn her professional eye on them, and admits herself
that this has been the ultimate exercise in combining
business with sheer unadulterated pleasure.

The Best of
British Country House
Hotels
and Restaurants

KATIE WOOD

Chief Researcher: Devin Scobie

FONTANA/Collins

First published in 1989 by Fontana Paperbacks,
8 Grafton Street, London W1X 3LA

Copyright © Katie Wood 1989
Sketches by Rhona Cunningham

Printed and bound in Great Britain by
Collins, Glasgow

In memory of
Leslie Wood

CONTENTS

NORTHERN ENGLAND

CENTRAL ENGLAND

INTRODUCTION

For many, and certainly for me, one of the most pleasant and civilized ways of spending a weekend is staying in one of Britain's Country Houses. It is wonderful to see so many of these enjoying something of a renaissance in recent years, adapting to the times and opening their doors to the public, either as 'Open Houses' or, better still, as de luxe Country House Hotels where almost anybody can spend a few days amid the sort of surroundings normally only enjoyed by the super-rich or aristocracy.

The sheer spoiling in store for you in a Country House Hotel weekend is wonderful. It is a chance to step back in time and indulge yourself in a 'Brideshead-style' existence you didn't think was possible in the 1980s and, for a few days at least, to see how the other half lives. Surprisingly this treat (worth far more in terms of enjoyment and relaxation than numerous weeks on the sun-drenched Costas) need not cost such a prohibitive sum that it must be the preserve only of the very rich. Young professionals account for a substantial share of the Country House weekend break market, and the recently retired are another significant group who treat themselves to breaks in these houses. And quite right too. For the same price as a room and dinner in one of the large, business-orientated hotel chains, where the furnishings, food, atmosphere and staff's smiles are all decidedly on the plastic side, you can drive an hour or so into the country and spend your time in one of these beautiful old, historic houses and enjoy the luxuries and special touches of a bygone era; the fresh linen sheets, the quality toiletries in your bathroom, flowers in the bedroom, views of the countryside from the window, home-produced food and courteous service.

Everyone has at least three or four special occasions in a year; birthdays, anniversaries and family celebrations, and it's at these times that it really matters where you eat out, and what type of weekend you have. It is for this very reason that I've put this book together. The hotels listed are not cheap, but for special occasions they *are* value for money.

We are very privileged in Britain to have such a fine collection of Country House Hotels. Our own particular history has left us this legacy, and I feel it is important that we patronize these houses so that they are not allowed to close their doors and admit defeat to either the taxman, or the advance of building renovation costs. Few of these houses make large profits as hotels: their overheads are far greater than the bed-factories in towns and cities which pick up passing trade and have lucrative deals with large companies with travelling executives. These houses invariably rely on word of mouth bringing people to their doors, and then they rely on people coming back again. The fact that so many do, and become hooked on Country House breaks, says a lot to recommend them.

Keeping a historic house watertight, heated, appropriately furnished, and maintaining staff who care about the house and the guests is a costly affair, and while I'm not suggesting we should patronize these hotels out of a sense of duty or charity, I do think they deserve our special attention, and that everyone should experience a Country House weekend at least once or twice a year.

Before I'm accused of an overdose of patriotism it must be said that our European neighbours, notably the French, Italians and Germans, do have their share of Châteaux, Villas and fine old Schlösse operating as de luxe hotels. However, by comparison with British Country Houses these are few and far between, and they can be exorbitantly expensive. They really *are* the preserve of the wealthy. Only the rich German industrialist could afford to treat his wife to a weekend in Schloss Buehlerhoehe, or the titled Count afford to take his favoured one to Villa San Michele, outside Florence, for their respective bed and breakfast prices are around the two hundred and fifty and three hundred pounds mark, and that's before dinner! Conversely, our hotels are within the reach of most people, even if it's just for the usually very reasonable set-dinners on offer, or the special winter break weekends which many houses run out of season.

It is in the kitchens of the old English manor houses and Scottish castles that our country's finest young chefs are working and training, and the *nouvelle cuisine* which has transformed Britain's culinary reputation owes more to the likes of Cromlix, Cliveden and Middlethorpe Hall than Langan's and the Savoy.

With the dramatic rise in popularity in Country House Hotel weekends (they now account for well over a thousand million pounds' worth of the British tourist trade), many hotels make claims to be 'Country Houses', but I have employed quite exacting standards as to what qualifies and what doesn't. Inglenook-fireplaces, converted in the 1970s, obviously reproduction 'antique' furnishings, gas-fuelled coal fires and fake brass, pleasant as they may be, are *not* the stuff of real Country House Hotels. To qualify for inclusion in this guide a house has to be the genuine article – a real country estate or house converted tastefully into a Country House Hotel. It must have high standards of accommodation, an outstanding restaurant, and be the sort of place where wedding nights should be spent.

Every hotel has been vetted by a team of professional travel journalists, with hundreds of hotel visits under their belts. All the tricks of the trade have been looked for and we think this guide is completely objective. No hotelier can buy his way in, and no advertising is taken.

This book contains, in my opinion, the best Country House Hotels in the UK in the year of publication. They are all places where I feel a memorable dinner or special weekend can be spent. Every establishment is vetted carefully, and everything from the cleanliness of the kitchens to the quality of the face cloths is taken into consideration. My research team and I are always open to new ideas, and any book like this lays itself wide open to criticism. It is almost inevitable some of you will disagree with my choices, or will hit a bad day in one of the hotels listed, but overall I hope this guide will be a useful

15

addition to your bookshelf and will offer suggestions which lead to some marvellous meals and memorable weekends.

Photographs of the houses have not been included because, quite simply, the book would have cost you three times as much to buy if they had, and I very much want this guide to reach as many people as possible. Black and white line drawings are included, however, to give you an idea of what to expect, and point out the architectural features of the buildings, without taking away too much from the moment you first see the house yourself, which is usually a very pleasant treat. The written description will tell you all you need to know about the house and should whet your appetite for it, while still leaving some of the tiny minor details as surprises for when you arrive.

The country has been divided into seven regions: Scotland; Northern England; Central England; Wales; London Area; Southern England and the Channel Islands. (Northern Ireland has not been included in this guide, but will appear in Katie Wood's second book on Country House Hotels.) Each hotel has been categorized into its price bracket. These are: up to £100; £100–£150; over £150. This is the price for two for dinner, bed and breakfast. Unless otherwise stated all the hotels have stressed to us the need to book ahead in high season (June–Sept.), and unless we state to the contrary children and pets should be allowed, but it is always advisable to check with the hotel before departing.

Overall marks out of ten are awarded and displayed at the top of each entry. The final mark comes from the percentages awarded for the five categories under which the hotels were graded. These were Food, Service, Decor, Atmosphere and Facilities.

Each category is divided into sub-headings. Food is marked for taste, presentation, value for money and originality. Decor for the overall effect, authenticity to the style of the house and state of repair. Service is marked for efficiency and friendliness, and any special little touches added for the guest's convenience, and Atmosphere was considered as an overall feeling, taking into account all of the other criteria. Do the guests feel at home, or is there an uncomfortable, stiff formality to the hotel? Have they a maître d' quietly orchestrating things or are the services offered erratic? Do you feel like a guest at a Country House weekend, or is it very obviously a paying hotel? Any jarring points? Overall, is it a happy place, offering value for money on all counts?

Facilities are marked more on how what is on offer is presented, rather than strictly what is or is not there. Hence a ten-bedroomed house with no more than a pool room and extensive grounds loses no marks to its neighbour boasting 30 bedrooms with Jacuzzis, even if it has a whole leisure complex at its disposal. Assuming the basics for comfort and enjoyment are all there (as they are in all hotels listed in the guide), it is more a case of the use to which the facilities are put. It is points off for having beautiful grounds which have been allowed to fall into disrepair, or for sacrificing a library to make a sauna and swimming pool. At all times the Country House tradition has been considered. You can find hotels with every available facility you can think of up and down the country, but that's not what this book is about.

Any outstanding extras are mentioned in the text, but overall when you're looking at the hotel's mark, bear in mind the points outlined here.

I sincerely hope you enjoy these special places. Please feel free to write to me with your comments on the hotels mentioned, and with any suggestions of your own. Address your correspondence to:

Katie Wood
Best of British Country House Hotels
Fontana Paperbacks
Collins Publishers
8 Grafton Street
London W1X 3LA

DRESS

As a rule, formal or smart evening dress is required for the dining-rooms of all the hotels listed in this guide. Dinner jackets and long dresses are not compulsory in any, though guests at Cliveden (see p.284) are encouraged to dress in this manner, as it is in keeping with the formal style of the house. The minimum accepted dress is jacket, collar and tie for a gent, and a dress for a lady; and this is required in all hotels listed.

Much of the pleasure in visiting a Country House comes from the after-breakfast stroll through the grounds, and for this a pair of Wellington boots or stout walking shoes are invariably necessary. Irrespective of the season, you will come across muddy corners in the estate grounds, and if you're visiting between October and April waterproof clothing and footwear really is an essential if you are to have the pleasure of exploring the grounds at all. Some hotels thoughtfully provide umbrellas, raincoats and even an odd pair of boots, but it's best to pack your own in the boot of the car, just in case. Many of the old estates date back to the period when specimen decorative trees were being introduced from abroad and consequently there are many fine examples of exotic and rare species in the grounds. If you are particularly interested in gardening, try to visit the house through the week and seek out the gardener for a chat. (If you're very lucky and will be returning home that day or very soon after, you may be allowed to take cuttings from some of the more unusual plants for your own garden!)

CHILDREN

Many Country House Hotels take the unfortunate view that children are not welcome. The reasons they quote are invariably those of safety for their antique furnishings and disturbance to the other guests, many of whom, they say, go there to escape the noise and problems of family life. There is some justice in all this, but personally, as a mother of two young children myself, I do baulk at this Victorian 'seen and not heard' attitude. If the ground rules are laid out from the start: no under 12s in the dining-room, any damages to be paid for, and so on, I do not see why children should be treated as outcasts. They are, after all, our next generations, and if they are not taught how to behave in civilized surroundings from an early age, how can we expect them to grow into balanced adults? This custom is rarely practised in the de luxe hotels of continental Europe, I'm happy to say. Particularly infuriating is the habit that some hotels have of allowing dogs, but not children. The little pooches can even be seen in the dining-rooms! Personally I find few things more off-putting than to watch an overfed lap-dog being passed scraps from the plate by a doting owner, and I think priorities have become decidedly confused when one can't bring a baby into the breakfast room, but the dog can come to dinner.

All the hotels I list as accepting children will. Those which specify they will not are very unlikely to change their policy.

HOTEL REPORTS

In many reports I have listed the house specialities or sample dishes to give an indication of the style and quality of cuisine to be expected in the house. I cannot absolutely guarantee, however, that these particular dishes will be on the menu when you visit. If there is a dish you particularly want, phone or write ahead and request that it be made available for you. Vegetarian dishes can be prepared at all the houses, though if it is one with a smaller kitchen, or one which normally operates a table d'hôte menu only, please phone or write ahead.

SCOTLAND

THE AIRDS HOTEL

Port Appin, Appin, Argyll PA38 4DF
Tel: 063173 236

Nearest towns Oban and Fort William.
Directions Twenty-five miles from both Oban
and Fort William; the hotel is three miles off the
A828 overlooking Loch Linnhe and the Morvern
mountain range.
Awards AA ** (red) plus rosette; Egon Ronay Star
graded recommendation; Michelin recommended;
winners of the first Scottish Field/Bollinger Best
Scottish Restaurant Award; 1986 Good Food Guide
Scottish Hotel of the Year; member of Relais et
Châteaux 1988; chef Betty Allen was Scotland's
first, and so far only, female Chef Laureate of the
British Academy of Gastronomes.
Open from mid-March until mid-November.
Price for dinner, with wine, bed and breakfast for
two – over £150.
Credit cards None accepted at all.
Children over 5 are welcomed, but dogs are not allowed.
The hotel is unsuitable for disabled persons.
Overall mark out of ten 9

For nearly three centuries since 1700, the Airds Hotel has stood as a welcoming Ferry Inn by the village of Port Appin overlooking the majestic Loch Linnhe. Current owners Eric and Betty Allen left Edinburgh some years ago and managed to transform the dull old inn into one of Argyll's most private Country Houses without destroying the wonderful eighteenth-century atmosphere. A number of standard concessions to modern-day hotel luxury have deliberately been passed over in order to keep that atmosphere intact. You will not find a colour television set in your bedroom, but you will receive a warm personal welcome and have an enviable opportunity to genuinely switch off and relax without worrying too much about the rest of the world.

There are fifteen bedrooms in all, each with private facilities, and comfortably, if not ostentatiously, furnished. Rather honestly, the owners say, 'We have no special facilities other than peace and quiet and good food.' The Airds' three large public rooms are spacious and comfortable; one is a particularly attractive sunlounge during the summer months – and a perfect retreat from the chilly Argyll autumn evenings if you choose to visit towards the end of the hotel's annual season.

Eating in the Airds' intimate dining-room, with its glorious views far across the loch, will undoubtedly be one of the highlights of your visit to the hotel. Indeed, such is the reputation of the hotel's fine cooking that it is the principle reason, even before the prospect of enjoying the uninterrupted solitude of the surrounding countryside is taken into consideration, for many visitors returning year after year.

Smoking is not permitted in the dining-room and there is approximately a four to one ratio between residents and non-residents in the dining-room at any one time. The restaurant has one of the best reputations of any Country House in Scotland and advance booking is strongly urged.

Presentation and service are immaculate, and dinner is served at a single sitting around 8 p.m. to ensure everything can be cooked and served as freshly as possible. The style of food is distinctly Scottish, although subtle continental influences are obvious on the fine-grey card menus which are changed

24

daily. All the food is locally produced and rigorously selected to ensure only the finest cuts of meat and fish are prepared. Most of the vegetables are grown in the large kitchen garden which the hotel owners look after themselves.

Locally caught seafood features mainly on the list of starters, although Betty's magnificent Poached Fillets of Sole with Prawns and Vermouth Cream Sauce is a mouthwatering exception on the main course options. Other recommended specialities are Breast of Duckling with Port and Orange Sauce and Roast Loin of Lamb with Crab Apple and Mint Jelly. All meals can be complemented with a wine selected from over 350 on the shrewdly prepared list. Although house wines start under £10 a bottle, the list includes most European favourites and some of the rarest modern wines available anywhere in Scotland – at a price, of course, but well worth the once-off extravagance to go with that special meal.

The hotel is well located for touring historic Argyllshire, and nearby attractions include the spectacular Glen Coe, the famous pass from the Moor of Rannoch to Loch Leven and site of the Glen Coe massacre in 1692. A poignant memorial stands in memory of the murdered Macdonalds and the area now acts as the beautiful setting for more peaceful activities including rock-climbing and skiing. You can also visit Castle Stalker, a Stewart hunting lodge used by King James IV before the Battle of Flodden Field in 1513. Other attractions include day trips to Fort William, or Oban, a busy little seaside resort from where you can sail to Mull for the day.

ARDANAISEIG

Kilchrenan, by Taynuilt, Argyll PA35 1HE
Tel: 08663 333

Nearest town Village of Kilchrenan, or the larger
Taynuilt a few miles further away.
Directions Turn south off the A85 at Taynuilt on
to the B845 to Kilchrenan. Head left at the
Ardanaiseig signpost when you reach Kilchrenan
and the hotel is four miles further on.
A member of the **Pride of Britain** consortium.
Awards AA *** (red) and rosette for food;
Michelin three (red) turrets; Egon Ronay 73% and
star for food; American Hideaway report: Scottish
Hotel of the Year 1986.
Open from Easter until mid-October.
No **special breaks**, but the hotel offers three- and
seven-day rates throughout the season.
Price for dinner, with wine, bed and breakfast for
two – over £150.
Credit cards Access, Visa and Amex.
Ardanaiseig is not suitable for the disabled and does not
allow children under the age of 8.
Overall mark out of ten 7

Nestling in the heart of mountainous Argyllshire, Ardanaiseig
is steeped in history and surrounded by acres of smooth

woodland and shrub. For centuries the Clan Campbell owned and controlled most of the region and it was a member of that clan, Colonel James Archibald Campbell, who built the present house in 1834. He spent over two years just laying out the grounds and planting the trees, many of which are fine examples and have grown to full maturity today, before the house itself was started. The house was built by William Burn, who was one of the leading architects of his time, and one of just four appointed to carry out Robert Adam's unfinished plans for Edinburgh's New Town in the decades after his death in 1793.

Sunday mornings at Ardanaiseig always witnessed an intriguing family ritual during the years when Colonel Campbell was in residence. He would sternly line up his ample collection of daughters and then choose one or two to row him across Loch Awe to church at Cladich. The rest of the sizeable family would follow in a flotilla of smaller boats at a discreet distance behind the head of the household!

Colonel Campbell died in 1879, by which time he had helped form the then 100,000 strong National Union of Agricultural Workers which later became the powerful National Union of Farmers. A hundred years later, the modern NUF still has a very considerable membership in Scotland alone. Ardanaiseig was sold in 1880 after the old man's death and, curiously, occupied in turn by two successive Members of Parliament for Argyll before being bought by the present owners in 1963 and transformed into a Country House Hotel.

Very little of the original house interior has been altered structurally, apart from the addition of a few extra bathrooms and fire safety requirements, and as a result the owners' attempt to retain the atmosphere of a private house has largely succeeded. All three public rooms, including the airy dining-room, have fine views across the loch. The hotel has a particularly attractive drawing-room, with a huge bay window looking out across the grounds and allowing you to savour every moment spent enjoying the views. Tastefully decorated, the drawing-room has a number of comfortable armchairs, a good grand piano and a constant supply of fresh flowers; almost too inviting to ignore.

Ardanaiseig has a total of fourteen bedrooms; twelve doubles and two singles. All are well furnished, centrally heated and with their own private facilities including colour television and direct-dial telephone. Rooms to the back of the house have the best views across the loch and up towards Ben Cruachan. The magnificent surrounding grounds are one of Ardanaiseig's most attractive features.

The hotel's dining-room has traditional decor, candle-lit in the evenings, and pink table linen accompanies the silverware at each meal. The style of cooking is best described as modern British with a strong emphasis on traditional Scottish specialities like Fillet of Beef Argyll and Fillet of Wild Salmon. A speciality of chef Lindsay Little is his 'Symphony of Seafoods', a delicious array of locally caught seafood gently poached then blended with a creamy Noilly Prat sauce flavoured with saffron and chervil. A number of speciality dishes have an additional charge of a few pounds, but the chef makes the bold pledge on the menu that, subject to a few days notice, he will be pleased to produce any dish of your choice.

The hotel offers a wide range of outdoor sporting facilities for residents; tennis, croquet, fishing, boating and shooting are all available throughout the season. Nearby attractions include Oban; Glen Coe, one of Scotland's most dramatic glens; the Mull of Kintyre, made famous by Paul McCartney's worldwide 1978 hit record of the same name; and Loch Fyne, a thirty-mile-long sea arm dividing Knapdale and Kintyre from the Cowal peninsula.

3

ARDSHEAL HOUSE

Kentallen of Appin, Argyll PA38 4BX
Tel: 063174 227

Nearest town Fort William.
Directions Follow A828 thirty miles north of
Oban; seventeen miles south of Fort William.
Hotel is clearly signposted by roadside.
Awards British Tourist Authority commended.
Open from April until November.
No **special weekend** or winter breaks available.
Price for dinner, with wine, bed and breakfast for
two – £100–£150.
Credit cards Access and Visa.
Children and dogs are welcomed but the hotel is
unsuitable for disabled persons.
Overall mark out of ten 6.5

A mile along a winding private driveway which skirts the
banks of Loch Linnhe and you will find yourself at one of the
most private Country House Hotels in Argyllshire and, indeed,
in all Britain. The hotel's history can be traced back to 1545, a
turbulent period in Scottish history when the infant Mary,
Queen of Scots, had already been on the throne for three
years and fragile negotiations were taking place for her possible marriage to the young Edward VI of England.

The Stewarts of Appin, one of the strongest noble families

in this part of Scotland at the time, occupied the original house for two centuries before it was brutally sacked in the wake of the last great Jacobite uprising in 1745. By 1760 the house was completely rebuilt, and it is that second-generation Ardsheal House which largely remains as a hotel today, although later generations of Stewarts added considerably to the house in 1814, and again at the start of this century. Interestingly, Ardsheal plays an important part in Robert Louis Stevenson's classic *Kidnapped* as it was just a mile or so from here that the infamous murder of Appin actually took place.

Resident proprietors Bob and Jane Taylor are natives of New York and quite how they came to own and run Ardsheal is an interesting tale which they will probably recount if you ask them. Ten years ago they came over to this part of Scotland on holiday and fell in love with it at once. Turning off a quiet country road to investigate an old 'For Sale' sign they came across Ardsheal in what was then a rather poor state of repair. A token effort to run the place as a hotel had failed because little routine repair work had been done for some years, and practically all the original furniture had been sold off and replaced with junk.

Within a few weeks Bob had given up his job as Vice-President of the Morgan Guaranty Trust, sold their house on West 78th Street, and taken the plunge to head back to Argyll for good. As a result, they fairly claim in their brochure, 'Ardsheal is not just an inn. It's our home, and we're looking forward to sharing it with you.'

An informal welcome is assured at Ardsheal, and the Taylors' American roots, not to mention considerable publicity their unique move has attracted in the States, means that half their clientele are Americans.

Even as you enter the main reception area, with its magnificent oak-panelling that is clearly well looked after, the relatively small size of the hotel at once gives it that 'at home' feel. Bob and Jane Taylor make a point of introducing new guests to everyone else, so giving them the opportunity to socialize if they so desire. Not everyone wishes to, of course, and the relative isolation of Ardsheal is one of its positive attractions.

There are fourteen bedrooms, none with colour television, but all have private bathroom facilities, together with ample heating for those late-summer and early-autumn visitors. Each one is individually decorated and offers a slightly different character to the one before it. In addition to a popular billiards room, there are three public lounges downstairs. Only one has a television set, allowing residents to enjoy the peace and tranquillity of the surrounding countryside, not to mention the quite breathtaking views far across Loch Linnhe, from the large windows of the other lounge.

A nice touch is the glassed-in extension to the dining-room, affording a greenhouse-type atmosphere with the surrounding garden if you choose to sit in this part of the restaurant for your breakfast or evening meal. Good food is a key feature of life at Ardsheal, although the rather limited set menu may not suit visitors more used to larger hotels offering a wider range. In addition to fine local cuts of meat, and fish, the style and presentation of side vegetables is particularly impressive. Braised rice, poached cucumber and baked onions are a few rather unusual favourites which you are likely to see accompanying your main course.

Attractions include day trips to nearby islands including Mull, Iona and Luing; popular Scottish castles like Cawdor and Inveraray; and some quite spectacular natural scenery. There are glens to explore, lochs to fish in or boat on, and magnificent walks in every direction. The hotel sits in over 900 acres of its own hillside, woodland and shorefront, so you will have no shortage of places to explore within easy walking distance.

4

ARISAIG HOUSE

Beasdale, Arisaig, Invernesshire PH39 4NR
Tel: 06875 622

Nearest town Fort William.
Directions Drive west from Fort William on the
A830. Arisaig House is clearly signposted after
thirty miles.
Awards AA *** (red) and rosette for food;
Michelin three red pavillons plus red M; BTA
commended Country House Hotel; Scottish Tourist
Board four Crowns; Egon Ronay 75% highly
commended.
Open from Easter until the end of November.
Special terms for stays of five days or over
provided booking is made direct to the hotel.
Price for dinner, with wine, bed and breakfast for
two – over £150.
Credit cards Access, Visa, Amex.
The hotel is not suited for disabled persons; children
under ten and dogs are not permitted.
Overall mark out of ten 7

Built in 1864 to the design of the great Victorian architect
Philip Webb, Arisaig House is a splendid old mansion ideally

situated for touring the Western Highlands or nearby islands. Offering perfect peace and tranquillity combined with luxury service, Arisaig was completely rebuilt in 1937 by Ian Hamilton after being gutted by fire. One of the most appealing features of the hotel today is the 1930s 'time-warp' atmosphere which you can feel throughout the hotel and, above all, in the airy dining-room.

Bonnie Prince Charlie is reputed to have hidden after the Battle of Culloden in a dank cave, still known as Charlie's Cave, located quite near the hotel. From there, the Young Pretender met a small French frigate on a dark night in 1746 and escaped back to France with the help of some of his remaining sympathetic countrymen. Few could have guessed at the time of this sad departure that he was destined to live there in exile from his native Scotland for the rest of his life.

As you approach Arisaig along the long gravel driveway you will be able to appreciate, for the first time during your stay here, the real beauty of the hotel's surrounding twenty acres of grounds. Arisaig is sheltered from the north and has sweeping views to the south and east of a great sea loch and mountain. At the height of summer the immediate garden area around the hotel is a delight, with broad terraces overlooking the gardens. Well-tended displays of azaleas, rhododendrons and countless varieties of wild shrubbery stretch from the hotel's outer walls up to the fringes of natural woodland which quite completes this charming scene.

Two additional walled gardens can be explored by residents, and it is from here that all of the fresh flowers which decorate the hotel's public rooms come. The house as a whole is distinctly stylish and the two main public rooms, the Morning Room and the Drawing Room, have great windows to take advantage of the amazing views. Roaring log fires on those chilly autumn evenings are ideal to help you relax and enjoy your after-dinner coffee.

Arisaig has a total of sixteen bedrooms, including two two-bedroomed suites. All have been individually designed to the specifications of current proprietors Ruth and John Smither, and offer private bathroom facilities, together with colour television and direct-dial telephone. Rooms have their own Scottish names – Nevis, Morar and so on – giving that little bit of extra individuality which is so sadly missed from more modern hotels in the same price bracket. All rooms offer particularly fine views of the surrounding woodland, sea loch or mountain, depending on which side of the house you find yourself.

One of Arisaig's most attractive features is its 1930s-style wood-panelled dining-room. The food is based on first-class local produce with a touch of *nouvelle cuisine*; indeed, most of the vegetables on your evening dinner plate come from no further away than the hotel's own walled gardens, which are lovingly looked after by the proprietors.

Dinner is served from a set menu which some residents may find a little restrictive as only minor variations are possible from any given evening's prepared fare. That said, of course, the standard of food is quite superb and there is a particularly fine range of hors d'oeuvres. For a typical main course of Duck Breast with Green Peppercorn Sauce or Fillet of Sole Vincent Bourrel you may care to whet your appetite beforehand with Smoked Venison with Asparagus and Fromage Blanc, Salad of Smoked Mussels, Oysters and Avocado, or even Bavarois of Smoked Salmon, Cheese and Cucumber. Dinner includes a soup course, which is likely to be an in-house speciality like Carrot and Orange or Tomato and Basil, and there is a modest wine list with eighty or so bottles to select from.

Attractions include day trips to nearby Mallaig, the northern end of the famous West Highland railway line; a visit to the Isle of Skye – regular car ferries make the short crossing from Mallaig to Armadale; boat trips across to the smaller islands of Canna, Rhum, Eigg or Muck from the village of Arisaig.

5

AUCHTERARDER HOUSE

Auchterarder, near Gleneagles, Perthshire PH3 1DZ
Tel: 07646 2939

Nearest town Auchterarder.
Directions Auchterarder House is fifty miles from
Edinburgh and sixty from Glasgow. Head for either
Perth or Stirling, whichever is nearer to your
departure point, and then follow signs for
Auchterarder. Following the B8062, the hotel is
about two miles north of Gleneagles Hotel.
A member of the **Prestige Hotels** consortium.
Awards Recommended by Michelin; Egon Ronay
71%; Ashley Courtenay recommended; Scottish
Tourist Board five Crowns – highly commended.
Open throughout the year.
Special breaks *from April until October*:
10% discount for stays of more than one night.
20% discount for stays of more than seven nights.
from November to March:
automatic seasonal reduction of 20% on all rates.
30% discount for stays of seven days or longer.
Note: None of these rates applies over Christmas
and New Year, the Easter week and weekend,

theme national weekends, private house parties, shooting and fishing functions, gourmet and wine weekends and musical weekends – so check well in advance to make sure your dates do not clash with any of the above.

No children under the age of 12 are allowed.

Price for dinner, with wine, bed and breakfast for two – £100–£150.

Credit cards Access, Visa, Amex, Diners, Mastercharge and Carte Bleu.

Overall mark out of ten 8.5

Within a couple of miles of the world-famous five-star Gleneagles Hotel lies a much less well-known Country House Hotel offering similar standards of luxury for substantially lower rates. Auchterarder House has an almost confusing array of discounts and bargain breaks, but their low-season rates make this hotel one of the best-value options in central Scotland if you can afford the time to travel away from the main summer months.

Auchterarder itself is an ancient Royal Burgh which was ideally situated on the road which lead from Scone Palace, home for generations of Scottish monarchs in medieval times and before, and historic Stirling Castle. By the early nineteenth century half of the burgh was in the possession of Lieutenant-Colonel James Hunter who commissioned Scottish architect William Burn to design an impressive new mansion house for him.

Within a year, by 1832, the oldest part of the present hotel was completed and today visitors still marvel at their first sight of Burn's asymmetrical two-storey design, with its crow-stepped gables built in the old Jacobean style, as they draw up to the front of the building. The south wing and terraces were added towards the end of the last century, by which time the house was no longer owned by the Hunter family, and the interior modelled in a rich Renaissance style, with elegant Victorian overtones, which is how it basically remains today. James Reid, the new owner after the Hunter family sold the house, was the great railway magnate responsible for a huge railroad construction firm which supplied locomotives throughout the world. He gave much of his wealth to the City of Glasgow in the form of donations of art treasures, and a statue of James Reid can be seen in Glasgow's Springburn Park.

The sumptuous interior of Auchterarder is emphasized by fine wood panelling and ornate ceilings in all the public rooms, and a number of the bedrooms. All the public rooms are furnished with reproduction Victorian furniture offering romantic, old-style comfort for even the most discerning. Light live entertainment is available every evening after dinner in the drawing-room, and is generally of a rather subdued mood to suit the peaceful atmosphere of the house, with background classical music being favoured.

The main dining-room is arranged to seat 25 people and has a distinct Scottish atmosphere. The quality of food served is very high. A complimentary glass of cocktail punch is served before dinner, and the menu overall has a strong Scottish emphasis. Your coffee, served with a *petit four*, is also complimentary after dinner, and the impressive à la carte menu will cost you between £20 and £35, depending whether you have three or five courses.

The hotel has six master bedrooms, four superior bedrooms and one very impressive suite with stunning views to the north. All eleven bedrooms are individually named and furnished to the highest standards with colour television, telephone, writing desk, trouser press and so forth. A few are not furnished in the best of taste, with rather out-of-place ornaments here and there, but the overall impression is good. All have their own private bathroom facilities which include a number of interesting 'extras', including a good range of soaps and complimentary toiletries. Nearby attractions include Scone Palace, where kings of Scotland were crowned for eight centuries; Glamis Castle, childhood home of Queen Elizabeth, the Queen Mother; Blair Castle; Strathallan Aircraft Museum; Crieff glassworks; the natural splendour of the Trossachs; and a number of major whisky distilleries.

6

BALCRAIG HOUSE

By Scone, Perth PH2 7PG
Tel: 0738 51123

Nearest town Perth.
Directions Three miles north-east of Perth, drive along the A94 Perth to Aberdeen road. The hotel is clearly signposted.
Awards AA *** (red) and rosette for dinner; AA Best New Scottish Hotel of 1984.
Open throughout the year, except the second and third weeks of January.
Off-season breaks are available.
Children of all ages are welcome and baby sitting services are available.
Price for dinner, with wine, bed and breakfast for two – £100–£150.
Credit cards Access, Visa, Amex, Diners Club.
Overall mark out of ten 8.5

Balcraig House was built in 1872 as a home for the McDuff family, doubtless direct descendants of the great Lord McDuff who defeated Shakespeare's evil king in *Macbeth*. A monument to the later McDuff responsible for building Balcraig can be seen on a nearby hill.

Remarkably for many Scottish Country House Hotels, this one was still home to the McDuff family right up to 1982 but within a couple of years the old family home had been transformed into one of Scotland's premier country retreats, and in 1985 was recognized as such when it played host to Prime Minister Margaret Thatcher and husband Denis for one night on the occasion of Denis's seventieth birthday.

The hotel is one of the smallest Country Houses in Scotland and so clearly a house of tremendous character. Accordingly it is not difficult to understand why the proprietors place so much emphasis on an informal appeal to visitors. It has a wealth of original period Scottish furniture and wide vistas of the extensive gardens make for memorable first impressions. This is enhanced by crystal chandeliers, impeccable service and fine home-produced food which truly deserves the coveted AA rosette for food. Crystal wine glasses are a nice touch and there are many more – the warmth of the welcome by your hosts being one.

The style of food at Balcraig reflects the best of Scottish traditions: venison, pigeon, Aberdeen Angus steak and salmon are usually on the menu. Menus change daily and there is always some choice. Particularly good value is the table d'hôte, and on the à la carte menu the steak and choice of fish dishes are exceptional. Balcraig has its own market garden to supply the restaurant, and chef Michael Wildman is a master of his profession. Some of the sweets are worth driving from London for: one favourite, the chocolate roulade, is exquisite and always on the menu.

A comprehensive wine list is available, offering vintages from every major wine-producing country. The new management of Derek and Lesley Makintosh has added many improving facilities including a bar in which to enjoy pre-dinner drinks, a conservatory dining-room, and also complimentary early-morning tea or coffee.

All ten bedrooms are individually furnished, each with private bathroom facilities which include an original hand-painted wall mural by Sally Anderson. Remote control colour television, direct-dial telephones, hair dryers, trouser presses and radio are all standard.

Nearby attractions are numerous and include the city of

Perth just three miles away, with its multi-million-pound leisure centre; the famous Caithness Glass factory; Scone Palace; Glamis Castle; Falkland Palace; Dunkeld cathedral; and an abundance of outdoor pursuits from fishing to hill-walking. From one nearby peak – Kinnoull Hill – it is reckoned that you can see nearly a sixth of Scotland on a clear day. A tennis court and croquet lawn are available in the hotel grounds, and pony trekking can be arranged if you fancy a gentle canter through the surrounding woodland. Golfers are particularly well catered for: among the choice of courses are Gleneagles, Rosemount, Carnoustie and St Andrews, to name but a few within an average twenty-minute drive. Clay pigeon shooting can also be arranged.

7

BANCHORY LODGE HOTEL

Banchory, Kincardineshire AB3 3HS
Tel: 03302 2625

Nearest town Banchory.
Directions Travel eighteen miles west of
Aberdeen on the A93. The hotel is situated on
Royal Deeside, beside the Rive Dee, at the
confluence of the River Feugh.
Awards AA *** (red) graded since 1977; RAC
***; British Tourist Authority commended;
Scottish Tourist Board four Crowns.
Open from the beginning of February until mid-
December.
The hotel welcomes children and dogs, but is unsuitable
for disabled.
Price for dinner, with wine, bed and breakfast for
two – up to £100.
Credit cards Access, Visa, Diners, Amex, Carte
Blanche.
Overall mark out of ten 7

A building of some description is reputed to have stood on the
site of the Banchory Lodge Hotel for over one-and-a-half
thousand years. Saint Ternan brought Christianity to the area
of Banchory in the fifth century AD, teaching the local Picts
the ways of European agriculture, arts and crafts, and building
a monastery at the point where the rivers Feugh and Dee met.

Ternan's white-coloured circular palace, or 'Ban Choire', stood as the beginning of modern Banchory.

Over the centuries the old monastery decayed and crumbled away and a modest lodge first appeared in its place. It was here that mail coaches used to halt while the horses were rested and watered before the last stretch up Deeside proper. A ferryman's house stood on or near the site of the present hotel long before the bridge over the Dee was built at Banchory.

Banchory Lodge as you will find it today was restored and greatly enlarged in the eighteenth century by General William Burnett. He eventually retired here after a lifetime of faithful service as equerry to both King George III, who died in 1820, and his son George IV, who reigned over Great Britain a further ten years before his own death in 1830. The Lodge used to include the lands of Arbeadie on which most of the present town of Banchory, and the immediate surrounding area, is built.

Present owners, Dugald and Margaret Jaffray, have made a number of substantial improvements to the property since they bought it in 1966. Even so, a modest Georgian atmosphere still prevails and much of the authentic period charm can still be appreciated. Open log fires and magnificent flower arrangements enhance the two spacious public lounges which offer grand views out across the River Dee which runs through the grounds of the hotel. Indeed, the Dee is one of the finest salmon rivers in the world and fishing is one of the central attractions of the Banchory Lodge. Bear in mind that the salmon fishing season only runs from February 1st to September 30th in this part of Scotland.

The main dining-room has a traditional design and is furnished with authentic Victorian tables and chairs. Lunch and dinner are served in this room and up to 80 can be seated at any one time. Breakfast is served in a smaller oak-panelled dining-room, which is also available for private functions.

Banchory Lodge has a brigade of chefs and cooks and preparation, planning and cooking are supervised by the owners. The table d'hôte menu offers a good range and is prepared almost exclusively from local produce. The range of starters is imaginative and the main courses, including, of course, Dee Salmon, and roast beef are good. When you reach the sweet course you are really spoiled for choice with almost a dozen calorie-filled options ranging from Water Melon in Ginger Beer to Irish Coffee Gateau. Whatever the course, the size of the portions is always more than generous.

Banchory Lodge has a total of 24 bedrooms, all with colour television and private facilities. Three offer the added luxury of four-poster beds for that added touch of romance. Eight bedrooms have been built in the south-facing wing, the most recent structural addition to the hotel. Two of the three four-poster rooms are in this wing, and the remaining six rooms have both a single and a double bed, making them ideal for families.

Nearby attractions are plentiful. Within an easy drive you can reach Crathes Castle, Craigievar Castle, Kildrummy Castle, Dunottar Castle, Drum Castle, Braemar Castle, Pitmedden Gardens, Leith Hall, Haddo House and, of course, the Royal Family's Scottish residence at Balmoral, the grounds of which are open throughout the summer when the family are not in residence.

8

BARON'S CRAIG

Rockcliffe, by Dalbeattie, Kirkcudbrightshire DG5 4QF
Tel: 055663 225

Nearest town Dalbeattie.

Directions The hotel is fifty-five miles west of
Carlisle. From there, or further north, head for
Dumfries then follow A711 to Dalbeattie. Baron's
Craig is seven miles south on the A710.

Awards AA and RAC *** graded; British Tourist
Authority commended Country Hotel; Scottish
Tourist Board four Crowns commended;
recommended by the following guides: Egon
Ronay, Ashley Courtenay, Signpost and Michelin.

Open from Easter until mid-October.

Special breaks Three-day Bargain Breaks are
operated when space permits.

*Facilities suitable for the disabled; children and dogs
welcome.*

Price for dinner, with wine, bed and breakfast for
two – under £100.

Credit cards Access and Visa.

Overall mark out of ten 8.5

The Baron's Craig Hotel has the distinction of occupying one of the most spectacular locations of any Country House included in this guide. It is a solid granite-built Victorian building standing high above the Solway coast in southern Scotland, an area which has been compared to the French Riviera when witnessed in all its glory on a sunny day. The hotel stands in wooded country overlooking the Solway and a tidal inlet, known as the Rough Firth, which cuts far into the surrounding tree- and heather-covered hills.

A comparatively 'young' Country House, Baron's Craig dates back little more than a century when it was first built as an imposing mansion retreat. The original family sold the house in 1928 and the new owners turned it into a hydro. It has been in the hands of the family of the present proprietor, Mr D. A. Richardson, for almost half a century, and the continuity and style of service over the years has been a positive attraction to three generations of visitors.

The hotel stands in a clearing amid twelve acres of private grounds. Well-groomed lawns and trim gardens are ideal for a relaxing stroll before or after dinner and are alive with colour if you are fortunate enough to visit in spring or early summer. The surrounding woodland shelters the gardens from the biting north and east winds.

Inside, the hotel has an exceptionally homely feel. Staff make an above-average effort to be genuinely helpful and friendly towards all guests and this results in a very pleasant, comfortable atmosphere. The high standards of staff training are obvious throughout the hotel, making the place particularly welcoming and relaxing for that special break.

Much of the interior decor echoes its Victorian origins although period wall-panelling has largely given way to modern paper or painted coverings. The bedrooms are bright and more 1960s rather than truly period, but if you are keen on a walking or sailing weekend, the appeal is to have the comfort of a Country House in the public rooms combined with not having to take off your shoes to walk across the carpets of your bedroom. If you have children, it's a boon not to have to worry over much about the bedroom furnishings, but still be able to wallow in your own idea of civilized comfort downstairs once they're safely in bed!

All the public rooms are on the ground floor and the hotel has five large ground-floor bedrooms with bathroom facilities suitable for disabled visitors. There are 26 bedrooms in all, of which only twenty have private bathroom facilities. All rooms have colour televisions, which include up-to-date in-house movies, and direct-dial telephones.

The hotel has a spacious dining-room with beautiful panoramic views far across the Solway Firth. It was completely refurbished in 1987 in a blend of soft greens, pinks and greys at a cost of nearly £20,000. Non-residents are welcome for evening meals, and make up approximately half of the diners.

A full four-course dinner, including coffee, is excellent value at under £15 for non-residents. A good range of hors d'oeuvres, including Smoked Salmon with Lemon or a rather unusual Cream of Cucumber Soup, is complemented by a wider range of more traditional British main courses. House specialities include locally caught Salmon Steak with Hollandaise Sauce and Baked Saddle of Rabbit with Lemon Sauce. A more adventurous suggestion is the delicious Roast Guinea Fowl in a rich Almond Sauce.

Nearby attractions include the sailing centre of Kippford, the towns of Dumfries and Castle Douglas, the ruins of Dundrennan Abbey (where Mary Stuart spent her last night in Scotland), Caerlaverock Castle, Thomas Carlyle's birthplace at Ecclefechan, Threave Castle and Gardens and a host of locations in and around Dumfries associated with Scotland's bard Robert Burns.

9

CALLY PALACE

Gatehouse of Fleet, Dumfries and Galloway DG7 2DL
Tel: 05574 341

Nearest town Gatehouse of Fleet.
Directions From Dumfries, take the A75 west
towards Stranraer. Turning off the bypass towards
Gatehouse you will see the driveway to the Cally
Palace clearly signposted on your left.
Awards AA and RAC **** graded.
Open from March until late December.
Special breaks Weekend breaks from 1st
October until the end of May (excluding Christmas
and New Year period).
Facilities are available to accommodate disabled guests;
children of any age and dogs are welcome.
Price for dinner, with wine, bed and breakfast for
two – £100–£150.
Credit cards Only Visa.
Overall mark out of ten 8

Hidden away in the heart of southern Scotland, Cally Palace
can accurately claim to be the 'complete resort' it advertises
on its impressive glossy brochures. An unhurried atmosphere
and elegant private grounds are assured, and if you have never
before explored this part of Scotland then a stay at this
particular Country House Hotel would be a good starting
point.

The hotel has a long and interesting history, with its origins dating back to the mid-seventeenth century when the village of Gatehouse itself first began to grow up. The Murray family who first built the present hotel owned it right up until the start of the Second World War. The current family representative, Mrs Murray Usher still owns an impressive town hotel in Gatehouse, once frequented by Robert Burns.

Cally Palace really took shape in 1835 when the existing modest country mansion underwent a great deal of alteration and improvement. A portico was added to the front of the house and four massive granite monoliths were erected, creating the impressive frontal exterior which can still be seen. The stone was quarried from Craigdeus near the town of Newton Stewart some fifteen miles away. It is hard to believe that the now quiet little village of Gatehouse contained, at that time, no less than four cotton factories, several tanneries, a brickworks, a soap factory, a brass foundry, a wine company, a busy brewery, and even a prosperous ship-building and repair yard.

Two huge oak front doors are one of the hotel's most striking features as you draw up to it. Behind these magnificent reminders of former glory, lies the great marble entrance hall which is almost certain to make the first-time visitor take a step back in admiration. No brochure illustration can do justice to this marvellous public reception area. Indeed, the splendour of earlier generations has been maintained throughout Cally Palace and it would be hard to criticize any aspect of the hotel's largely authentic period decor. All the spacious public rooms have intricately ornate ceilings, outsize marble fireplaces and reproduction period furniture. The main dining-room was refurbished in 1987 in elegant blue and pink. Well over a hundred can be seated at any one time, so most of the year it remains surprisingly uncrowded. Cally Palace is one of the most popular 'society' choices for smart local weddings and as a conference location from further afield.

The hotel reckons about 95 per cent of their dinner guests are residents, which is a pity for non-residents staying nearby, considering the outstanding value of their four-course table d'hôte menu. Roast Sirloin of Beef, one of Scotland's finest specialities (and Cally Palace is no exception), is a main course alternative every evening. Other recommended main dishes include Julienne of Chicken cooked in Lemon and Cream Sauce, finished with strips of smoked salmon, and Poached Fillet of Plaice served with a White Wine and Prawn Sauce. An à la carte menu and extensive wine list are also available.

The hotel has a total of 67 bedrooms, including two suites, one family suite, and a sumptuous honeymoon suite. As you might expect, all rooms have private bathroom facilities, colour television, telephone and so forth. Residents may find the hotel's size rather intimidating as it is rather larger than the average Scottish Country House establishment, but where Cally Palace really comes into its own is when taken as a self-contained resort rather than 'just' a smart Country Hotel.

Offering itself as the perfect all-round retreat, the hotel has facilities available for tennis, golf (or more leisurely putting), swimming in its large outdoor heated swimming pool, forest walks and bird-watching in the surrounding private grounds, sauna, sun bed – and there's even a nursery to let those with young children have a real break for an hour or two.

Nearby attractions include the picturesque Galloway coast, with the towns of Dumfries, Castle Douglas, Kirkcudbright and Newton Stewart. Also within a short drive you can visit Cardoness Castle, Dundrennan Abbey, Drumlanrig Castle, and a number of places associated with Robert Burns in and around Dumfries.

10

CRINGLETIE HOUSE

Peebles, Peeblesshire EH45 8PL
Tel: 07213 233

Nearest town Peebles.
Directions From Peebles, Cringletie House is just
two miles north on the main A703 Edinburgh
road.
Awards AA ** (red) rosette for food; British
Tourist Authority commended; recommended by
Egon Ronay and Ashley Courtenay.
Open from early March until late December.
Special breaks for stays of five days or more are
available for dinner, bed and breakfast inclusive.
Price for dinner, with wine, bed and breakfast –
£100–£150.
Credit Cards Access and Visa.
Overall mark out of ten 8

Just twenty miles from Edinburgh, in the heart of the Scottish
Borders, Cringletie House is ideally situated for touring most
of east-central and southern Scotland. A distinguished old red-
sandstone mansion house, Cringletie sits in 28 acres of private
grounds and was originally designed by Scottish architect
David Bryce in the middle of the last century. The pink stone
house was built in 1861 for the Wolfe Murray family and,

indeed, it was Colonel Alexander Murray from Cringletie who accepted the surrender of Quebec after General Wolfe was killed.

All the hotel's public rooms are tastefully decorated in Victorian style, and furnished to a very high standard of comfort. The main lounge area is decorated with magnificent dark panels, and the Victorian portrait framed above the marble fireplace quite completes the period image. The house's former library has been turned into a second lounge bar area, and log fires are the order of the day in both public lounges whenever the east coast weather turns chilly. Views from this room are particularly attractive, stretching out far across the surrounding grounds. The bar is particularly well stocked with Scottish malt whiskies so you will probably never find a more relaxing setting in which to experiment with the drink Gaelic speakers aptly term 'the water of life'.

The dining-room is another Victorian-style panelled room and seats a total of 50 people, about half of whom are non-residents at any one time. The present proprietors, Stanley and Aileen Maguire, have owned the hotel since 1971, and in that time have established a strong reputation for good cuisine with the emphasis on imaginative home-produced food. The full Sottish breakfasts are guaranteed to ensure you will not leave the table feeling hungry.

Aileen Maguire takes charge of the cooking herself and her distinctive home style has won an impressive number of awards over the last seventeen years. Much of the produce comes from Cringletie's huge two-acre kitchen garden. The range of hors d'oeuvres has a strong local flavour, including fresh Smoked Salmon and an interesting Mushroom Tartlet with a steaming Garlic Sauce. Mrs Maguire's expertise in the kitchen really comes into its own, however, when you sample her range of main course options. Traditional dishes like Roast Loin of Pork and Casseroled Haunch of Venison vie for your palate with a wider selection of more unusual house specialities. Two particular favourites are Lemon Stuffed Chicken Supreme with Cream Sauce and Seafood Crepes filled with Prawns, Scallops and Monkfish in a Seafood Sauce. Sauces with intriguing alcohol bases feature prominently: you can have your Venison bathed with Guinness and Prunes, or your Lamb Kidney cooked in Brandy and Cream. One above-average touch is the fried banana which is served as a garnish to the Grilled Fillet of Sole St Lucia – coated in buttery coconut. After your choice of sweets, coffee can be taken in the lounge and is served with home-made *petit fours*.

Cringletie has a total of sixteen bedrooms, including four singles, although one or two do not yet have private bathroom facilities and none has television. Bedrooms are all different and each has a distinctive identity. One right at the upper corner of the house has a peculiar turret window, a very rare sight even in Country House Hotels. Advance booking is essential if this particular room appeals to you.

Nearby attractions are almost too numerous to name. First and foremost, of course, if the city of Edinburgh, about half an hour's drive away, with all that has to offer. Local castles and stately homes within easy reach include Traquair House, Bowhill, Abbotsford (once home of Sir Walter Scott), Floors Castle (still home to the Duke and Duchess of Roxburghe) and Thirlestane Castle. The surrounding countryside is among Scotland's finest and a few suggested local highlights which you can see near here are St Mary's Loch, Grey Mare's Tail and the Moorfoot Hills.

As a hallmark of recommendation, let me just say that I spent my own wedding night and first day of honeymoon in this hotel back in 1984!

11

CROMLIX HOUSE

Kinbuck, Dunblane, Perthshire FK15 9JT
Tel: 0786 822125

Nearest town Dunblane.

Directions From both Glasgow and Edinburgh follow the M9 to Dunblane then follow the B8033 to the village of Kinbuck. Cromlix House is half a mile north of here and signposted.

A member of the **Pride of Britain** consortium.

Awards AA *** graded and rosette for food; 1984 Diners Club Luncheon of the Year award; 1984 Egon Ronay Hotel of the Year; 1984 Country House Hotel of the Year (awarded by Andrew Harper's Hideaway Report); 1986 Restaurant of the Year award from *Decanter* magazine; British Tourist Authority commended hotel; Scottish Tourist Board's highest commendation – five Crowns.

Open all year round.

Not suitable for visitors with severe physical disability; children and dogs welcome.

Special breaks Bargain winter breaks available from 1st October; also Fly-Drive weekends throughout the year.

Price for dinner, with wine, bed and breakfast for two — over £150.
Credit Cards Access, Visa, Amex, Diners Club.
Overall mark out of ten 9.5

Some of the highest standards of international luxury combine with an elegant Country House atmosphere to make Cromlix one of the most outstanding Scottish hotels included in this guide. Originally built as a family house in 1880, Cromlix was altered and extended around the turn of the century. Much of the south-west of the house can be seen as it was when first occupied, and the Cromlix House which King Edward VII came to visit in 1908 is basically the modern-day hotel which awaits you.

The hotel stands on land which has been in the continuous ownership of the same family for an amazing five centuries. Formerly owned by the Hays and the Drummonds, the house and 5000-acre surrounding estate now belong to the related Edens. As you might expect, an abundance of outdoor activities, including tennis, riding, hill-walking, bird-watching, croquet, shooting (both clay and live game by prior arrangement), fishing (trout, salmon and sea), is available on the estate.

The hotel has a number of elegant public rooms including three separate dining-rooms. One such room, the library, can accommodate up to twelve people for private dinners around a rather unusual round table. After-dinner liqueurs can be enjoyed in the same room around a log fire. The original family dining-room can seat up to sixteen people separately or together as a party around one huge table.

The main dining-room is the hotel's old drawing-room, and offers superb views through the French windows across to the conservatory, back lawns and wide gardens. Non-residents are welcome for dinner but advance booking is essential as Cromlix is generally full most of the year. By the time of publication, the hotel's two Victorian conservatories will have been dismantled and rebuilt to an original design to allow an extra twelve non-residents to be served for dinner.

The high standards of cooking at Cromlix embrace a mixture

of many ideas and influences. It is not so much *nouvelle cuisine* as Country House or Modern Classic style, though the presentation is beautiful and the quality absolutely first class. As far as possible everything edible comes from the Cromlix estate itself, and this includes the bread and all pastries. The emphasis on freshness throughout the menu is very noticeable and much of the produce is grown or reared in the grounds around Cromlix.

A set menu is provided each night although alternatives are always available, and a strong point in the hotel's favour is the kitchen's ability to adapt to meet special dietary requirements. During the season, the hotel uses a wide variety of game from the surrounding estate, including hare, rabbit, pheasant, woodcock, venison and wild duck. Salmon and trout often come from estate lochs or nearby rivers. Two of the most popular main dishes at Cromlix are Breast of Duck in a Four Fruits Vinegar Sauce, Glazed Apples, Schupfnudeln and Baby Vegetables, and Loin of Scottish Lamb, Charlotte of Aubergine, Gratin Dauphinoise and Rosemary Sauce. The hotel has a very comprehensive wine list, with over 400 vintages to suit all palates regardless of your choice of starter and main dish.

Cromlix House has a total of fourteen bedrooms, including eight suites which are all furnished to the highest standard with period-style furnishings and which enhance the atmosphere of Victorian luxury in the hotel. A visiting *Glasgow Herald* correspondent wrote, in a recent profile of the hotel: 'I am still waiting to be persuaded that the Upper Turret at Cromlix is not the finest suite of rooms in Scotland.' As you might expect, bookings for the best suites are essential – at least nine months in advance.

Nearby attractions include the Stuart Strathearn glassworks; Doune Motor Museum; Loch Lomond (and loch cruises on the popular *Countess Fiona*); Blair Castle; Dunblane Cathedral; and, of course, the cities of Edinburgh and Glasgow, and the town of Stirling, which can all be reached within an hour's drive.

12

CULLODEN HOUSE

Inverness, Invernesshire IY1 2NZ
Tel: 0463 790461

Nearest town Inverness.
Directions From Inverness or Nairn, take signs to
Culloden off the A96 Inverness/Nairn, adjacent to
Culloden village. Do *not* follow the Culloden signs
on the A9.
A member of the **Prestige Hotels** consortium.
Awards AA **** graded; Egon Ronay
recommended; Scottish Tourist Board five Crowns;
British Tourist Authority commended.
Open throughout the year.
Special breaks Winter breaks are available.
The hotel has stairs everywhere so is not suitable for
disabled visitors.
Price for dinner, with wine, bed and breakfast –
over £150.
Credit cards Access, Visa, Amex, Diners Card.
Overall mark out of ten 8

The very name Culloden evokes so many colourful images of
Scotland's tragic history that it would be a bitter disappointment if Culloden House did not have an outstanding historical
pedigree. As it happens, this imposing Georgian mansion was
originally built as a Jacobean castle, and served briefly as the
headquarters for the Young Pretender, Bonnie Prince Charlie,

in the early eighteenth century, as he continued his ultimately hopeless quest to reclaim the Scottish throne. The surrounding land is Culloden Moor – the very ground where so much Scottish blood was shed and where the young prince made his last great stand in 1746 before fleeing to France to spend the rest of his life in broken exile. The actual battlesite is now in the care of the National Trust for Scotland, and the small headstones which mark individual clan graves are a poignant sight.

Culloden House itself was partly destroyed by fire later in the eighteenth century, and subsequently remodelled and rebuilt as a traditional-style Georgian mansion. It had a relatively undistinguished past from then until 1981 when the present owners, Ian and Marjory McKenzie, took over, promising to restore it to something approaching its former glory. The traditional Scottish feel to Culloden House is particularly appreciated by American visitors, and a staggering 70 per cent of those who stay at the hotel come from the United States.

Culloden House retains much of the 'olde worlde' elegance which generations of earlier visitors would have known. Surrounded by 40 acres of private parkland and majestic forest, the hotel is a particularly attractive example of Georgian architecture in this part of northern Scotland. Its central three-storey block is flanked by two further two-storey wings which are all connected together by covered period passageways. A large lawn in front of the house is a popular site for wedding marquees; indeed, Culloden House is one of the favoured hotels in the Highlands in which to hold a society wedding reception. The lawn also doubles as a helicopter pad should guests choose to arrive in that manner.

The hotel's numerous public rooms, including a billiard room, retain a striking Georgian atmosphere, and subtle lighting enhances the elegant antique furnishings and writing-tables which sit alongside deep armchairs for that relaxing after-dinner coffee. The house has a good collection of antique books which are not chained or caged in, but freely available for residents to read. In eight years running the hotel, Ian McKenzie says not one has ever been stolen. Conference facilities are particularly good at Culloden House and director level and senior management meetings are encouraged by the resident proprietors.

Culloden House's most appealing public room *has* to be its restaurant. With seating for 45, it is decorated in traditional Adam style, and is reputed to be an authentic Adam design, although documentary evidence cannot be traced to prove this. The decor is dark green with white plaster relief and medallions – very elegant, and a more romantic setting than this room, when set and candle-lit at night, is hard to find.

Chef Michael Simpson serves a wide range of food in a combination of classical, *nouvelle cuisine* and Scottish Country House styles, and Ian McKenzie himself, resplendent in his traditional kilted Highland dress, presides over dinner each evening. Predominantly local produce is used in the preparation of all meals, and prime Scottish beef and fresh seafood are central features of the menu. An interesting speciality which was highlighted by *Gourmet* magazine was their (very fresh) locally caught Smoked Salmon served with an original Broccoli and 'Red Bell Pepper' which the chef makes with purple cauliflower and serves chilled with a dressing enhanced by a little finely chopped green chilli pepper. A very detailed wine list is also available.

The hotel has a total of 21 bedrooms, including one large family room and a four-poster. All have private bathroom facilities, colour television and direct-dial telephone. Leisure facilities available at Culloden House include a hard tennis court, sauna and billiard room. Nearby attractions include the Culloden battlefield; Loch Ness; Clava Cairns (best described as a mini-Stonehenge complete with Neolithic burial chambers); Cawdor Castle with strong Macbeth connections, and the town of Inverness.

13

DALHOUSIE CASTLE

Bonnyrigg, Edinburgh EH19 3JB
Tel: 0875 20153

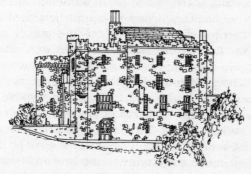

Nearest town Edinburgh.
Directions Take the A7 from Edinburgh for
seven miles until you reach the village of Eskbank.
Continue along the A7 at the roundabout for one
mile, turn right under a bridge towards Carrington
then head left at the first crossroads by the church.
After 200 yards turn left at the hotel sign and right
again.
Part of the **Crown Hotels** group.
Awards AA **** graded; recommended by Egon
Ronay; Birnbaum's Guide to Great Britain and
Northern Ireland; Worldwide Hotel Guide; British
Tourist Authority commended.
Open throughout the year.
Winter breaks are available from November to
March.
Not suitable for disabled visitors; children are welcome
and dogs are allowed, but not in public areas.
Price for dinner, with wine, bed and breakfast for
two – £100–£150.
Credit cards Access, Visa, Amex, Diners Club.
Overall mark out of ten 6.5

Lying just on the outskirts of Edinburgh, Dalhousie Castle has the distinction of being one of the oldest Country House Hotels, not only in Scotland but in Great Britain as a whole. It is superbly situated for those first-time visitors to Scotland keen to explore the capital city and, indeed, central Scotland and the beautiful nearby Borders region. Dalhousie's historical pedigree is outstanding. A four-page history is included in all hotel-room information packs and makes fascinating reading if you choose to really savour the moment and relax with a long drink in one of the spacious public rooms.

The castle was originally built in the thirteenth century by the Ramsay Family which, remarkably, still owns the present hotel, and has retained possession of the castle longer than any other family-owned castle in Scotland. As far back as 1140, one Simudus de Ramseia, a freeman who followed David I to Scotland from the Huntingdonshire village of Ramsay, was settling in these parts and is said to be the founder of the whole Ramsay line, and the first to have land at 'Dalwolsey'.

By the end of the thirteenth century the castle was built, and the English monarch Edward I spent a night within its walls before going on to Falkirk where he defeated William Wallace. William Ramsay, then owner of Dalhousie, later joined forces with Lord Robert Bruce and was present at Bannockburn in 1314 when the future Scottish king heavily defeated the English oppressors. The foundations of the enormous thick walls of the original thirteenth-century castle and the vaulted dungeons still remain as an integral part of the present hotel, just as they were seven centuries ago.

In 1400 Dalhousie was besieged by the vigorous young English monarch, Henry IV. The siege lasted six bitter months, and this proved the last occasion a Scottish castle was attacked by an English king in person. The history of the castle in later centuries is no less colourful. Oliver Cromwell spent some time here in October 1648, a critical period in the English civil war and just three months before he authorized the execution of Charles I. In the last century Queen Victoria and Sir Walter Scott both stayed a while at Dalhousie Castle.

Now, of course, Dalhousie is a busy luxury hotel, richly decorated and open to all throughout the year. Most of the exterior dates from 1450 and the public rooms inside have striven a little too hard to echo that period feel which is essential in a good Country House Hotel. There is little of the homely atmosphere associated with Country House Hotels, and no public bar, so pre-dinner drinks are served in the library.

The panelled ceilings, ornate wood-polished walls, thick curtains and reproduction period furniture in all the public rooms might be considered a little over-the-top, but there is no doubting their comfort. The most notable public room is the hotel's Dungeon Restaurant, constructed out of medieval barrel-vaulted dungeons. Complete with stone walls and subtle lighting, this has to be one of the most unique locations for that special candle-lit meal anywhere in Scotland.

The menu is long and comprehensive, although there are surprisingly few house specialities on the list of main dish options, which is a little disappointing. Prime beef, lamb, chicken, pork and veal feature prominently, but the most interesting choice is the Châteaubriand, served in two-person sized portions: tender Scotch Fillet is cooked in a rich Crayfish Sauce and garnished with Fresh Lobster. The list of hors d'oeuvres is much more impressive, but sadly the wine list with a choice of 60 wines offers practically nothing older than 1978 for the connoisseur. Live music is occasionally provided in the restaurant – and can be a distraction if you've come here specifically for that 'special evening'. Still, as it tends to be a discreet lute player or harpist, it's usually a pleasant diversion.

Dalhousie Castle has 24 bedrooms in all, offering every modern facility including colour television and private bathrooms. Bathroom fittings, however, are very average and some of the bedrooms are a far cry from 'luxury', and a little out of keeping with the rest of the hotel. The interior decor of several needs to be improved if the hotel wishes to maintain its high-price-bracket room rates. When booking, be sure to ask to see your room first. You may be very lucky and come

61

away with glowing impressions, but you should check before accepting the room that it's not one that needs refurbishing.

The hotel has a number of leisure facilities available, including a games room offering table tennis and billiards. Nearby attractions include the city of Edinburgh, including the Castle, Holyrood Palace, the Royal Mile, the Royal Botanic Gardens and (during August) the banquet of music and drama offered by the Edinburgh International Festival. Sporting facilities, including dry-slope skiing, golf, clay pigeon shooting and horse riding can all be arranged nearby through the hotel.

14

DRYBURGH ABBEY

St Boswells, Roxburghshire TD6 ORQ
Tel: 0835 22261

Nearest town St Boswells.
Directions Take the A68 to St Boswells then
follow Dryburgh Abbey signs along the B6404 for
about three miles, then turn left into Clintmains
and from there continue on for approximately
another mile.
Awards AA *** RAC graded.
Open throughout the year.
Special weekend breaks are available from
November to May.
The hotel is suited for disabled visitors; children and
dogs are welcomed.
Price for dinner, with wine, bed and breakfast for
two – £100–£150.
Credit cards Access, Visa, Amex and Diners
Card.
Overall mark out of ten 7

In the heart of the Scottish Borders, the Dryburgh Abbey
Hotel was originally built around 1845, and subsequently
modernized in 1875 by Lord Jerviswood, brother to Lady

Grisell Baillie. Prior to that the Baillie family had rented the then Dryburgh Abbey House from the Biber-Erskine family, having moved from Maxpoffle near St Boswells proper. Alice and Mary Teressa Baillie spent the remainder of their long spinster lives at Dryburgh, and shortly after Mary's eventual death in 1929 the house was purchased by the Scottish Motor Traction company (SMT) – owners now of the largest Scottish bus group. A new wing was then added and the house officially became the Dryburgh Abbey Hotel, first opening its doors to visitors in 1932. The stylish ballroom was added in 1937, and the present cocktail bar opened in April 1981.

Dryburgh is unusual among Scottish Country House Hotels because it is still furnished in a manner which the original owners would recognize, rather than being subject to a determined effort to make it 'appear' old. In their detailed brochure, the proprietors make a bold claim to take visitors 'back to an age when the comfort of each guest was considered to be rather more important than the number of names in the hotel register' – a claim the well-trained staff strive hard to live up to.

The more traditional of the hotel's two public lounges is furnished like a smart Victorian parlour, with red leather armchairs and sofas laid out around hand-carved oak coffee tables. The attention to detail is a credit to the proprietors; even the coal fireplace furnishings are authentic brass.

A basement cellar lounge has been well renovated to make a warm and welcoming hideaway. Complete with log fire, subdued lighting and an assortment of period armour adorning the walls, this popular nook is one of the most relaxing spots in the entire hotel.

The dining-room is light and airy, with good views far out across the River Tweed. Local artwork decorates the walls (also well lit) and extensive conference facilities can be made available if required. Service is prompt and reassuringly attentive. The style of cooking is traditional Scottish, although the chef has sensibly allowed himself to be influenced by the best in French and Italian cuisine.

There is a strong emphasis on fine cuts of locally reared beef and fresh Borders salmon, and in summer most of the vegetables come straight from the hotel's large walled garden. Two favourites are Supreme of Chicken Princess, served with a light White Wine and Fresh Cream Sauce, and the delicious Fillets of Fresh Lemon Sole Meunière garnished with Prawns and Lemon. Fresh strawberries, also from Dryburgh's garden, are an irresistable treat for summer guests.

Dryburgh Abbey has a total of 29 bedrooms, all with central heating and several with four-poster beds. Private bathroom facilities are provided with most rooms and, by the time of publication, it is expected that all rooms will have the additional facilities of colour television and direct-dial telephone.

A number of leisure facilities are available in the hotel grounds, including an eighteen-hole putting green, croquet and indoor games room. Several full-scale golf courses are in the surrounding area and both this and trout and salmon fishing can be arranged on request. Another feature which should be available by the time of publication is a full-size tennis court, and a five-hole pitch and putt area.

Nearby attractions are plentiful. The most obvious one is the magnificent Dryburgh Abbey itself, founded in 1140 and within easy reach of the hotel. Many similar abbeys are dotted around the Borders and an interesting day's excursion is an exploration of the better-known ones towards which any local guidebook will point you. Other attractions include Scott's view, Mellerstain House, Manderston House, Abbotsford House (former home of Sir Walter Scott), Floors Castle, and countless local woollen mills and small museums.

15

FERNIE CASTLE

Letham, near Cupar, Fife KY7 7RU
Tel: 0337 81381

Nearest town Cupar.

Directions From Edinburgh, follow the A92 from the Fife side of the Forth Road Bridge towards Cupar. Shortly after Glenrothes turn-off follow the A914 and Fernie Castle is signposted about four miles past Cupar. Do not detour via Cupar itself.

Awards AA *** RAC graded; Egon Ronay recommended; British Tourist Authority commended.

Open throughout the year.

Special two- and three-day dinner, bed and breakfast breaks are available all year.

The hotel is unsuitable for the disabled; children and dogs are welcomed.

Price for dinner, with wine, bed and breakfast – £100–£150.

Credit cards Access, Visa, Amex, Diners Club.

Overall mark out of ten 6

A small Country House Hotel a few miles inland from St Andrews, the present L-shaped Fernie Castle dates back to the sixteenth century. The ancient Castle of Fernie can be traced back much further: indeed, the original castle, in the parish of Monimail, four miles west of the little town of Cupar, was first recorded in 1353 when it belonged to the Earl of Fife, Duncan the thirteenth. Two centuries later Wester Fernie was retained by a family known only as Fernie of that ilk before changing hands to the more powerful Arnott family by the start of the sixteenth century. It was they who built the present building and, later that century, in 1680, the castle changed hands once again when bought by the Balfours of Burleigh. Their descendants kept the tenure on the castle until 1965 when it was finally turned into a hotel.

The Balfour family felt the impact of the Jacobite uprisings in the eighteenth century, like so many of their noble contemporaries in Scotland. Colonel John Balfour had his entire estate, including the castle, confiscated because of his active support for the rebels. These were restored to his brother in 1720 after the colonel's death, when support was pledged to the English king's forces. The duties of Forester of Falkland and Constable of Cupar, largely honorary titles to the nobles concerned, were related to the Barony of Castle Fernie.

Many later alterations have been made to Fernie Castle, but its medieval origins are unmistakable even today. One of the castle's most interesting features – inside and out – is the sixteenth-century tower, complete with slit windows, from the days when it was necessary to protect castle archers from enemy arrows. You should also look out for the rather unique water tower. One or two other features of interest to visitors keen to investigate the castle's former glory are an original lead bath and the old Ice House at the rear of the castle which is said to be one of the best preserved in Scotland.

Fernie Castle's public rooms are furnished to high standards, and the decor strives hard to retain an authentic period atmosphere. The bedrooms, however, are a little disappointing. The reception area is set in an open hallway, behind an antique desk, and visitors generally find this rather more welcoming than the shop counter style office reception which many similar hotels have adapted. One room of note is the historic Keep Bar, with its armour-type decor and barrelled stone ceiling.

The main restaurant is in a round dining-room, of dubious decor, but fully bedecked with cut crystal, polished silverware and candelabras on each table. Up to 60 people can be seated here at any one time, and conference visits are encouraged. The hotel places much emphasis on the quality of its cooking and proprietors Arthur and Judy Watt searched for almost two years before they found a chef suitably well qualified, imaginative and skilled.

Daniel Martelat was the top chef they eventually engaged, and his style is neither classical nor outright *nouvelle cuisine*. By his own definition, it falls more into the bracket of classical French, but finished and presented to modern British standards. The best of local produce is used in its preparation – with only a few 'special' ingredients being imported from Paris and elsewhere. Two magnificent main dish specialities are Noisettes de Venaison aux Framboises, tender roast venison flavoured with gin and garnished with hot raspberries, and Paupiettes de Sole Farcies, poached fillets of local sole with a green peppercorn and tomato sauce and garnished with a hint of caviar. The wine list is reasonable but offers few surprises. The food is good, but the à la carte menu is *not* cheap (£60 for two with wine).

Fernie Castle has sixteen bedrooms, all decorated to a respectable level but decidedly lacking the top luxury feel associated with many Scottish Country House Hotels. All have private bathroom facilities and come complete with colour television and direct-dial telephone. Some are furnished with four-poster beds and an elegant Honeymoon Suite is available – complete with complimentary half bottle of champagne.

Nearby attractions include the historic town of St Andrews, and the city of Edinburgh within an hour's drive. Endless country walks are possible within a short distance of the hotel and its surrounding estate, and excellent golf facilities are only a short drive away. Ladybank Golf Course is just two miles away and is one of the best courses in the Fife area, offering reasonable charges to visitors. Slightly further afield is the world-famous St Andrews golf course – a must for any serious golfers staying at Fernie Castle.

16

GLEDDOCH HOUSE

Langbank, Renfrewshire PA14 6YE
Tel: 0475 54711

Nearest town Glasgow.
Directions From Glasgow, follow the M8 towards
Paisley and turn off when you see the sign for
Langbank and Houston. Follow the B789 and signs
to the hotel.
Awards AA *** graded and rosette; British
Tourist Authority commended; Taste of Britain
national food award – Scottish outright winner;
Scottish Tourist Board four Crowns.
Open throughout the year.
Special weekend breaks are available
throughout the year.
Price for dinner, with wine, bed and breakfast for
two – £100–£150.
Credit cards Access, Visa, Amex, Diners Club.
*Children and dogs are allowed. The hotel is suitable for
disabled persons.*
Overall mark out of ten 7.5

Gleddoch House enjoys the distinction of being the youngest
Scottish Country House Hotel included in this guide. Built just
62 years ago, in 1927, by the great Scottish shipbuilder Sir
James Lithgow, the house has retained strong links with the
shipbuilding industry ever since. The hotel was sensibly situated in 250 acres of idyllic west coast countryside, enjoying

some truly spendid views across the River Clyde estuary and the hills surrounding Loch Lomond. A small advantage of the hotel's location is the fact that just ten minutes will take you to or from Glasgow Airport.

The hotel has a total of 33 bedrooms, all of which are named after Scottish bird-life and each with distinct individual characteristics. They vary considerably in size, and a number of the single rooms are a little on the small size. The hotel offers two types of single rooms: a standard single and an executive single which is specifically aimed at business visitors who might require that extra space. These bedrooms have the attractive advantage of leather-inlaid writing desks, all well lit, and telephones that can be moved from their normal bedside table location to the desk if you so desire. At the top of the range, there is an executive suite where up to eight people can be accommodated for a meeting if necessary.

All bedrooms are furnished to impeccable standards and include the luxuries you would expect in a hotel of Gleddoch's character, including private bathroom facilities, colour television, tea and coffee making facilities and even four-poster beds if you feel like splashing out on that little extra.

The public rooms have obvious attractions to the business clientele, and this market is central to the hotel's trade. The large Garden Room offers unrestricted views across the terrace to the gardens and both lunch and dinner can be arranged here for up to 40 guests. The house's original drawing-room has a wide marble fireplace and richly ornate plasterwork all round, and accordingly makes a truly superior venue for a top-level business meeting where impressions are important.

Gleddoch House is blessed with an outstanding chef in Charles Price, and his bold promise to cook whatever dish you fancy (given a few days' notice) has yet to be beaten. Few residents, however, will want to stray far from his elegant à la carte menu which relies heavily on the best of local produce. Fresh Artichoke with Lobster, served warm on a bed of Spinach Noodles, is an extravagant opener (at over £10 per person) but easily the best hors d'oeuvre for what is to follow. But most wait for the main course before really spoiling themselves, and what better way to do so than by ordering Prime Aberdeen Angus Beef, or perhaps Breast of Partridge, served pan-fried with Woodland Mushrooms on a Truffle Essence, or maybe even Loin of Veal cooked with Stem Ginger and served with a Crisp Potato Cake bathed in a Cider Sauce. The menu prices are not cheap, even for a hotel of this calibre, so bear in mind a first-class meal for two, eating four courses and accompanied by a reasonable wine, is likely to leave you with little change from £80. The quality, presentation and surroundings, however, will be excellent.

Leisure facilities for the sportsman are plentiful at Gleddoch House. As a hotel guest, you will have access to some of south-western Scotland's finest golf courses, and membership of the Gleddoch House Country Club where, in the Golf and Country Clubhouse, you will find a squash court, sauna facilities, plunge pool, international-size snooker table as well as the club lounge bar and restaurant. You can go horse riding from the hotel's own riding school without ever having to leave the spacious grounds.

Nearby attractions are almost too numerous to mention, but the most obvious attraction is the city of Glasgow itself just half an hour away by car. No more the dirty, run-down industrial city of the 1940s and '50s, Glasgow has undergone a major regeneration programme and is now a serious challenger for Edinburgh's crown as Scotland's cultural capital. Scotland's number one tourist attraction, the Burrell Collection, is twenty minutes away by car. To the north you have the breathtaking beauty of Loch Lomond and the Trossachs and, to the south, the Ayrshire coast. Further west, down the coast, are the yachting centres of Gourock and Inverkip.

17

GREYWALLS

Muirfield, Gullane, East Lothian EH31 2EG
Tel: 0620 842144

Nearest town Gullane.
Directions From Edinburgh, follow the A198 to Gullane. Greywalls is clearly signposted at the east end of the town.
A member of the **Pride of Britain** consortium; member of the Association of Britain's Leading Family Owned Hotels.
Awards AA *** (red) graded and rosette; Egon Ronay recommended.
Open from April until the end of October.
No **special breaks** are available.
The hotel is suitable for disabled visitors and there are ground-floor rooms; children and dogs are welcome.
Price for dinner, with wine, bed and breakfast for two – over £150.
Credit cards Access, Visa, Amex, Diners Club.
Overall mark out of ten 8

If you are a golf fanatic, or keen to find a peaceful retreat within striking distance of Edinburgh, or just curious to look at the small house which was once King Edward VII's bathroom, then Greywalls is where you've been looking for. This tranquil Country House Hotel was originally built in 1901 by one of Britain's greatest Edwardian architects, Sir Edwin Lutyens, and considered a model mansion for its period even then.

The house's most famous guest was King Edward VII, who made regular visits here towards the end of his nine-year reign, between 1901 and 1910. Ostensibly the king came to relax and enjoy the views far across the Firth of Forth and the Lammermuir Hills, but the real reason was his desire to visit Mrs Willy James, his mistress and wife of the house's owner. Such was the king's attraction to the house that they even built him a large private bathroom with a view across the garden! The two-room 'King's Loo' remains one of the hotel's most charming attractions, and is now a delightful bedroom, with en suite bathroom, overlooking the Rose Garden.

In 1924 the house was sold to Lt Colonel Sir James Horlick, grandfather of the present owner, Giles Weaver. It remained an upmarket holiday home until the Second World War when it saw service as an officer's mess for the RAF, and subsequently as a hospital for the Polish forces and their wives. Finally, in 1948, it was turned into a hotel and over the four decades which followed gradually improved and built up to the informal luxury standards you can expect today. Golf has been one of the central themes of life at Greywalls and its location at the very edge of the world-famous Muirfield golf course makes it an obvious favourite with golfers the world over. Many top professionals stay here during British Opens at Muirfield – and Tom Watson is known to have so loved the place that he's sneaked back a few times since.

The impressive hotel gardens were laid out by Sir Edwin Lutyens' imaginative friend and partner Gertrude Jekyll, and were lovingly tended for an incredible 60 years by the same gardener, James Walker. The house itself, garden walls, paths and hedges are all geometrically interlinked and plans are well in hand to recreate the small vegetable garden just as Mrs Jekyll had planned all those years ago.

Greywalls has a number of fine public rooms inside, but the panelled library is easily the most appealing and furnished in authentic period style right down to the last detail. On both sides of the big open fire there are shelves and shelves of books; ironically, many of the libraries in Country House Hotels today no longer have any books and have been converted into lounges instead. Refreshingly, the library at Greywalls still serves its original purpose. The Sunday papers, of all description, are laid out in the library and are an added treat to your huge Sabbath breakfast.

With seating for 70, the dining-room was once the courtyard of the house and now serves food in top *nouvelle cuisine* style. When it was constructed care was taken to ensure that Lutyens' original concept for the house's interior design was adhered to. Non-residents are welcome for dinner, but the management strongly urges advance booking, particularly during the month of August when the Edinburgh Festival is in full swing. The menu has a set price for four courses, with a small number of options and an additional charge if you wish to have a fifth course.

Greywalls has one of the youngest top chefs in the business, Andrew Mitchell, and he has managed to create some intriguing specialities that verge on the adventurous. Starters are more interesting than the main course options and include a Chilled Galantine of Chicken and Magret Duck layered with Strips of Opal Basil and finished on a Black Grape Dressing. The remainder of the Magret Duck, served in a rich Cherry Sauce, appears as a main course option, oven-roasted and thinly sliced. The quality is excellent.

The hotel has 23 bedrooms, five in a more modern extension and all furnished as closely to original period authenticity as possible and with their own private bathroom facilities. Most have views over the gardens or Muirfield golf course. When the house was first built there was a single bathroom so the renovations over the last few decades have made a tremendous improvement to the whole place.

Nearby attractions are obvious if you are a golfer: ten courses within a five-mile radius. A hard tennis court and croquet lawn are also available within the hotel grounds, but further afield you can visit Edinburgh and all that it has to offer, or the ancient castle of Tantallon, or the renowned bird sanctuary on the Bass Rock. Facilities for just walking and exploring are excellent and both the surrounding Lammermuir hills and the long sandy beaches nearby offer perfect opportunities for the inquisitive walker.

18

INVERLOCHY CASTLE

Torlundy, Fort William, Scotland PH33 6SN
Tel: 0397 2177

Nearest town Fort William.
Directions Follow the A82 to Fort William and
continue on the same road for a further three
miles north. Inverlochy is located at the village of
Torlundy.
A member of the **Relais et Châteaux** consortium.
Awards AA **** (red) graded and two rosettes;
awarded Gold Plate Hotel of the Year award in
1971 by Egon Ronay; recommended (with rosette)
by Michelin guide. Awarded maximum five Red
Turrets by Michelin in 1986, the only Country
House Hotel outside London area to receive this
distinction.
Open from March until mid-November.
The hotel is unsuitable for the disabled. Children are
permitted but dogs are not allowed.
Price for dinner, with wine, bed and breakfast for
two – over £150 (will be nearer £250).
Credit cards Access, Visa, Amex, Diners Club,
Mastercharge.
Overall mark out of ten 9

Definitely one of Britain's top Country House Hotels, Inverlochy Castle is a romantic old Victorian building surrounded by a quite idyllic baronial estate. Queen Victoria herself spent a week here in 1873 and hit the nail firmly on the head when she wrote in her diaries: 'I never saw a lovelier or a more romantic spot'.

The castle was commissioned in 1863 by William Scarlett, third Baron Abinger and a former soldier, when he took the bold decision to sell the previous family seat of Abinger Hall in Surrey. By 1870 the first part of the new castle was complete and the family moved in, spending most of the year at their new home before returning to London for the winter. A huge staff was retained to look after Inverlochy Castle and its surrounding 39,000-acre estate throughout the year. Abinger retired from the army in 1877, fifteen years before his death, and became a local magistrate and much more actively involved in local affairs.

The castle remained in the Abinger family's possession until 1944 when it was sold to one Mr Hobbs of Vancouver, British Columbia. His family still own and run the hotel today, although it was as late as 1969 before the decision was taken to turn it into a luxury hotel.

Almost everything about Inverlochy Castle will amaze and, no doubt, impress you. A long elegant driveway, filled with well-tended shrubbery and floral displays and, in season, the rich smell of rhododendrons, makes for a welcome few hotels in Scotland can match. Inside the impression is no less striking. From the moment you enter the huge Great Hall, with its intricately decorated domed ceiling, you will be met by one of many smart, friendly and efficient staff who will make your stay here as smooth and trouble-free as possible. A staff of around 50 are on duty every day to look after a maximum of 28 guests at any one time.

When you do enter the hotel, take a few moments to savour that first sight of this grand hallway, complete with authentic crystal chandeliers, large oil paintings and a handsome carved wooden stairway which cascades down from the first floor. The high quality of the furnishings throughout the hotel befit the vast proportions of the public rooms, and accurately reflect the atmosphere of a former era.

The vast main public lounge is furnished in a style of timeless elegance rather than specifically Victorian or later. Every piece of furniture is of exceptional quality and the hotel's colour brochure can only struggle to do justice to any of the public rooms illustrated. Do look out for the billiard room, with its dark period table and traditional deer-antler wall hangings which quite complete the 'feel' of the place.

The main dining-room has glorious views out across the nearby loch, and with a head chef trained and recruited from London's prestigious Connaught Hotel you are unlikely to be disappointed with the menu. The choice is not extensive, but the quality of food, standard of service and presentation are of the highest international standards. A couple of recommendations from the varied range of starters are Warm Salad of Quail and Artichoke served with Walnut Dressing, and Paupiette of Smoked Salmon with a Dill and Mustard Sauce.

Main course specialities are always prepared from the finest local produce and include Poached Fillet of Baby Turbot with Vermouth Sauce and – a rarely seen main course option anywhere now – Roast Saddle of Hare with Juniper Berries. From their list of sweets, do watch out for the delicious Hot Minted Strawberries in Puff Pastry. As you might expect from a hotel of this class, an extensive and balanced wine list is available.

The hotel has a total of sixteen bedrooms, most of which are extra-large and all of which have an impeccable range of private facilities. A nice touch is the Malvern mineral water and Rochas soaps provided as standard in all bedrooms. Room service is particularly comprehensive at Inverlochy.

Nearby attractions include the town of Fort William and Britain's highest peak, Ben Nevis; the West Highland Museum; a vitrified fort three miles up Glen Nevis; old fort walls behind Fort William's travel centre; Tor Castle (on the B8004 two miles north-east of Banavie); and a wealth of sporting and outdoor facilities within the hotel grounds, and in Fort William itself.

ISLE OF ERISKA

Ledaig, by Oban, Argyll PA37 1SD
Tel: 0631 72371

Nearest town Oban.
Directions From Oban, follow the A828 to Fort William. The hotel is located four miles to the west, at the mouth of Loch Creran, and is clearly signposted.
Awards AA *** (red) graded; Egon Ronay recommended; British Tourist Authority commended; Scottish Tourist Board five Crowns award and very highly commended.
Open from February to November.
Special breaks Discounts for stays of seven nights or more; advance reservations are only accepted for a minimum of two nights.
Price for dinner, with wine, bed and breakfast for two – over £150.
Credit cards Access, Visa, Amex and Diners Club.
Suitable for the disabled. Children are welcome and dogs are allowed if kept in bedrooms.
Overall mark out of ten 8

If you're seeking a truly private retreat, and at the same time want to be surrounded by the highest standards of traditional

Country House comfort, then you should seriously consider a visit to the Isle of Eriska. This is a perfect honeymoon hotel and indeed, with the owner doubling as a Church of Scotland minister, you could even tie the knot while there and turn your visit into an unexpected honeymoon!

As its name suggests, the sandstone and granite hotel is situated on a 300-acre private island right in the middle of Loch Linnhe. A good road bridge is the sole connection with the mainland and the rest of civilization for however long you may choose to escape here. Much of the sprawling estate is left to mother nature's care so that guests can really enjoy the 'get-away-from-it-all' atmosphere to the full.

Enthusiastic proprietor Robin Buchanan-Smith has run the hotel since 1974 and his heavy personal and financial investments have long since begun to pay off. The house was built 90 years before his arrival in true Scottish baronial style for one of the Stewarts of Appin, a distant branch of the ancient Scottish Royal House of Stewart. The architect was really the last one of significance to flourish in Scotland before Robert Lorimer, and rejoiced in the name of Hippolyte Blanc. He was responsible for the Argyll Tower in Edinburgh Castle, probably his best-known commission.

The original owner died suddenly around the end of the last century while standing as a Unionist candidate in an Ulster election. Shortly afterwards his dubious business interests went bust and creditors came in to take over the house! The Clark Hutchison family eventually bought the house and lived here for a generation or so until circumstances caused its resale in 1930. Two sons, Sir Ian and Michael, entered Parliament for Scottish constituencies and still maintain contact with the hotel by visiting separately each summer, despite their advancing years.

The house fell into a state of neglect from 1930 until 1973, when the present owners took over and it took the Buchanan-Smiths over eight months, with a team of 30 workmen, to get the house smart enough to open as a Country House Hotel the following year. The results speak for themselves.

The various public rooms are spacious and elegant, typifying

Victorian craftsmanship at its very best. Log fires are lit when the temperature outside demands it (which is quite often with Scotland's brisk west coast breeze) and deep wall-panelling and rich plasterwork are delights to admire as you sit back, relax and enjoy your after-dinner coffee in the drawing-room. Even the reception area is large and open with the emphasis on creating a warm and informal atmosphere. More than one guidebook has said that the personality of Robin Buchanan-Smith, a burly former university chaplain, quite dominates the hotel and this is certainly a fair assessment. He pledges that the island belongs to his guests and strives to make sure each visitor to Eriska will remember their stay long after the memory of most hotels would have worn off. He usually succeeds.

The dining-room is decorated with pine panelling and a thick plaster-modelled ceiling. The emphasis is placed firmly on a traditional Scottish Country House style of cooking and presentation, under the expert eye of Robin's wife Sheena. Menus are changed nightly and centre around the carving trolley for dinner. The food served is wholesome and simple, with large servings, rather than fancy continental cuisine. On Sundays a traditional Sunday lunch, complete with roast beef and Yorkshire pudding, is the norm, although increasingly fish dishes are becoming more popular as main course alternatives through the week. Breakfasts are a particularly elaborate affair, with every conceivable alternative from porridge and bacon and eggs to snap, crackle and pop cereals being available. The freshly baked home-made bread prepared by Sheena Buchanan-Smith is reason enough to undertake the long drive from London. You might be disappointed if you come to Eriska expecting luxury continental cooking, but you will certainly not leave hungry.

Eriska has built its reputation on very high standards of comfort, faithful to the original Country House style rather than going overboard for pampered luxury. There is no sports complex, heated swimming pool or even a discreet sauna; indeed, leisure facilities are limited to gentle exploration of the 300-acre island and an assortment of watersports for the more energetic. All eighteen bedrooms have private bathroom facilities and include the standard extra of colour television.

Nearby attractions include the Isle of Iona, Glen Coe and surrounding countryside, and Inveraray Castle. Most guests prefer not to leave the island throughout their stay, and for the more adventurous there are a number of Icelandic ponies, and even a couple of donkeys, which can be taken on a ride round the mile-and-a-half-long island.

20

JOHNSTOUNBURN HOUSE

Humbie, near Edinburgh, East Lothian EH36 5PL
Tel: 087533 696

Nearest town Edinburgh.
Directions Take A68 through Dalkeith and
Pathhead to Fala. Turn left on to B6457. After one
and a half miles, turn right at T junction.
Part of the **Mount Charlotte** hotel group.
Awards AA *** and British Tourist Authority
commended.
Open throughout the year.
Special breaks Details on application. Pheasant
and grouse shooting and clay pigeon shooting
breaks by arrangement. Special winter breaks are
also available.
Not suitable for the disabled.
Price for dinner, with wine, bed and breakfast for
two – over £150.
Credit cards Access, Visa, Amex and Diners Card.
Overall mark out of ten 7

Johnstounburn is a charming country retreat within easy
driving distance of Edinburgh. It really is, as it claims, one of

Scotland's most 'charming historic houses' – a turreted mansion house with all the classical features of an eighteenth-century estate – walled garden, parkland, outhouses – and it is now returning to its former splendour under the managership of the Mount Charlotte group after the rather sad period in its history when it was closed down due to bad management and local council bureaucracy. The only reminder of this now are the still somewhat neglected gardens, though plans are afoot and gardeners now employed to remedy this, and by the time of publication this should no longer be a problem.

Everything else to be said about the house is good. The food is superb, the rooms beautifully furnished and the facilities well cared for. With the strength of the Mount Charlotte group behind it, Johnstounburn House is going out to market itself on a more commerical line than many other Country House Hotels. The benefit to the guest is the low prices on the special breaks offered. The owning hotel group is not looking on this hotel to make huge profits for them, so prices are reasonable.

Among its more interesting claims to fame is that in the 1950s the estate was owned by the uncle of John Hunt, one of the chaps who conquered Everest in 1953 with Sir Edmund Hillary. After the descent Hunt telegrammed Johnstounburn to let his family know the good news about the conquest, thus making Johnstounburn the first to know of the conquest before the news leaked out to the rest of the world. It was also the home of the brewery baron, Andrew Usher, who was the first man in Scotland to blend whisky and start the new trend away from the traditional malts.

The main part of Johnstounburn was built in 1625, with the panelled dining-room dating back to 1740. The house, as you see it today, was finished in 1840, with the most attractive stable conversions having been added in the last couple of years. Among the treasures of the house are several noteworthy oil paintings by the artist Robert Norris. However, the showpiece of this house stands outside in the gardens, the Dovecot, dating back to the eighteenth century and listed as a Historic Monument.

There are twenty bedrooms which by time of publication will have been completely refurbished. The recently converted stables, which are situated a five-minute walk from the main house, are particularly good for families or couples wishing a greater degree of privacy. They are more spacious, and give the occupant the benefit of having his own front door! The rooms in the house are more traditional, so if it's a romantic four-poster weekend you are looking for these would be more suitable.

The food is described as French/Scottish. Certainly it features all the best Scottish specialities, such as prime Scotch beef, venison, game and seafood. The quality is first class, presentation good and service attentive without being fussy. The wine list is small but reasonably priced and particularly good value is the set menu – still under £20 at the time of publishing. The sweets are particularly good; well worth saving room for before retiring to the log-fired lounge for coffee.

Nearby attractions are plentiful: the city of Edinburgh; the famous golf courses of East Lothian; fourteenth-century Tantallon Castle; bird-watching on the Bass Rock; Sir Walter Scott's home Abbotsford; and Traquair House, the oldest inhabited house in Scotland.

21

KILDRUMMY CASTLE

By Alford, Aberdeenshire AB3 8RA
Tel: 03365 288

Nearest town Ballater.
Directions From Aberdeen, follow the main A97
Ballater to Huntly road. Kildrummy Castle is
signposted.
A member of the **Best Western Hotels**
consortium.
Awards AA *** RAC graded; Scottish Tourist
Board four Crowns and highly commended;
British Tourist Authority commended.
Open from mid-March until early January.
Special early/late season rates are offered for
stays of two nights or more.
*The hotel is unsuitable for disabled visitors; children
and dogs are welcome.*
Price for dinner, with wine, bed and breakfast for
two – £100–£150.
Credit cards All major cards.
Overall mark out of ten 7

Kildrummy Castle is a little unusual in its origins, as it was
deliberately *not* built on the site of, or even from the ruins of,
a much older building. In fact, the present hotel dates only

from 1900 when it was built as a private mansion house for Colonel James Ogston and it was inhabited as a family home right up to 1956 when it became a hotel. The origins of the first Kildrummy Castle go back a lot further, and the graceful ruins of the original thirteenth-century structure can be seen from the upper floor of the present hotel. Your first glimpse of them will be as you turn round a wide bend in the long rhododendron-lined driveway leading off from the main A97 up to the front of the hotel.

It is difficult to imagine the tall, roofless ruins of the old castle back in the days of its full glory, but it must truly have been an outstanding fortress when it was the family seat of the Earls of Mar, one of medieval Scotland's great noble families. It has lain abandoned now for centuries, but remains subtly looked after to ensure its timeless charm doesn't crumble away altogether, like so many of Scotland's ruined castles.

A strong feature of Kildrummy Castle is the proprietors' obvious intention to retain the intimate family house atmosphere as much as possible. The temptation to build on suites of new bedrooms has been resisted, although all sixteen bedrooms have been gradually upgraded to their present high standards. In addition to private bathroom facilities, all have colour television, direct-dial telephone, trouser press and tea and coffee making facilities as standard. Most of the bedrooms are comfortable without being remarkable, although a number of master doubles are available (and generally need to be booked further in advance). The master doubles represent excellent value and cost only a couple of pounds more per person – well worth the investment for that little bit extra space.

The hotel's public rooms are pleasing rather than luxurious with their period-style furnishings and oak panelling. The one truly outstanding public area is the main reception/hallway, with its criss-cross wood-panelled ceiling and superb Edwardian staircase. The dining-room is light and airy with seating for 42. Both à la carte and table d'hôte meals are available and there is a strong emphasis on local game produce, together with the fine traditional cuts of meats, fish and fresh produce which Aberdeenshire is rightly famous for.

The à la carte menu is impressive, containing seventeen main course options; you will not be disappointed with the Breast of Pheasant or Roast Country Chicken, gently cooked with a subtle Whisky Sauce. The range of appetizers has few surprises, and for somewhere with a tradition of a ready supply of freshly caught Don fish, the Smoked Scotch Salmon starter served with nothing more than a wedge of lemon was rather unimaginative.

The restaurant's fish course options, however, are as a whole, much more encouraging, with Grilled Fillets of Lemon Sole served with Fried Bananas and Mango, and a superb Poached Scotch Salmon served in a Lobster and Prawn Sauce. The additional option of a vegetarian pasta in the middle of the soup and fish options is an unusual addition to the menu, though no doubt a welcome one to vegetarians who should be able to eat here from the fish courses happily. The accompanying wine list is respectable but, again, had few surprises other than a particularly well-chosen house white.

Nearby attractions are plentiful. For the golfer there are approximately 30 golf courses within an hour's drive of the hotel, and for the angler, three and a half miles of prime River Don on which to cast his rod. For the less energetic no fewer than seven well-preserved castles or stately homes in the care of the National Trust for Scotland lie within easy reach – Fyvie, Craigevar, Castle Fraser, Leith Hall, Haddo House, Drum Castle and Crathes Castle. The Royal Family's official Scottish residence, Balmoral Castle, is approximately thirty minutes' drive from Kildrummy and the gardens are open all summer, whenever the Family is not in residence.

22

LOCKERBIE HOUSE HOTEL

Lockerbie, Dumfries and Galloway DG11 2RG
Tel: 05762 2610

Nearest town Lockerbie.
Directions From the north or the south, follow
the A74 to Lockerbie. Bear left at the War
Memorial in the centre of town and about 600
yards further on take the B723. The hotel is clearly
signposted on the right about a mile down this
road.
A member of the **Consort Hotels** group of
independent hotels.
Awards AA and RAC *** graded. Michelin
recommended.
Open all year except over the Christmas and New
Year period.
Special breaks Good value two-day packages
offering dinner, bed and breakfast for under £75
per person any two days of the week throughout
the year.
Price for dinner, with wine, bed and breakfast for
two – under £100.
Credit cards Access, Visa, Diners, Amex.
Suitable for the disabled; children and dogs welcome.
Overall mark out of ten 8

Lockerbie House's close proximity to main road and rail links, combined with its extremely well-priced dinner, bed and breakfast rates, help make this one of the most appealing Country House Hotels in southern Scotland. A compact family mansion, Lockerbie House was first built in 1814 and today still stands amid its 78 acres of tranquil park and woodland which made the original site so attractive to its first owners.

It is said that Dame Grace Johnstone, wife of Sir William Douglas of Kellhead, drew the original plan of Lockerbie House on the ground with her walking stick, and from that the idea for their new country home was born. Whatever the case the solid family house is typical of Georgian architecture and has lost little of the charm which endeared it to the first owners.

Sir William and Dame Grace's more famous great-grandson, John Sholto Douglas – better known as the 8th Marquis of Queensbury (1844–1900) – was largely responsible for drawing up the Queensbury rules for modern boxing. The hotel's present owners, the Smaile family, believe the rules were first drafted in the public area that is now the reception.

Although the Johnstone-Douglas family sold Lockerbie House in 1888, it remained a private home for another couple of generations before changing hands again in the 1920s to become the smart Country House Hotel it is today. Thankfully the long tree-lined driveway retains few of the troublesome potholes which doubtless caused coachdrivers of earlier times more problems than those encountered by modern-day visitors arriving by car. Then, as now, the secret is to drive very slowly up to the car-park just in front of the main door.

Inside, Lockerbie house has managed to retain an uncannily private feel. As you relax in the elegant Adam Lounge with your after-dinner coffee or liqueur you can quite easily imagine Sir William walking in to join you after a hard day's shooting on the adjoining estate.

The two spacious public lounges are the hotel's best feature. Both are generously furnished in largely authentic period furniture, with the notable exception of the dark wood-cased Teletext television set which sits discreetly in the corner of the smaller lounge. The Adam Lounge, complete with original Adam fireplace, is the larger of the two, featuring prominently on the hotel's publicity brochures, and sumptuously furnished right down to the Edwardian writing desk for guests' use, complete with brass inkwell, and a vintage Scottish gazetteer lying casually on top of the Victorian bureau. The good table and ceiling lighting still fails to do justice to the impressive gallery of oil paintings adorning all the lounge walls.

There are 26 bedrooms, most of which have been completely refurbished in the last few years. All offer private bathrooms and tea or coffee making facilities together with colour television and direct-dial telephone. Most are contained in the main body of the house except for the single rooms and one or two of the smaller doubles which have been added in a modern extension. The facilities and standard of decor are equally high in all rooms, but the first-floor older doubles have a definite 'feel' to them and if you have the chance to book at least a couple of clear months in advance then ask for one of the corner double rooms. With their two huge windows the sun streams in by late afternoon just as Dame Grace planned all those years ago.

The food is a mixture of English and French cuisine. A set menu offers four courses, plus coffee, for under £15 per person at the time of publication. Non-residents are welcomed and usually don't need to book. Garlic mushrooms are one of the recommended speciality starters, but the presentation and quality of the generous main course will surely be one of the highlights of your stay here. Local salmon and trout are available, or alternatively the healthy cut of sirloin steak 'Balmoral' served with the chef's selection of vegetables will leave you struggling to find space for a sweet.

In addition to a reasonable wine list, Lockerbie House has a fine list of clarets available to complement your meal. Two highlights are the 1969 Château Haut Brion, at around £60 a bottle, and the 1967 Château Pichon for about two-thirds of that price.

The dining-room was originally one of the house's more intimate public rooms, with thick wall panelling and glorious views across the lawn to the surrounding estate. The atmosphere is restrained and private without any feeling of being rushed to finish your meal and make your table available for later guests.

Nearby attractions are numerous. In addition to free golf at Lockerbie and Moffat Monday to Friday, horse riding and tennis can be arranged nearby. Within the space of a short drive you can visit the beautiful Galloway coast; Drumlanrigg Castle; Maxwellton House in Moniaive; Threave Gardens and Castle near Castle Douglas; and Thomas Carlyle's birthplace at Ecclefechan.

23

PITTODRIE HOUSE

Pitcople, Aberdeenshire AB5 9HS
Tel: 04676 444

Nearest town Inverurie.
Directions From Aberdeen, follow the A96
Inverness road. Once through the town of
Inverurie take the first road off to the left
signposted 'Chapel of Garioch'. The village bearing
that name is about two miles down the narrow
road, and the hotel is signposted through the
village.
Belongs to the **Scotland Heritage** group of
privately owned hotels.
Awards British Tourist Authority commended.
Open throughout the year.
Special breaks Winter breaks are available for at
least two nights, dinner, bed and breakfast.
*Both children and dogs are welcome, but the hotel is
unsuitable for disabled guests unable to manage one
flight of stairs.*
Price for dinner, with wine, bed and breakfast for
two – £100 to £150.
Credit cards Access, Visa, Amex and Diners
Club.
Overall mark out of ten 7

The Pittodrie House Hotel is situated at the heart of a huge fertile 3000-acre Highland estate which comprises mixed arable, forestry and hill land. Surrounding the building there is a three-acre walled ornamental garden which is at the disposal of residents to explore and enjoy. The hotel itself has a long history, dating back as far as 1480. Sadly, though, there is little remaining of the original medieval building, which was burnt to the ground by the Marquis of Montrose in the mid-seventeenth century. The Marquis did not have long to gloat on his triumph, however, as he was executed for high treason in 1650 during the Interregnum period.

The main ivy-covered hotel building which you can see today is a Z-plan castle which was rebuilt in 1675. Substantial Victorian improvements were made in the middle of the last century under the watchful eye of Aberdeen architect Archibald Simpson. The house remained in the possession of the Erskine family, a branch of the Earl of Mar's family, until the turn of this century, when the grandfather of the present owner bought it. Many of the original paintings and antiques from this time, and before, have been retained in the public rooms, and a few of the bedrooms.

The library, and main dining-room particularly, have achieved an Edwardian atmosphere, with solid mahogany furniture, enormous original paintings (many of which have hung on these walls for over a century), large open fires and, of course, the beautiful views far across the surrounding grounds and distant hills which have pleased generations of visitors and residents alike. The library is occasionally used for private dinner parties for up to sixteen guests, and the subtle smell of antique books is a gentle reminder of the age of the hotel.

Wherever you choose to eat, it is unlikely that you will be disappointed by the quality of food served. The style is a combination of classical French and traditional Scottish, with emphasis on using only fresh local produce. The restaurant seats up to 40 persons and, as tables are always kept available for residents, weekend booking for non-resident diners is essential.

The menu is limited but changes daily and the chef specializes in game and salmon dishes. For openers, a typical menu would include the choice of Haggis with Whisky Cream Sauce, or Smoked Woodpigeon Bagration. If you wish to have a soup and/or fish course there is no choice, and the option can be fairly unimaginative: Celery, Apple and Walnut soup, for example, followed by Poached Plaice with Mussel Sauce. For your main course, though, the range is better and you may care to try out the marvellous Roast Haunch of Roe Deer with Cassis Sauce or the top speciality, Baked Darne of Salmon *Maître d'hôtel*.

Pittodrie House is one of Scotland's smallest Country House Hotels, with just twelve double bedrooms. As a result, advance booking is strongly recommended. All have private bathroom facilities, television, telephone and so forth – and more often than not there is an extra piece of furniture in your room that will remind you that not all that long ago the hotel was still an elegant private home. Perhaps a piano, or an antique writing desk, or even a Victorian children's toy chest: you never can tell, but whatever the 'extra' happens to be, it is a lovely touch.

Leisure and recreation facilities at Pittodrie House are excellent. In addition to a billiard room, with international-size snooker table, there are two squash courts, a tennis court, and facilities for table tennis, croquet, clay pigeon shooting and endless possibilities for long, rambling hill walks from the hotel grounds. Horse riding and 18-hole golf can be easily arranged nearby.

Other nearby attractions for the less energetically inclined include the cities of Aberdeen and Inverness; the National Trust for Scotland's famous Castle Trail, which includes seven of Scotland's most famous castles and houses; Braemar; and Balmoral Castle, during the summer months when the Royal Family is not in residence.

24

ROMAN CAMP

Callander, Perthshire FK17 8BG
Tel: 0877 30003

Nearest town Callander.
Directions Follow the A84 as far as Callander.
Enter the hotel drive directly from the A84 at the
east end of Callander Main Street at the hotel sign
between two pink cottages.
A member of the **Historic and Romantik** hotel
group.
Awards AA *** and rosette for food; RAC ***
graded; British Tourist Authority commended;
Scottish Tourist Board four Crowns commended
hotel; Egon Ronay recommended.
Open from mid-March until early November.
Special breaks Two-day breaks from March until
early May, and again from mid-October until
November. Three-day 'Trossachs' breaks
throughout the summer months.
The hotel is particularly well suited for disabled visitors
with one ground-floor room specially adapted for the
physically handicapped. Children of all ages and dogs
are welcome.
Price for dinner, with wine, bed and breakfast for
two – under £100 (just over for large room).
Credit cards None accepted.
Overall mark out of ten 7

Despite its name, the Roman Camp Hotel and Restaurant has nothing particularly Roman about it. The present house was, in fact, given its name from the conspicuous earthwork which you can clearly see across the meadow to the south of the gardens. This is thought to be of Roman origin, and there is certainly evidence of the site of a proven Roman fort at Bochcastle on the west side of the nearby town of Callander.

The owners of the hotel describe it rather honestly as a 'modest seventeenth-century manor house' in the detailed history which they make available to all guests. The house was built on the estate of the Earl of Mar, who was responsible for quite a number of the Scottish Country Houses included in this guide. Probably the Earl's best-known ancestor was the Regent of Scotland in the middle of the sixteenth century during the infancy of Mary, Queen of Scots.

The hotel's history is sketchy prior to 1897 when it is known that the house was acquired by the remarkable 2nd Viscount Esher, friend and confidant of several prime ministers and both King Edward VII and his son George V. In his time Esher became Governor of Windsor Castle and father of artist Dorothy Brett, perhaps best known for her 'Bloomsbury Set' of friends which included Virginia Woolf and eventually D. H. Lawrence as well.

In his time, Lord Esher employed a team of Glasgow architects and had added considerably to the structure of the house by his later years. The present-day library, drawing-room and the guest house, which is connected to the main building by a long passage, were all his responsibility. The highlight of the walkway are the tapestries of English cathedrals which date from between 1937 and 1939.

The hotel's most striking public room is the ornate library which Lord Esher commissioned and so obviously loved towards the end of his long life. It has featured in a number of travel guides and press articles – particularly American ones – and has a curious 'lived-in' feel which many similar such hotel rooms lack. With its very ornate plaster ceiling, dark wood panelling, and shelf upon shelf of predominantly modern tomes, this room is a must to enjoy that informal morning coffee, or relaxed after-dinner liqueur, when you happily remember there is no need to rush home.

The other public room, apart from the spacious drawing-room, is the dining-room. It has a soft pink decor but is rather a disappointment compared to the library. It's modern appearance and lack of subtle lighting make it a touch on the unromantic side. Admittedly it features tables made from the strongest European mountain maple and all the (numerous) oil paintings which decorate the room are Scottish originals, but it is more suited to a business meeting than a romantic dinner. An interesting feature, though, is the painted ceiling, based on traditional Scottish painted ceiling design of the late sixteenth and early seventeenth century. Advance booking, up to a week ahead, is essential for weekend dinner for non-residents.

Food concentrates on standard Scottish Country House style and the owner/chef, Sami Denzler, is a Swiss national who came to the hotel seven years ago, having previously owned and run his own restaurant in Edinburgh. As you might expect, the menu concentrates heavily on local game and fish, although Scotch beef and lamb feature most evenings as well.

The owner's Swiss origins mean that you can expect the rather odd spectacle of a fairly traditional Scottish menu written in French, with English translations underneath, a style of menu presentation usually reserved for more adventurous continental styles. A strong speciality is the chef's Filets de Sole aux Crevettes: Fillets of Sole with Shrimps in a White Wine Sauce. The wine list contains a few pleasant surprises including one or two seldom seen Swiss and Australian bottles which are well worth trying.

When you're finally ready to call it a day you can retire to one of the hotel's fourteen bedrooms. Seven are on the ground floor and particularly suited to the elderly visitor. All rooms have private bathroom facilities, colour television and direct-dial telephone.

Nearby attractions include endless possibilities for hill walking, golf, fishing – the hotel has its own stretch of the River

Teith available – and a number of obvious targets for sightseeing like Stirling, with its historic castle, Loch Lomond and the Trossachs, the site of the Battle of Bannockburn and Doune Motor Museum.

25

SUMMER ISLES

Achiltibuie, by Ullapool, Highland Region IV26 2YG
Tel: 085 482 282

Nearest town Ullapool.
Directions Follow signs on the A835 from
Ullapool to Achiltibuie, then continue for ten miles
north of Ullapool on the same road. Turn left on to
a single-track road towards Achiltibuie, which you
will reach after fifteen miles. 100 yards past the
post office you will find the hotel on the left.
Open From Easter until mid-October.
Special breaks None available at present.
*Not suitable for the disabled; children under the age of
eight are not allowed.*
Price for dinner, with wine, bed and breakfast for
two – £100–£150.
Credit cards None accepted.
Overall mark out of ten 7

If there was an award for the most private and secluded
Country House Hotel in Scotland, it is certain that the Summer
Isles hotel would be a strong contender, if not the outright
winner. So well hidden is its idyllic comfort that not even the
AA guidebook has uncovered this Highland gem of a hotel.

The Summer Isles is largely self-contained and, assuming you have managed to find it in the first place, one of the most relaxing 'away-from-it-all' Country House Hotels you will ever come across.

The Summer Isles differs from other Scottish Country House Hotels in a number of rather obvious ways. The building is not a historic listed building, nor was it ever an ancient Scottish castle or even a modest baronial mansion in the last century. It was built in 1900 as a fishing lodge on the banks of Loch Broom and is typical of the style of Highland lodges which were being built by wealthy landowners from further south throughout the latter part of the last century, and early years of this century. Over the last couple of decades, the old lodge has been transformed from little more than a rundown shack into the comfortable hotel it is today.

The hotel has been run by Mark and Geraldine Irvine since the early 1970s. An interesting little aside is that Mark's sister is author Lucy Irvine, famous for her best-selling *Castaway* and *Runaway* books which were written in the small cottage at the foot of the hotel garden. In 1987 a film of the *Castaway* story, made by United British Artists, was released worldwide. Lucy was clearly attracted by the peace and tranquillity which the hotel's isolated position offers and that is undoubtedly the top attraction of the Summer Isles today.

Few other Country House Hotels could have hens, geese, ducks and quail wandering tame and contented around their four walls, yet it is for little touches like these that people come to Summer Isles year after year. Eating the food, sleeping well and generally relaxing in peaceful surroundings is a strong tonic for many lethargic city-dwelling visitors to this part of Scotland.

The hotel markets itself with the delightful claim: 'There is a marvellous amount of nothing to do in Achiltibuie' and nothing could be closer to the truth. For the 'energetic' there is the option of sea trout and salmon fishing from the end of June until the end of September. Boats are available on either Loch Oscaig, or Lochs Badagyle and Lurgain. The former is the more expensive option with the daily charge a few pounds more than the £20 fee for Badagyle and Lurgain. Right- and left-bank fishing of the River Garvie is also possible for a considerably smaller fee and, wherever you choose to fish, experienced ghillies are available for around £20 a day.

Another delight of this part of Scotland is the endless variety of walks and rambles which are available. At the end of your bed you will find a handy home-produced booklet with details of a collection of favourite tried and tested walks. These vary in length from three to 30 miles, and if you plan to do a lot of walking then you would do well to bring a good range of accessories – midge cream, Wellington boots, comfortable old clothes and so forth – which you will need to make the best of the natural countryside round about you. Bear in mind that, despite a gulf stream literally at the foot of the garden, the climate can vary from Arctic to Aegean within the space of a few days.

The hotel has a total of fourteen bedrooms, most with private bathroom facilities and magnificent views of sea, islands and mountains far in the distance. There is little evidence of pampered luxury anywhere in the hotel, however, particularly in the bedrooms, so don't come here for a hedonistic time. This is a place for the upmarket outdoor crowd. Wherever you go the decor is never pretentious and the dining-room is no exception.

The walls are decorated in a rich moss green, and the woodwork in brilliant white. The table decor echoes this colour scheme, with its white tablecloths and moss-green linen napkins. Wherever you sit, the views are stunning as they sweep far across Loch Broom to the Summer Isles themselves. Few who have the pleasure to see one can deny that a Summer Isles sunset is one of the most beautiful sights possible in this part of the world.

Food is typical of Scottish Country House style and all the vegetables come straight from the hotel's own gardens, being picked no more than an hour before serving. The choice of shellfish is impressive, and locally caught trout and salmon are obvious specialities. Dinner is served from a set menu, offering virtually no option, but it is changed nightly and the five-course meal is excellent value at around £20 per head at the time of publication. The presentation is as simple as it is immaculate.

Nearby attractions include the wealth of natural countryside all around, and one of the best ways to take advantage of this is to cruise on the local boat, the Hectoria, which takes people round the nearby islands to see the natural seal colonies and rare birds. In addition, Inverewe gardens, the Inverpolly nature reserve and the coast of Sutherland can all be visited quite easily from the hotel.

26

SUNLAWS HOUSE

Kelso, Roxburghshire ED5 8JZ
Tel: 05735 331

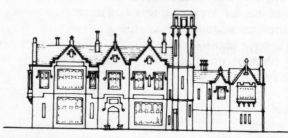

Nearest town Kelso.

Directions Sunlaws is situated three miles south-west of the town of Kelso on the main A698 Kelso to Jedburgh road at the south side of Heiton village.

An independent hotel owned by the Duke and Duchess of Roxburghe.

Awards AA *** graded and rosette for food; Egon Ronay 74%; Michelin two Black Towers recommended.

Open throughout the year.

Special breaks A good variety are available throughout the year including Weekend breaks, While-Away breaks, and both Shooting and Fishing breaks.

Facilities for disabled visitors are excellent, including several ground-floor rooms and a specially adapted toilet; children and dogs are both welcome.

Price for dinner, with wine, bed and breakfast for two – over £150.

Credit cards Access, Visa, Amex, Diners Club – Visa Travel Vouchers also accepted.

Overall mark out of ten 7.5

One of very few Country House Hotels in Great Britain which is still owned by a titled member of the aristocracy, Sunlaws is part of the estate of the Duke and Duchess of Roxburghe, and can fairly claim to be one of the Border's top hotels. The present hotel is actually the third building which has been constructed on this site in the last two centuries, as a combination of fire, fair wear and tear and general expansion have taken their toll since then.

The hotel you can see today dates from the 1860s, but just over a century earlier, on 5th November 1745, it is reputed that Bonnie Prince Charlie stayed at the house which was then Sunlaws, and planted a white rose-bush somewhere in the surrounding grounds whilst the Jacobites were amassing in Kelso before their march south. Then owners, the Scott-Kerr family, were known supporters of the Stuart cause, so the story is certain to contain some grain of truth. Two residents from former times are still said to haunt part of the house; one sad lady is reputed to walk the ground floor of the hotel, and an old soldier can still occasionally be heard on the turret battlements. Sightings are very rare, though, and pretty certain not to interrupt the enjoyment of your stay here.

Set in 200 acres of fine country estate, the hotel retains the feel of a converted country gentleman's retreat, offering much of the traditional comfort visitors in earlier generations would have known and appreciated. It is smartly furnished throughout and although the high standards of comfort offered are never in doubt, the choice of furnishings in some of the public rooms tends a little too much towards the modern.

However, this is a small niggle and the very striking wood-panelled Library Bar more than compensates for this. As you sit by the roaring log fire, with its ornate Victorian fireplace, it is all too tempting to cast your mind back to the days when the local gentry used to meet here to discuss such weighty matters as where to head for their next fox-hunt, or even the vintage of the house port!

The restaurant seats some 45 people, although for luncheon guests have the opportunity of dining in the Library Bar and so savouring its atmosphere that bit longer. On warm days, and there *are* a few during the early summer months, particularly in this part of Scotland, a fixed price Country Luncheon is also available in the large Conservatory. Both are served from 12.30 p.m. until 2 p.m. throughout the week.

The cuisine is typically Scottish Country House style, with the emphasis on local produce, as you might expect. The menu is respectable without being ostentatious, and doesn't quite enter the luxury bracket. As a welcome result, non-residents (who generally make up about one third of the clientele on any given evening) can enjoy dinner for around £15 a head – slightly more if you add a modest wine from the hotel's youngish wine list.

The range of hors d'oeuvres is deceivingly adventurous if you look at it closely. Baked Fillets of Local Trout with a creative Orange and Cucumber Sauce; Chilled West Coast Oysters with Guinness; and even Eyemouth Langoustine Tails grilled with Garlic Butter are just three of the possibilities. From the main course options, East Coast Lobster and Scallops in a Cream and Drambuie Sauce, served with rice, stand out as outstanding value at around £10 at the time of publication. Equally the chef's Grilled Angus Sirloin with Anchovy Butter is good value at a few pounds dearer, although the generous portions of vegetables will set you back another couple of pounds.

Sunlaws House has a total of 21 bedrooms, including two well-appointed singles and all with private bathroom facilities. Most bedrooms are pleasantly spacious, although not all are to the generous extent of the blue-carpeted double featured on the hotel's advertising brochure. Six are located in the Stable Courtyard and all have colour television, radio alarm and direct-dial telephone.

Nearby attractions include Floors Castle, a magnificent stately home and private residence of the hotel's owners, the Duke and Duchess of Roxburghe. Complimentary admission is available to hotel residents during the summer season. Other attractions include a range of leisure facilities like croquet, shooting, hard court tennis, salmon and trout fishing, and both golf and horse riding within the immediate area of the estate. More leisurely attractions include Abbotsford, former home of Sir Walter Scott, Bowhill, Mellerstain, Thirlestane Castle, and the magnificent collection of ancient abbeys at Dryburgh, Jedburgh, Melrose and Kelso itself. The city of Edinburgh is just over an hour's drive away with all that it offers visitors to Scotland.

NORTHERN ENGLAND

27

ARMATHWAITE HALL

Bassenthwaite Lake, Keswick, Cumbria CA12 4RE
Tel: 059 681 551

Nearest town Keswick.

Directions From the M6, exit at junction 40 signposted Penrith. Follow the A66, bypassing Keswick, and branch off on to the A591 (signposted Carlisle) at the major roundabout. Travel for about eight miles to a crossroads; turn left at the Castle Inn Hotel for 200 yards.

Awards AA **** graded, Egon Ronay and Michelin recommended.

Open throughout the year.

Special breaks Winter breaks available from the beginning of November until the end of April, excluding Bank Holidays; also special Christmas and New Year programme.

The hotel has specially adapted rooms for the disabled; children and dogs are accepted.

Price for dinner, with wine, bed and breakfast for two – £100–£150.

Credit cards Access, Visa, Amex and Diners Club.

Overall mark out of ten 9

Twenty miles from Carlisle, sitting by the edge of Bassenthwaite Lake, Armathwaite Hall is one of Cumbria's best hotels and one of the best-value upper price-bracket Country House Hotels featured in this guide. As the proprietor states, Armathwaite Hall offers a type of holiday associated with English life at its best: good food, luxurious surroundings, and acres of natural beauty all around you.

Armathwaite Hall was built in the late eighteenth century, and was a grand country house even then. For centuries the original building on the site of the present house was home to a convent of Benedictine nuns, and although the convent was 'wretchedly poor' it was frequently plundered and finally dissolved during the Reformation.

The current house was purchased in 1796 by one Sir Frederick Fletcher Vane, and it remained the Vane family seat for generations. Prior to then the surrounding grounds and Bassenthwaite Lake had been the subject of considerable controversy when the Earl of Egremont and Sir Wilfred Lawson fought each other in the assize court of Carlisle for the rights to the area. It was swiftly decided that: 'The lake and every part thereof is of the freehold of the Earl of Egremont . . . and the said Earl and his tenants are entitled to the privilege of drawing and landing nets.'

Wherever you wander in the public areas of the hotel, you will appreciate it has been built to baronial proportions. The main lounge area has an enormous fireplace, usually set with a welcoming log fire, and is oak panelled all around. Antlers, pewter plates from earlier generations and dainty little wall lamps enhance the feeling that this really is one of northern England's most authentic Country House Hotels. The hotel's large wood-panelled restaurant can seat up to 80 people at any one time. The ceiling is one of the most intriguing features of the whole hotel, with its deep square-set octagonal pattern contrasting with the more modern furnishings. A huge wooden carved fireplace dominates the longer wall, opposite the large windows which look out across the lake.

Both an à la carte and a table d'hôte menu are available

each evening; their popularity is reflected by the management's earnest request for bookings as far in advance as possible by non-residents. Several menus are available: dishes include favourites of English Country House fayre like Duckling Montmorency and Beef Wellington; another offers *haute cuisine* française with a more adventurous range, including a magnificent double fillet steak Châteaubriand for two, and a Carré d'Agneau St Michel, also for two and served pink unless you request otherwise. Finally you have the choice of local fayre 'from river, sea and lake' which, as you might expect, includes local salmon, monkfish, lobster and a house speciality scampi dish, cooked at your table.

The hotel has 42 bedrooms, including a Honeymoon Suite, Hartley Tower Suite and Four Poster Suite – all of which are extremely popular and require considerable advance booking. All rooms are a good size, and comfortably furnished. Standards are being improved all the time, but all have private bathroom facilities and colour television which includes an in-house video service changed daily.

Armathwaite Hall has an extensive range of leisure facilities to suit all tastes. The hotel's leisure club has an indoor heated swimming pool, sauna, solarium, spa bath and gymnasium and hairdressing salon. Other attractions include facilities for tennis, darts, golf, snooker and squash. For the less energetic resident, an old-style games room has a good range of board games which can be played in here or in your room.

Nearby attractions are plentiful: Lingholm Gardens, near Keswick; Lowther Wildlife Adventure Park; Munchester Castle; Windermere Steamboat Museum; the town of Kendal, with its popular museum of natural history and archaeology; Dent Craft Centre; the Haverthwaite Railway, near Newby Bridge; the city of Carlisle; and the surrounding natural beauty of the Lake District as a whole.

28

BREAMISH HOUSE

Powburn, Alnwick, Northumbria NE66 4LL
Tel: 066 578 266

Nearest town Alnwick.
Directions The hotel is approximately thirty-eight miles north of Newcastle-upon-Tyne, leaving the A1 for the A697 Wooler to Coldstream road.
Awards AA ** (red) graded plus rosette for food; British Tourist Authority commended; Egon Ronay and Michelin recommended.
Open from February until the end of December.
Special breaks Mini-breaks available from February until April, and again from mid-October until 30th December.
Only the restaurant is suitable for the disabled; children under twelve not permitted, and dogs by arrangement in advance.
Price for dinner, with wine, bed and breakfast for two – under £100.
Credit cards None accepted.
Overall mark out of ten 7.5

Set amid five acres of gardens and woodland on the edge of a national park, Breamish House has an extremely peaceful, rustic setting which understandably attracts dozens of repeat visitors each year. The hotel was built in the seventeenth century, and was originally a large farmhouse. In the nineteenth century it was extended to become a Georgian-style hunting lodge and, this century, converted from a private home into a small luxury hotel.

The resident proprietors have striven hard to achieve a balance of comfort and period charm. They pride themselves on a friendly and caring service, where it is possible to relax and feel at home from the moment you arrive at the hotel. From the exterior, the hotel looks rather unspectacular; it is a standard-design Georgian house, with symmetrical stonework and identical rectangular windows. Inside, though, the house has been furnished in the style of the period when it was a private residence, but it would be fair to say the emphasis is more on informal comfort than pampered luxury.

Two main public rooms, a sitting-room and a drawing-room, offer excellent views across the surrounding Northumbrian countryside. It might be worth bearing in mind if you smoke that the sitting-room is strictly non-smoking.

Breamish House is recognized as one of the best small hotels in Northumberland, and its bright public rooms and quality of cuisine justify this. The hotel has not attempted to enter the upper league of luxury Country House Hotels, and this is reflected in the fact that the AA have awarded Breamish two red stars, for outstanding quality within its given class, but just two stars nevertheless.

Breamish has ten bedrooms, all with private bathroom facilities, colour television and telephone, and a number of pleasing little touches like quality toiletries to make your stay that little bit more comfortable. The courteous staff are very attentive to small details, particularly where culinary preferences are concerned. Indeed, this attention to detail was one of the principal attractions highlighted by the Consumers' Association in their write up of this hotel in their guide.

The dining-room is wonderfully informal. Your typical day begins with a hearty Northumbrian breakfast, which can include the famous locally smoked kippers, but is guaranteed to give you a good start whatever you have planned for the rest of the day. A wonderful 'traditional' Sunday lunch is available each weekend. In the evening, though, whatever day of the week it is, dinner is selected from a standard price table d'hôte menu – excellent value at around £15 per person at the time of publication. The choice is limited to around three or four dishes for each course, but the presentation and quality of food is excellent. Popular starters include Mushrooms marinated with Red and Green Peppers, or an interesting cocktail of Melon, Grapes and Pineapple in a Vinaigrette Dressing. A home-made soup, which is generally a chef's favourite, like Cream of Parsnip or Cauliflower follows before the main course – which usually contains at least one fish choice from locally caught produce. Non-fish specialities include Roast Loin of Lamb with a Purée of Onion, Thyme and Celery, served with stuffing and mint salad; or perhaps Fillet of Pork cooked with fresh Marjoram, Parsley, Rosemary and Garlic, served with the succulent pan juices and glazed oranges.

Leisure facilities at Breamish House are rather limited, although all the usual outdoor sporting activities – golf, fishing, horse riding, hillwalking and so forth – can be arranged nearby. The hotel lies at the foot of the Cheviot Hills, and the Coquet and Ingram Valleys lie nearby. To the east lies the dramatic and secluded Northumbrian coastline, perfect for long walks and gentle exploration. Nearby attractions include Holy Island and the Farne Islands bird sanctuary, as well as Floors Castle (stately home of the Duke and Duchess of Roxburghe), and the Borders towns of Kelso, Hawick and Selkirk with the countless attractions they have to offer the visitor to this region.

CAVENDISH

Baslow, Derbyshire DE4 1SP
Tel: 024 688 2311

Nearest town Chesterfield.
Directions Leave the M1 at junction 29 and take
the A617 to the Chesterfield bypass. Then follow
the A619 to reach the Cavendish.
Awards AA *** graded; British Tourist Authority
commended.
Open throughout the year.
Winter breaks available from 1st October until
the end of March.
Children are welcome; access difficult for disabled guests;
dogs are not allowed.
Price for dinner, with wine, bed and breakfast for
two – £100–£150.
Credit cards Access, Visa, Amex and Diners
Club.
Overall mark out of ten 8.5

Set on the enormous estate belonging to Chatsworth, the
magnificent stately home of the Duke and Duchess of Devonshire, the luxury Cavendish hotel enjoys one of the most

desirable locations of any hotel in northern England. There has been an inn on the site of the present hotel for centuries, but the present building dates back only a couple of centuries to the 1780s. Known as the famous Peacock Inn for generations, it was for a long time the property of the Duke of Rutland, providing a vital service as an alehouse to the turnpike between industrial Chesterfield and the quieter spa town of Buxton.

Around 1830 the building first became the property of the Duke of Devonshire, but was not restored properly until 1975. Major renovations took place in 1984 when the hotel was extended, and throughout the renovation period the operation was carefully supervised by the Duchess of Devonshire who has also taken a keen interest in the choice of interior decor and the selection of furnishings and fittings.

Guests are always welcomed personally on their arrival at the Cavendish, more often than not by the enthusiastic proprietor Eric Marsh, who seems to be almost permanently on call to chat with guests and sort out any minor queries or problems they may have. Nearly all the public rooms are enhanced by huge beams, open log fires when the season demands it and vases of freshly cut flowers to add that all-important 'lived in' touch.

Dining at the Cavendish has been highly commended ever since it opened, and once you have sampled the food here (which is, after all, the hotel's principle attraction) you will know that top chef Nick Buckingham, and his young deputy Eamonn Redden, thoroughly deserve the major culinary awards which they have attracted. It would be an unkind understatement to describe the cuisine as French, or English or *nouvelle cuisine* or anything else as, in actual fact, it is an outstanding combination of most modern influences. And the result is magnificent.

A closely typed à la carte menu greets residents and non-residents in the Paxton Room restaurant, and the additional touches of Wedgwood china and silver cutlery make the difference between a fine meal and an outstanding culinary experience which has few rivals in northern England. The range of dishes is extensive and varies with the season. A typical opener might be a Rabbit and Pine Nut Terrine with Cucumber Sauce, or a Warm Salad of Smoked Duck Breast with Cranberry Dressing, or perhaps something lighter like Monkfish and Tomato Soup with Garlic Croutons. An intermediate course follows: the Cavendish House Salad is a favourite here, but you might prefer a half dozen salty Normandy Oysters served in a unique Shallot Vinegar. Whatever you choose, be sure and leave plenty of room for your choice of main course. It would be difficult not to recommend more traditional specialities like Fillet of Salmon and Char-Grilled Trout, but if you really wish to sample the type of cuisine for which the Cavendish is justly famous then try something a little more unusual – like Braised English Ox-Tongue with Mushroom and Madeira Sauce. You will not be disappointed and, whatever you choose, an international and carefully selected wine list is always available.

The Cavendish has 23 bedrooms, all individually furnished but varying considerably in size. All overlook the sprawling Chatsworth estate and the surrounding Derbyshire Peak District. Bedrooms are extremely comfortable, furnished with private bathroom facilities, colour television, direct-dial telephone, and refrigerated mini-bar.

Leisure facilities at the Cavendish are putting and golf practice within the hotel grounds itself and exclusive fly-fishing is available on over ten miles of the Rivers Derwent and Wye which run through the Chatsworth estate. The waters are managed by bailiffs and they will advise on the quality of fishing available on individual stretches of the river. Local fishing expert Arnold Mosley is available for private coaching by arrangement.

Nearby attractions include shopping in ancient Sheffield, a visit to the famous crooked spire at Chesterfield, convenient access to Chatsworth itself, climbing and walking on the surrounding peaks and the Pennine Way, gliding from Hucklow, open mines and show caverns at Castleton, and the chance to explore the origins of British Rail, Rolls Royce, and Crown Porcelain at Derby.

CRATHORNE HALL

Crathorne, Yarm, Cleveland TS15 OAR
Tel: 0642 700398

Nearest town Yarm.
Directions Crathorne Hall is close to the A19
trunk road on the way from Thirsk to Yarm; follow
the signs to Crathorne village.
Awards AA **** graded; Egon Ronay grade 1
hotel; Michelin recommended.
Open throughout the year.
Special breaks Weekend breaks are available;
breaks are possible via tour operators Bonus
Breaks and Golden Key.
The hotel is unsuitable for the disabled; children are
welcome but dogs are not allowed.
Price for dinner, with wine, bed and breakfast for
two – £100–£150.
Credit cards All major cards accepted.
Overall mark out of ten 8

Crathorne Hall has the distinction of being the largest Country
House built during the nine-year reign of Edward VII, which
lasted from 1901 until 1910. The hotel is set amid fifteen acres
of rolling green countryside, just by the little Yorkshire village
of Crathorne. Just as in the days when the hotel was first

built, visitors can appreciate its prime location right above the Leven Valley, with wide panoramic views to the Cleveland Hills beyond.

The interior of the house has lost little of its Edwardian style and elegance. The huge drawing-room is one of two spacious public lounges, and contains a number of impressive oil paintings dating back to the era when the house was built, and before. The room is dominated by an enormous wood-carved coat of arms mounted above the fireplace, and is furnished with a combination of period furniture and comfortable modern armchairs which blend well with the Edwardian feel of the room.

The hotel is a popular venue for business seminars, conferences, society functions, weddings and so forth, and on these occasions the large ballroom, with its great views across the Leven Valley, is used. For particularly grand functions the drawing-room, ballroom and dining-room all interconnect, providing a most impressive setting which allows up to 200 people to be accommodated in style at any one time.

The dining-room is another magnificent old room, its size and enormous stone fireplace typical of Edwardian lavishness in the decade or so prior to the outbreak of the First World War. Half-wall wood panelling goes all the way around the room, adding to the 'warm' feel. Cast your eyes heavenwards for a few moments while you are waiting for your meal to be served and enjoy the elaborately decorated ceiling, its raised square pattern marked out in rich gold leaf against a brilliant white background.

Despite its size, the restaurant offers a surprisingly intimate atmosphere. The chairs are comfortable and of modern design, crafted in an uncomplicated fashion which will not detract from the splendour of the room around you. Food is served in a French style, although some of the best features of English cooking (such as the traditional Sunday lunch) have not been forgotten. Local game specialities are particularly popular during the appropriate season, and the restaurant is as popular with non-residents as it is with residents throughout the year. Advance booking, particularly at weekends, is essential.

Crathorne Hall has a total of 39 bedrooms, and each room is unique in style and design. Much of the original Edwardian charm remains: the ornate friezes where the walls meet the ceiling, pieces of antique furniture, long flowing curtains and so on. Each room has a limited edition graphic print on its walls and, in addition, all bedrooms have their own private facilities. Each one has been fitted with the sort of modern comforts you would expect in a quality hotel like this, such as colour television, telephones, and an assortment of complimentary toiletries. All rooms have large windows and splendid views across the grounds and surrounding countryside.

In a determined effort to offer guests peace and quiet in the most comfortable surroundings, the hotel has deliberately not yet developed any recreational facilities other than a games room which includes a full-size snooker table and a number of card tables. Crathorne Hall has no designated sporting areas, but most popular sporting facilities, including golf, fishing and shooting, can be arranged locally. Nearby attractions include Leven Valley and the Cleveland Hills beyond, the coastal towns of Whitby and Hartlepool, and the city of Newcastle within an afternoon's drive.

CROSBY LODGE

Crosby-on-Eden, Cumbria CA6 4QZ
Tel: 0228 73618

Nearest town Carlisle.
Directions Leave the M6 at junction 44 – the last junction on the motorway, or first if travelling from Scotland. Follow the B6264 and you will soon see the hotel signs.
Awards AA *** graded; British Tourist Authority commended; English Tourist Board four Crowns; Egon Ronay and Michelin recommended.
Open late January until Christmas Eve.
Weekend breaks are available from October until the end of March.
The hotel is unsuitable for disabled guests; children and dogs accepted by prior arrangement.
Price for dinner, with wine, bed and breakfast for two – under £100.
Credit cards Visa, Amex and Diners Club.
Overall mark out of ten 7.5

Just a few miles into England from the Scottish border, Crosby Lodge is an extremely popular stop-over point for business-men and tourists alike travelling either north or south on the busy M6 motorway. Even so, the hotel has a wonderfully secluded location which also makes it popular for couples looking for that informal romantic hideaway to enjoy a second (or even a first) honeymoon, or just a special weekend.

The Lodge is a converted country mansion, originally built at the beginning of the nineteenth century by a wealthy local magnate. It was a private residence until 1969, although was allowed to run down considerably during the earlier part of this century. Present owners Michael and Patricia Sedgwick bought the house in 1970, and after an extensive programme of renovation and redecoration finally opened the Lodge as a Country House Hotel in 1971.

Crosby Lodge sits in a beautiful pastoral setting near the village of Low Crosby. Several acres of neatly tended gardens encircle the hotel, and a particularly well looked-after walled garden is marvellously peaceful and the perfect place for a leisurely stroll before dinner or after a full Sunday lunch.

As far as possible, authentic antique furnishings have been retained throughout the hotel. Wherever you go inside Crosby Lodge you are likely to be struck by a feeling of space. All the public rooms, and the bedrooms, are large and airy, and the atmosphere is as informal as it is unhurried throughout your stay. The hotel is popular for weddings, anniversary and birthday parties, and can suit a wide range of business functions. The large Cocktail Bar is a popular local social spot, although the influx of non-residents at the weekend is seldom obtrusive. A good range of bar snacks are available.

The restaurant has an uncluttered feel, with more than enough space around each table and chair to allow resident and non-resident diners the opportunity to relax and enjoy their meal, and never will you get the sensation of being hurried along to finish your coffee and go. Michael Sedgwick himself takes charge of the kitchen, along with two assistant chefs and son James who joined him in 1987.

Crosby Lodge's menu is a successful mixture of traditional English and French cuisine, although it is increasingly drawing on *nouvelle cuisine*, with lightly cooked vegetables and herby sauces. All the baking is done on the premises, including home-made scones, biscuits, *petit fours*, and all your morning jams and marmalades come from the kitchen here.

A table d'hôte and an à la carte dinner menu are available each evening, with a most impressive range of starters which clearly gives away Michael Sedgwick's area of culinary speciality. There is an emphasis on fish-based dishes, and two succulent treats really stand out: Grilled Large King Prawns with a Mild Garlic Dip, and Prawns Thermidor, served in a Cream Sauce with Wine, Mushrooms and Cheese. Both are exquisite. Unfortunately the choice of main dishes is much less adventurous, concentrating on popular traditional dishes like Roast Farm Duckling and Grilled Solway Salmon. Nevertheless, the taste and presentation are excellent.

There are eleven bedrooms, including one family room and one single, which have all been individually designed and furnished to very high standards of comfort. *En suite* bathrooms, direct-dial telephones, colour television and hairdryers come as standard. Most have superb views across the surrounding grounds, and a number have massive antique half-tester beds. These are almost always more comfortable than standard doubles, to say nothing of being at least a foot higher off the ground, and if you are coming to Crosby Lodge for that special romantic break, it would be a sensible idea to reserve a half-tester room when you book.

Crosby Lodge has nothing to speak of in the way of leisure facilities, other than an extensive range of walks and strolls around the spacious grounds. Nearby attractions include the city of Carlisle, including its imposing castle and famous cathedral (said to be one of the smallest in the world); the beautiful Galloway coast, or Scottish Borders, are only an hour or so away by car; the city of Edinburgh makes an excellent day trip if you have never visited Scotland; and, of course, the breathtaking Lake District all around you in Cumbria.

32

FALCON MANOR

Skipton Road, Settle, North Yorkshire BD24 9BD
Tel: 07292 3814

Nearest town Settle.
Directions Follow the A65 trunk road and the
hotel is at Settle, mid-way between Skipton
(sixteen miles) and Kendal.
A member of the **Consort Hotel** group of
independent hotels.
Awards AA *** RAC graded.
Good value half-board **special breaks** for two
days or more available all year round.
Open throughout the year.
*The hotel is suitable for disabled visitors; children and
dogs are welcome.*
Price for dinner, with wine, bed and breakfast for
two – under £100.
Credit cards Access, Visa and Diners Club.
Overall mark out of ten 7

Falcon Manor is not a Country House Hotel in the strictest
sense because of its location on the fringes of the bustling
market town of Settle. However, it does offer the standards of
comfort and cuisine which are a fair match to any rival hotel
in northern England. The hotel dates back to 1841 when it
was built as a private residence for the first vicar of the parish

of Settle after it had separated from the much older parish of Giggleswick. It became a hotel in 1926 and was requisitioned by the RAF during the Second World War. Present owners, Mr and Mrs Chris Riley, have owned and run Falcon Manor since 1978.

The imposing façade is a superb example of early Victorian architecture, its pointed cornices a legacy from Georgian times, though already showing the traditional solidity associated with Victorian. Everything about the house from the outside is as it was in the nineteenth century: the exterior has changed little in the last 450 years, but the interior has been completely modernized since the Rileys took over the hotel. When they first bought the property, neither the AA nor the RAC would consider the hotel worthy of even a one-star rating. The fact that Falcon Manor now holds three stars from both organizations is testament to the improvements which have taken place over the last decade or so.

The hotel's main bar, the Falconers' Bar, is one of the most popular up-market bars in Settle. Understandably non-residential custom is brisk because of the hotel's town centre location, but the preponderance of non-residents most evenings is a drawback only to those looking for a completely isolated break and, frankly, if getting away from it all to the point of seclusion is your main motive for taking a Country House break, then Falcon Manor is not for you.

The Inglefield Room is the public room where residents are likely to spend most time, and few can enjoy more than one meal in this palatial restaurant without falling in love with it. Its size feels beautifully out of proportion with the rest of the hotel, and it really is one of the most attractive public rooms of any hotel in northern England. As you walk through the grand-sized doorway, pause for a moment to admire the elegant muted orange tones on the walls, delicately bathed in a warm electric light which enhances the ornate pillars and long drapes. Take a few moments to enjoy the view across the hotel bowling green and gardens against the backdrop of craggy limestone fells. This sight at sunset is magnificent.

You will be delighted to discover that the quality of the

127

food, to say nothing of the efficient, courteous service, more than matches the surroundings. A fresh table d'hôte menu is available each evening, representing outstanding value at around £11 per head. It is not a gourmet's menu, and at that price it is hardly surprising, but it is uncomplicated, traditional English cooking at its best. Starters range from the standard to the subtle, from Smoked Salmon and Watermelon with Yoghurt Sauce to a delicious Cocktail of Prawn, Apple and Celery Panache with Cottage Cheese. The choice of a home-made soup or fruit juice follows before your main course, and for that you will have up to half a dozen choices. It was a disappointment to see nothing more adventurous than ome-lette 'with a filling of your choice' available for vegetarians, but meat-eaters can expect to be looked after considerably better. One highlight is the main course dish made up from Diamonds of Plaice in a White Wine and Chive Cream Sauce.

Falcon Manor has 21 bedrooms, including one marvellous twin room on the ground floor of the Coach House (the extension to the main building), which has been specially widened and adapted in order to meet the needs of a visitor confined to a wheelchair. Two of the four other bedrooms in the Coach House feature four-poster beds, and all 21 bedrooms in the hotel have private bathroom facilities, colour television, direct-dial telephone and a number of other trimmings asso-ciated with a quality hotel.

In addition to its own bowling green, the hotel can arrange for golf, fishing and horse riding nearby. Local attractions include Castleberg Rock, Malham Cove, Settle Market, Bolton Abbey, Ingleton Waterfalls, Langcliffe Tops, Gordale Scar, the White Scar caves and, for railway enthusiasts, the famous Carlisle to Settle railway, so often threatened with closure and yet still running a regular daily service.

33

HACKNESS GRANGE

North Yorks Moors National Park,
near Scarborough YO13 OJW
Tel: 0723 82345

Nearest town Scarborough.
Directions Follow the A64 from York and turn
left at Staxton roundabout. Continue until Seamer,
taking first left at roundabout there to village of
Ayton. Just past a garage on the left there is a
sharp right turn to Firge Valley and Hackness. Four
miles along this road turn left at T-junction and
the hotel is 400 yards down this road in the village
of Hackness.
A member of the **Best Western Hotels**
consortium.
Awards AA *** graded; Ashley Courtenay
recommended.
Open throughout the year.
Details of **special breaks** available on request
from the hotel.
The hotel is suitable for the disabled; children are
allowed, but dogs are not permitted.
Price for dinner, with wine, bed and breakfast for
two – £100–£150.
Credit cards All major cards accepted.
Overall mark out of ten 7

The most exceptional feature of this delightful Country House Hotel is its location. Hackness Grange is located in the picturesque Yorkshire village of Hackness, six miles inland in the North Yorks Moors. The hotel itself stands in eleven acres of private grounds on the banks of the River Derwent, enjoying fine views across the surrounding countryside, and is popular with nature-lovers and city-dwelling guests alike.

Hackness Grange was built near the beginning of the nineteenth century, and in 1890 the property was enlarged to be occupied by the second Lord Derwent, and subsequently by the Earl of Listowel. Extensive modernization has taken place over the last decade or so, and the result has sadly meant that much of the Victorian charm of the place has been replaced by concessions to modern comfort: plush wallpaper where wood panelling would have looked more in place, and so forth.

All the public rooms have blazing log fires during the winter months, adding to the warmth and enthusiasm which will greet you from the hotel staff. Throughout your stay, the management work hard to develop a house-party kind of atmosphere, something which naturally relies very much on the cooperation of the residents, but on the whole the atmosphere is convivial, relaxed and informal.

There are 26 bedrooms, all with *en suite* bathroom facilities, refrigerated minibars, colour television and so on. A number of rooms are a little lacking in character, and although all are individually styled, one or two of the twin rooms are fitted with rather modest-quality furnishings. One positive point about bedroom facilities is the fact that there are nine ground-floor bedrooms available, in the Courtyard Wing, which are ideal for disabled visitors.

Hackness Grange has a bright Regency-style dining-room, offering good views across the hotel lake and surrounding valley. The brown and gold striped decor is a little overpowering, but the thick drapes around the wide bay windows do neutralize the effect considerably. A full silver service is on offer, and a reasonable wine list complements the table d'hôte menu which offers four or five choices for each course nightly.

A number of wines are exported exclusively for the hotel and bottled on the estate. Pre-booking is essential during the summer months.

The menu restricts itself to traditional English cooking. Dishes are filling and wholesome, with few culinary surprises but at least three or four choices per course. Cheese and Pear Salad or Mushroom and Ham Pancakes are among the more original starters available. A sorbet or modest salad-style intermediate course follows, and that may include something like poached fillet of plaice or similar. Lamb, pork and sirloin steak all feature as main dishes and seafood vol-au-vents, more commonly seen as a starter, are occasionally available as a main dish. One luxury which shouldn't be missed, if possible, is the delicious Fresh Strawberry Pavlova to round off your meal. This dish is extremely popular, and positively overflows with fresh strawberries and cream — it is even available when strawberries are out of season.

The hotel has a small indoor heated swimming pool, and other leisure facilities include a nine-hole golf course, a pitch and putt area, croquet lawn, all-weather tennis court, and facilities for fishing on eleven miles of the River Derwent. For the real enthusiast, special game fishing weekends are occasionally available — details on request. Nearby attractions include Scarborough Castle (and the busy seaside resort of Scarborough itself), the North Yorkshire Moors Railway, Whitby Castle, the historic city of York with its famous Minster, still being lovingly restored after a serious fire in 1984, and, of course, the North Yorks Moors National Park all around you.

34

JERVAULX HALL

Ripon, North Yorkshire HG4 4PH
Tel: 0677 60235

Nearest town Masham.
Directions The hotel is fourteen miles from
Ripon, so follow the A6108 from Masham to
Middleham and you will find Jervaulx Hall next to
Jervaulx Abbey.
A member of the **Historic and Romantik** hotel
group.
Open from March until mid-November (except
for parties of eight persons or more).
Spring breaks available from time of March
opening until Easter.
The hotel is suitable for the disabled; children are
welcome, and dogs by prior arrangement, but they must
never be left alone in the bedrooms.
Price for dinner, with wine, bed and breakfast for
two – under £100.
Credit cards None accepted.
Overall mark out of ten 7

Beautifully secluded in the heart of the Yorkshire Dales, yet
only twenty minutes' drive from the main A1, Jervaulx Hall

has achieved an enviable combination of rural charm and homely luxury. It sits on the edge of the Dales National Park, an area of 680 square miles containing some of the most spectacular scenery in northern England.

Despite the hotel's ancient name, taken from the adjoining Jervaulx Abbey which dates back to 1156, the house was built no earlier than the middle of the last century by the Earl of Ailesbury. He wanted a manor house on his 10,000-acre estate and could find no better site than that adjacent to the ruined twelfth-century abbey whose crumbling walls, even in the 1850s, were a veritable riot of brightly coloured marjoram and sunflowers.

The eight-acre garden surrounding the hotel is sheltered from the winds by a tree-covered mound to the north. The main lawn faces south and enjoys the best views across the old abbey and encircling Jervaulx Park. The remainder of the hotel's garden consists of a range of grassed walks and woodland paths which are almost entirely on level ground, offering a good range of strolls and wanders before dinner or after Sunday lunch.

Inside, the hotel has retained much of the informal private house atmosphere which distinguished it in the days before it became a hotel. Both reception rooms have open fires when the weather dictates, and are deliberately furnished in a manner which looks – and feels – more like a private drawing-room than a public lounge. The emphasis is on informality throughout the hotel.

The dining-room has a soft apricot decor, and a period blue carpet which creates a restful blend of colours. Non-residents are welcome but not encouraged, so one or two days' notice should be given. Dinner is served promptly at eight each evening; there is a single sitting, and you must be down for dinner at least thirty minutes beforehand to place your order. More flexibility of timing would be very welcome, particularly since however long you choose to stay here, dinner, bed and breafkast are included in your tariff. No allowance is made if you want to stay for just bed and breakfast, although the cost of dinner will be deducted from a stay of several nights if you decide to eat elsewhere on one occasion.

Dinner is chosen from a limited set menu, from which there is a choice of just two or three dishes for each course (plus a vegetable risotto or similar for vegans). The food is simple English fare, opening with something like a Salmon Mousse or Chicken Liver Pâté, and followed by Roast Leg of Lamb or Haddock Barrie with a selection of vegetables. In keeping with the style and informal atmosphere of the hotel as a whole, the wine list is very limited. Neither the gourmet nor the wine connoisseur should consider Jervaulx Hall unless they plan a weekend 'off duty', but for those looking for a more simple kind of English comfort, then this might be the place for you.

Jervaulx Hall has eight bedrooms, all doubles including one ground-floor room opening on to the garden which is suitable for disabled or elderly visitors, or those with dogs. All rooms are spacious and individually furnished and have private bathrooms and shower. All eight have tea- and coffee-making facilities, but the usual luxuries of colour television and direct-dial telephone have been dispensed with in an attempt to ensure residents' holiday breaks really are a completely relaxing 'switch-off'.

The hotel has no leisure facilities of its own, but riding and pony trekking are available at Masham. Golf courses are located at Masham and Bedale, and fishing can be enjoyed locally as well. Nearby attractions include Jervaulx Abbey itself, Middleham Castle, Castle Bolton, Newby Hall, Castle Howard, Bramham Park, Fountains Abbey, Beamish Museum, and the towns of Ripon, Harrogate, Richmond, Helmsley, Durham and, of course, the historic city of York.

35

KILDWICK HALL

Kildwick, near Skipton, North Yorkshire BD20 9AE
Tel: 0535 32244

Nearest town Skipton.
Directions Kildwick Hall is three miles south of
Skipton. From there, travel along the A629
towards Keighley. From Keighley A650 to
Kildwick roundabout in Kildwick and right at the
White Lion. Turn left at top of hill.
Awards AA *** graded; RAC ***; Egon Ronay
and Michelin recommended.
Open throughout the year.
Special breaks of at least two consecutive nights,
half-board, are available all year round.
The hotel is not suitable for disabled visitors; children
and dogs are welcome.
Price for dinner, with wine, bed and breakfast for
two – £100–£150.
Credit cards Access, Visa, Amex and Diners
Club.
Overall mark out of ten 7.5

Kildwick Hall lies three miles south of the Yorkshire town of
Skipton, often called the Gateway to the Dales. It is a stately
old house, with its origins in the early seventeenth century

when it was built by the Currer family. The Currers had close connections with the Brontë family, whose literary genius in the nineteenth century has put them among the most renowned former residents of this lovely part of England.

Emily Brontë, probably the most famous member of the family, used the pseudonym 'Currer Bell' on her published works in order to disguise the fact that she was a woman, women authors being frowned upon in highly conservative early Victorian society. A member of the Currer family who still owned Kildwick Hall in the last century used to be Emily's teacher and it was from this connection that the first half of her pseudonym originated. The more common 'Bell' surname is believed to have been inspired by the old bell which still hangs over the side entrance to the present hotel to which Emily was a frequent visitor.

The hotel today still has the imposing Jacobean façade which distinguished it in earlier centuries. A weather-beaten coat of arms is sculpted into the red brickwork above the main door, and two huge stone lions stand guard nearby. Inside, the public rooms are large and rather formal. They have lost rather too little of their period 'stiffness' and as a result can feel a bit austere. The dining-room, though, is an outstanding example of a traditional English restaurant where formality and discreet personal service are very much part of the enjoyment. Your break at Kildwick Hall can, of course, be as formal or informal as you choose, but for many guests it is precisely for this atmosphere that they come here year after year.

Polished wood panelling dominates the lounge, and richly ornate plasterwork adorns the dining-room. The decor is 'busy', with an assortment of oil paintings never failing to catch the eye wherever you glance. French modern cuisine is served from an impressive à la carte menu, and the hotel's growing reputation as one of northern England's best kitchens is not difficult to understand. Kildwick Hall also has a particularly well-stocked cellar.

All evening meals begin with a small complimentary appetizer which changes nightly – a very pleasant little consideration. Hors d'oeuvres proper include a comprehensive range of

French specialities, all explained in considerable detail to reflect the painstaking amount of time and effort which has gone into their preparation.

The cuisine is very imaginative and the menu changes monthly. At the time of going to press one of the favourite main dishes is Fresh Breast of French Duckling, roasted in Fresh Garlic, served on a bed of sugared limes and lemons and accompanied by a light Madeira sauce.

Kildwick Hall has sixteen bedrooms, including four large Honeymoon Suites which are extremely popular with newly-weds and romantic couples with memories to celebrate. All the rooms have private bathroom facilities, and two have four-posters. Advance booking is recommended especially if you want to be sure of a Honeymoon Suite.

The hotel has close links with Ilkley Tennis Club, which has indoor and grass courts available, and golf can be enjoyed at a number of local courses through personal introductions by the hotel management. Croquet can be played within the hotel grounds, and horse riding can also be arranged nearby.

Nearby attractions are plentiful, with the most obvious being the magnificent Yorkshire Dales right on your doorstep. Haworth, the area in which the Brontë family lived, is just fifteen minutes drive away, and also within easy reach by car are Skipton Castle, Ilkley and the surrounding Ilkley Moor, the cities of Leeds and Bradford, and the beautiful Lake District within an hour's drive.

36

KIRKBY FLEETHAM HALL

Kirkby Fleetham, Northallerton, North Yorkshire DL7 OSU
Tel: 0609 748226

Nearest town Northallerton.
Directions From the A1, follow signs to Kirkby
Fleetham, about eight miles south of Scotch
Corner. From the village follow a small sign on the
green to 'Kirkby Hall' and the hotel is one mile
north of the village, by the church.
Awards AA *** graded; British Tourist Authority
commended; Egon Ronay 76%; Michelin and
Ashley Courtenay recommended.
No **special breaks**.
*The hotel is not suitable for the disabled; dogs accepted
only by prior arrangement, and only 'well-behaved'
children allowed.*
Price for dinner, with wine, bed and breakfast for
two – £100–£150.
Credit cards Visa and Amex.
Overall mark out of ten 9

Easily one of the best Country House Hotels in northern
England, Kirkby Fleetham Hall has received generous commendation from practically every major British hotel association and guide in the eight years or so it has been open. Much

of this is due to the skill and shrewd business acumen of former marketing man David Grant who recognized potential in the near-derelict old building in 1980. If anything, the hard work he and wife Chris have lavished on the hotel has increased as the reputation of Kirkby Fleetham Hall has grown, with the result that guests can be assured of an enthusiastic personal welcome and first-class service throughout their stay here.

The Manor of Kirkby dates back to before the Norman Conquest of England in 1066. Originally it grew up as a Viking settlement on the banks of the River Swale and in the Domesday Book, in 1086, it was revealed that the manor was then held by one Alfred the Saxon. The estate passed through the hands of several families, including that of Sir Nicholas Stapleton, a knight of the great crusading Order of the Templars who died in 1290. The present house dates back as far as 1600 when the Smelt family built a small manor house that was enlarged considerably towards the end of the seventeenth century.

In 1740 the estate was sold to John Aislabie who, with his son William, improved the gardens considerably, adding both the present lake and terracing, and making cost-effective agricultural units out of the surrounding estate farms. Descendants of the family owned the house up until the end of the last century, and new owners made a number of major structural improvements. Sadly, the interior was allowed to deteriorate in the second half of this century to such a point that the house was completely run down by 1980, although painstaking effort on the part of David and Chris Grant has saved the building.

There is a fine dividing line between a Country House Hotel and a larger house which is now a luxury hotel that happens to be in the country. Yet if any hotel in this guide had to be nominated as the one which bridged the two definitions, then Kirkby Fleetham would have to be it. The public rooms are elegantly furnished without being ostentatious, and the Grants have deliberately avoided the use of the words 'bar' or 'reception' for any of them. Instead drinks are served in the spacious sitting-room, and reception formalities conducted at a huge antique writing desk. Informal luxury is the order of the day throughout the hotel.

The traditional dining-room at Kirkby Fleetham is not one of the leading Country House restaurants in Britain, but it does offer some of the highest standards of cuisine within the middle- to upper-class hotel bracket. Quality modern British-style food is served in relaxing surroundings, on fine Wedgwood china, and accompanied by a refreshingly informative wine list which helpfully tells non-connoisseurs a little about the most impressive range of wines available.

Chris Grant supervises the kitchen personally while David mingles with guests. Meals are ordered from a table d'hôte menu which changes nightly, and consists of a soup, a choice of three starters, then a choise of three main courses, and finally a choice from about seven sweets. A typical menu includes delicious specialities such as maize-fed chicken, lightly sautéd then flamed in Pernod, adding just a hint of aniseed to the dish.

Kirkby Fleetham Hall has fifteen bedrooms, all quite distinctly furnished in a refreshing period style, and all very spacious. Fresh flowers and antique fittings enhance the more modern comforts, such as private bathroom facilities, colour television and direct-dial telephones, which earlier occupants of the house did not have the opportunity to enjoy. All round, this hotel is delightfully different in so many little ways that it is not hard to see why virtually every guide book published has included it.

Most outdoor and indoor sports are available locally. As David Grant rather succinctly puts it: 'We stick to being a Country House and not a sports centre or a health farm. I feel so strongly about this that I do not do such things as wedding receptions because they destroy the tranquillity of the place.' Nearby attractions include James Herriot country (the North Yorkshire moors and dales), Castle Howard, Harewood House, and the cities of Durham and York.

37

MALLYAN SPOUT

Goathland, Whitby, Yorkshire YO22 5AN
Tel: 0947 86206

Nearest town Whitby.
Directions The hotel is located nine miles from
the coastal town of Whitby and ten miles from the
market town of Pickering. It is signposted two
miles off the main road between the two.
Awards Egon Ronay and Ashley Courtenay
recommended.
Open throughout the year.
Special breaks Two-day (or longer) special half-
board rates apply all year round.
*The hotel is unsuitable for disabled visitors; children
and dogs are welcome.*
Price for dinner, with wine, bed and breakfast for
two – under £100.
Credit cards Visa, Amex and Diners Club.
Overall mark out of ten 6.5

Mallyan Spout is an appealing little hotel lying about 40 miles
north-east of the historic city of York. Its rather unusual name
comes from a small waterfall which flows into a wooded valley
just a short walk below the hotel. Unlike virtually every other
Country House Hotel included in this guide, Mallyan Spout
has never been a private residence. It was built during the last

years of the nineteenth century as a small hotel, and despite several changes of owner and minor alterations has operated as a hotel ever since.

The exterior of the building is almost completely covered by dense green ivy; only a small corner of red brickwork can still be seen on the façade, and even the main chimney stack at the right-hand end of the building is obscured. Wherever you go in the hotel, you can see that this house was purpose-built. The public areas, of just the correct proportions, remain simply but comfortably furnished, with velvet armchairs and an interesting selection of old prints rather haphazardly arranged all over the walls. A portrait of Sir Winston Churchill dominates the wall above the smoke-stained stone fireplace in the main living-room.

The simple comfort which typifies Mallyan Spout is retained in the dining-room, which overlooks the garden and can seat up to 60 people. The room is modern in design and decor, with one or two clashes of style, like the all too obvious radiator beneath an ornate gold-framed mirror (which even features in the hotel's brochure) and the crystal-like chandeliers against an uncomplicated plain ceiling, but the overall effect is pleasing.

Mallyan does its utmost to cater for guests' individual requirements at dinner, and concentrates on providing good home-produced food made from fresh local produce. The chef's speciality is fresh Whitby fish which is bought direct from the quay at Whitby Bay. A set menu and a modest à la carte menu are available each evening, both with an emphasis on fish, and two of the highlights from the set menu include a delicious Mallyan Seafood Terrine to start with (a mousse of local whiting, monk fish, and salmon caviar, all served with a tangy mayonnaise), followed by Whole Grilled Lemon Sole with Parsley Butter. Two popular highlights from the à la carte menu are Breast of Chicken, filled with Herb and Garlic Butter and panfried, and Butterfried Moorland Trout, served with Nut-Brown Butter and Almonds. The choice of wines is reasonable, but the house white at around £6 a bottle is excellent value.

Mallyan has 22 bedrooms, all with television and private bathrooms facilities. The rooms are simply furnished and have few of the little extras which tend to make Country House Hotels that bit special — such as quality toiletries, a bowl of fruit, and so on. A number of the rooms are rather small, the main exceptions being the deliberately larger doubles which also serve as family rooms. However, most have glorious views across the surrounding Yorkshire countryside which is a reasonable consolation.

The hotel does not have any leisure facilities to speak of, but golf, tennis, sea and freshwater fishing and horse riding can be arranged locally. Mallyan emphasizes the fact that it is an ideal centre for people to come just to relax, get away from town or city life, and enjoy the rural beauty of the surrounding countryside. And indeed it is. The local tourist authority produces a very detailed brochure containing details of things to see in the immediate area. Nearby attractions include the rugged coastline and resorts of Scarborough and Whitby, and the city of York.

38

MIDDLETHORPE HALL

Bishopthorpe Road, York YO2 1QP
Tel: 0904 641241

Nearest town York.
Directions Middlethorpe Hall is situated 1.5 miles outside York, alongside York racecourse. From the south by car, Middlethorpe is reached by following the signs 'North' on the M1, and M18, A1 (M), A1 and A64, leaving at the exit marked 'York/West A1036, racecourse and Bishopthorpe'. A member of the **Prestige Hotels** consortium.
Awards AA *** (red) graded and rosette for food; RAC Blue Ribbon; British Tourist Authority commendation; Queen's Award to Industry for Export Achievement 1987.
Open throughout the year.
Special breaks Two-day half-board Champagne Breaks available from November until March.
The hotel is not suitable for the disabled; children under eight years and dogs not permitted.
Price for dinner, with wine, bed and breakfast for two – over £150.

Credit cards Access, Visa, Amex and Diners
Club.
Overall mark out of ten 9.5

With its magnificent location just one and a half miles from
the historic city of York, overlooking York racecourse, Middlethorpe Hall was the second decaying old manor house to be
rescued by Historic House Hotels and transformed into a truly
first-class luxury Country House Hotel within the space of a
decade. The other one, Bodysgallen Hall, is located in north
Wales and also featured in this guide.

Middlethorpe was positively wrested from the hands of
vandals when bought in 1980. The previous owners had
turned it into a 1960s nightclub. Paint was layered over the
oak panels, disco lights erected on the cornices, and the
seventeenth-century walls resounded to the blare of pop.
Numerous acts of architectural vandalism had to be undone
in lengthy and expensive operations before the glories of this
magnificent home could again be enjoyed in 1984. Thankfully
they were, and the end result is one of Britain's finest Country
House Hotels.

Although a few outbuildings date back to the 1680s, and
traces of timbers going back as far as a couple of centuries
before that have been found, the main structure of Middlethorpe Hall was built in 1699 by local industrialist Thomas
Barlow. He was not spared long to enjoy his attractive new
property as he died whilst on a Grand Tour of Europe with his
son in 1713.

From the moment visitors to Middlethorpe Hall are greeted
at the door by the uniformed doormen on their arrival at the
hotel, they invariably get the impression that time has stood
still – an impression which lingers throughout their stay. The
hotel is exceptionally well maintained, and the public rooms
resemble those tantalizing rooms in a stately home where
you'd love to sit down but are never allowed to because of
infuriating rope cordons.

The large main drawing-room is a positive treat, with its
elegant crystal chandelier and oil portraits all around. This is

where pre-dinner drinks are served by the footmen. Whatever room you are in, little touches like potted plants and open magazines make it feel so much more like a home than a hotel. The staff are discreet but attentive; nothing is ever too much trouble at Middlethorpe.

The hotel has two restaurants, the main Dining Room on the ground floor, the more formal of the two with magnificent views overlooking the gardens, and the Grill Room downstairs. Reservations are compulsory, dress must be formal, and ten days to a fortnight are recommended for advance bookings to be sure of a table. The Grill Room serves a three-course table d'hôte menu, representing a more traditional approach to the bill of fare, and a pianist provides a gentle background music most evenings.

For some of the finest gourmet cooking in northern England a visit to the main Dining Room really is a must. Guests have the choice of a four-course gourmet meal or a selection from the extensive à la carte menu. Exquisite sauces enliven even the most traditional of dishes, and more luxurious options, such as lobster and prime sirloin of beef, are cooked to perfection by chef Kevin Francksen. Particularly recommended are the Veal Kidneys, grilled and sliced, and served with Honey and Lemon Sauce on Creamed Endive. Whatever your choice, the presentation and style of service are impeccable. An extensive wine list is available, although the only real minus point so far as the main Dining Room is concerned is the fact that some of the more common wines are a little overpriced.

Middlethorpe Hall has 31 bedrooms, eleven in the main house, the rest in the adjacent eighteenth-century stable courtyard or beautifully restored Gardener's Cottage. All are individually designed, and the standard of furnishings, attention to detail and overall quality are outstanding. Each room has colour television, direct-dial telephone and its own bathroom facilities, complete with brass fittings, wooden toilet seats and high-quality toiletries.

The house is set in 26 acres of secluded woodland and garden, offering endless possibilities for evening strolls or, for the less energetic, a croquet lawn is available. Golf, horse riding and fishing can also be arranged nearby. Nearby attractions are numerous, although the most obvious is historic York with its famous Minster, narrow little streets and crowded antique shops. Other places of interest are Castle Howard, architecturally one of the most splendid houses in England, Beningborough Hall (a National Trust property), Selby Abbey, Fountains Abbey (one of the most important medieval abbeys in Europe) and Newby Hall, with its remarkable interiors crafted by Robert Adam in the late eighteenth century.

39

PEACOCK HOTEL

Rowsley, Matlock, Derbyshire DE4 2EB
Tel: 0629 733518

Nearest town Bakewell.
Directions Follow the A6, heading to or from
Manchester. The hotel is located just off the A6
shortly before you reach Bakewell (or just after if
you are travelling from Manchester).
A member of the **Embassy Hotels** group.
Awards AA *** RAC graded; British Tourist
Authority commended.
Open throughout the year.
Special breaks Hushaway Breaks, Businessman's
Rates, and half-board special rates for two nights
or more are available.
The hotel is unsuitable for disabled visitors; children are
welcome, as are dogs, but only on the understanding
that both are well behaved.
Price for dinner, with wine, bed and breakfast for
two – £100–£150.
Credit cards Access, Visa, Amex and Diners Club.
Overall mark out of ten 7.5

Although you are unlikely to see many of the peacocks today
which gave the Peacock Hotel its name, you can be assured of

a welcome at least as enthusiastic as that which has greeted visitors over the last century and a half that this solid old seventeenth-century manor house has been operating as a hotel.

Dating back to 1652, when local magnate John Stephenson decided to build himself a new manor house, the Peacock has been fashioned in a semi-Tudor style which was already considered old-fashioned in southern England by the mid-seventeenth century. After Stephenson's death the house became a farm for a while before someone, in 1820, recognized its potential to be turned into an early Country House Hotel – as opposed to an inn which happened to be in the country.

In its early days, the Peacock was popular because of the bathing in the nearby River Wye, which was said to have a beneficial effect on one's health. Long after the advent of transatlantic air travel, visitors from the United States used to come over to England for a couple of months in order to visit the hotel. Among its more famous visitors in the last century were the poet Longfellow and the ill-fated Emperor Maximilian of Mexico who spent one night here in 1867, shortly before his death.

The hotel's public rooms have been considerably renovated since the last century, and in many respects the move towards comfortable lounge chairs and central heating has meant that a little too much of the original hotel's nineteenth-century charm has been lost forever. The move towards greater conference trade has eroded the tranquillity that little bit more – although rest assured, this is anything but a noisy hotel.

Up to 45 can be seated in the hotel's intimate dining-room, which is easily the Peacock's most appealing public room. The decor is of soft colours, elegantly contrasted with traditional English oak tables and chairs made by the carpenter Robert Thompson. The table d'hôte menu is prepared daily and has a good selection of British Country House-style dishes. Quality starters include a delicious Smoked Fish Mousse, slightly flavoured with Worcester Sauce and Dill, moulded into a Creamy White Wine and Dill Sauce; and several outsized

149

Prawns served in their shell with a small Seasonal Salad and a pot of Garlic Mayonnaise.

Main dishes are generally accompanied by a rich, home-made sauce which really is an integral part of the meal, but of course this is not to everyone's liking and the chef notes on the menu that main dishes can be served without the usual sauce if so desired. Scottish salmon, roast venison, and a mint-enhanced pink-served double loin of lamb are among the wholesome options available most evenings.

The sweet course can be selected from a separate, folded postcard-style menu which has a lovely old sepia photograph of the hotel such as it was in the last century. From half a dozen suggestions, one delicious speciality of the chef stands out. Fresh Whole Strawberries, gently warmed in a Grand Marnier Syrup and arranged on to a round plate before being served with a ball of Vanilla Ice-Cream and sprinkled with Zest of Orange.

The Peacock Hotel has 20 bedrooms, although surprisingly only fifteen have private bath or shower facilities. All rooms have tea- and coffee-making facilities together with colour television, although in most cases this is a portable-size set. The style of decor varies from room to room, and most have at least one or two pieces of antique furniture as a reminder of more restful times when the old manor house first became a hotel.

Nearby attractions include Chatsworth, the stately home of the Duke and Duchess of Devonshire; the River Dove, an area so loved by Isaac Walton; the nearby graveyard, one of the most peaceful places in northern England and containing the graves of many famous people including President John F. Kennedy's sister, and Mary Queen of Scots' loyal chamberlain; Hardwick Hall, reckoned to be the crowning achievement of the infamous Bess of Hardwick who is buried nearby; and Haddon Hall, a restored medieval manor owned by the Duke of Rutland.

40

RIVERSIDE

Fennel Street, Ashford-in-the-Water, Bakewell,
Derbyshire DE4 1QF
Tel: 062981 4275

Nearest town Bakewell.
Directions From Bakewell, follow the A6 for
about two miles to the village of Ashford-in-the-
Water. The hotel is at the top of the main street.
Awards British Tourist Authority commended;
English Tourist Board four Crowns; recommended
in Egon Ronay and Michelin guides.
Open throughout the year.
Bargain breaks for two nights or longer; half-
board is available all year.
The hotel is not suitable for the disabled; children are
welcome, by arrangement; only small dogs allowed, and
then by prior arrangement at the proprietors' discretion.
Price for dinner, with wine, bed and breakfast for
two – around £100.
Credit cards Access, Visa and Amex.
Overall mark out of ten 7.5

Situated in the middle of the Peak District National Park, the
Riverside Country House lies amid an array of quaint cottages
in the attractive little Derbyshire hamlet of Ashford-in-the-
Water. The hotel has an ageless feeling about it, and is set in

an acre of mature garden with much of its exterior covered by dense green ivy. The gardens lead down to the River Wye, and there can be few more peaceful pre-dinner strolls in this part of northern England than the short walk from the rear of the hotel down to the water's edge.

Parts of the main building date back to the mid-seventeenth century, but it is essentially a typical Georgian-style Country House. Resident proprietors Roger and Sue Taylor take pride in the attentive personal service on offer at the Riverside. Both dining-rooms, the sitting-room and the cocktail bar are tastefully furnished in a traditional modern decor which, refreshingly, has not tried to emulate any given period style, with the result that guests can sit back and relax in timeless comfort. The main sitting-room has long windows and the view stretches down to the river, overlooking the garden.

Great care has been taken, however, to ensure that all the hotel's original beams, together with the polished oak panelling which adorns most of the public area, have been carefully preserved and looked after. Roger Taylor himself has taken charge of all the recent renovation work to ensure that the comfortable and elegant interior which distinguished the house when it was a private residence is altered as little as possible.

There are two dining-rooms, both furnished with polished antique tables, and the main restaurant can seat up to 40, of which a maximum of fourteen are residents at any one time. A Regency-style crystal chandelier dominates the room, and the use of silver cutlery and quality chinaware enhances the exceptionally high standard of cuisine at the Riverside. This is one of the most popular places to eat out in northern England, so advance booking by at least a week or two really is essential.

The ever-changing menu is very imaginatively presented, and the style is distinctly *nouvelle cuisine*. Two favourite starters are Fresh Mushrooms Stuffed with home-made Duck Liver Pâté, deep fried in batter; and fresh Chilled Watermelon dusted with Ground Black Pepper served with Quenelles of home-made Smoked Salmon Sorbet and garnished with Lemon and Cucumber.

Main dishes are no less imaginative and include Carved Roast Breast of Goose, stretched out on a bed of Crispy Stuffing made from Apples, Sultanas, Bacon and Thyme, all complimented by a tangy Juniper Berry Sauce garnished with Segments of Citrus Fruits. If local game is a dish you enjoy, then one of chef Jeremy Buckingham's favourite dishes is a delicious combination of rabbit, hare, pheasant, steak and kidney all cooked in Guinness and topped in pastry before being served with a rich gravy.

At present the hotel has seven bedrooms, five individually styled doubles and two twins, although there are plans to have a further nine rooms available within the next year or two. The bedrooms really are a delight, each one with its own antique bed, and a number have either four-posters or half-testers which are draped in fine Nottingham lace. All have private bathroom facilities, complete with antique brass and gold fittings, together with the more modern conveniences of colour television, direct-dial telephones and high-quality furnishings.

The Riverside really is an ideal place to escape to for that special break. The hotel doesn't go overboard with special sporting facilities, but if you are keen to indulge in some gentle exercise then golf, fishing, shooting and guided walks can be arranged quite easily. For nature-lovers the Peak District National Park is all around, but other nearby attractions include Chatsworth, the stately home of the Duke and Duchess of Devonshire, Haddon Hall, Hardwick Hall and the historic city of Derby 40 miles away.

41

ROOKHURST

Gayle, Hawes, North Yorkshire DL8 3RT
Tel: 09697 454

Nearest town Hawes.
Directions Leave either the M6 or the A1 when
you see signposts for the A684. Rookhurst is
located half a mile south of the little town of
Hawes, midway between the two main roads.
Awards Voted Hotel of the Year 1987 by Les
Routiers members; British Tourist Authority
commended; Ashley Courteney recommended.
Open throughout the year – but weekends only
from January until March.
Special **winter breaks** available.
The hotel is unsuitable for the disabled; children are
welcome but dogs are not allowed. No smoking in the
bedrooms or restaurant.
Price for dinner, with wine, bed and breakfast for
two – under £100.
Credit cards Amex only.
Overall mark out of ten 9

When the combined membership of the prestigious Les Routiers organization voted Rookhurst Hotel of the Year in 1987,
they recognized a small Country House Hotel of outstanding

class. Resident owners Brian and Susan Jutsum have worked hard to develop and maintain a reputation for luxurious country comfort, and Rookhurst's superb location in the tiny hamlet of Gayle on the edge of the Yorkshire Dales does much to enhance the traditional appeal of the hotel.

Rookhurst looks like a solid old manor house but, in fact, it was originally built as a farmhouse in 1670. An exterior stone inscription bears the date 1734, but recent research has revealed that this was when most of the internal walls, wood panelling and the rear of the house were added. For a couple of centuries the old farmhouse was known as the West End House, and was owned by the Whaley family whose local origins date back to the early fifteenth century.

The house was derelict for a couple of generations prior to 1869 when barrister Henry Whaley retired from the City of London and found that he 'required a residence in Gayle befitting his position'. He commissioned a firm of local builders to add the present eastern wing to the house, in a grand Victorian neo-Gothic style which turned out to be quite unique to the Yorkshire Dales. Henry Whaley also adoped the name Rookhurst, and his family remained in the house until 1973.

The house lay in disrepair until 1984 when the Jutsums bought it and, since then, they have worked hard to restore Rookhurst back to its original charm and interior splendour. All the public rooms are furnished with antiques; the decor is discreet and the atmosphere relaxed. The view across the gardens from the large bay window in the main lounge has changed little over the last couple of centuries, and the charm of the place remains as strong as ever.

The dining-room is run by Brian Jutsum and is small and informal, and it is here that the attentive personal service which attracts many visitors to Rookhurst really comes into its own. Susan Jutsum herself takes charge of the kitchen, and since 1984 has developed a unique style of cooking that is as cosmopolitan as it is original. No particular style of cuisine is adhered to, French, English, *nouvelle cuisine* or whatever, but the result is an exciting table d'hôte menu (excellent value at

155

around £12 per head for non-residents) which changes nightly.

A typical meal would open with a starter like Pasta Shells Stuffed with Fresh Salmon Mousse, or Fresh Pear with Tarragon Mayonnaise. The main course can be chosen from about three or four options, unfortunately offering nothing specifically for vegetarians, but including specialities like Fillet Steak topped with Blue Stilton, or Fillet of Plaice Stuffed with Spinach and served with a Veronique Sauce. Vegetarian meals are available on request.

Rookhurst opened with six bedrooms, but by the time of publication there will be nine, as a new East Wing is built on to the original farmhouse part of the hotel. An additional dining-room and public lounge should also be in operation by then as well. All the bedrooms have private bathrooms and colour television and have been furnished in an individual style, with authentic period furniture, either Georgian or Victorian. The Georgian rooms are smaller than the spacious Victorian rooms, but the effect is intimate rather than cramped. All rooms have antique or unusual beds. One double has a brass four-poster, and another room has a magnificent walnut four-poster which dates from the end of the eighteenth century. The Bridal Suite has the additional luxury of an authentic Royal Doulton bathroom suite, with its original brass and mahogany fittings, which dates back to 1903.

The owners have deliberately tried not to alter the original charm of Rookhurst by adding a plethora of leisure facilities; quite simply, peace and quiet are the main attractions of the hotel. Most sporting facilities – golf, shooting, sailing, hill-walking and even pot-holing or hang-gliding – can be arranged locally. Other nearby attractions include Middleham, once home to the famous English usurper, Richard III; Jervaulx Abbey; Barnard Castle; Bolton Abbey; the Carlisle to Settle railway; and the historic towns and cities of York, Ripon, Harrogate and Appleby.

42

ROWLEY MANOR

Little Weighton, near Hull, North Humberside HU20 3XR
Tel: 0482 848248

Nearest town Beverley.
Directions From the M62, follow the A63 until
the junction signposted for Beverley. Head for the
village of South Cave, and turn right at staggered
junction opposite clock tower. Follow the road up
through trees, go across Riplingham crossroads and
take next left. The hotel is signposted just at the
top of a steep bend.
Awards AA and RAC *** graded; recommended
by Egon Ronay and Ashley Courtenay guides.
Open throughout the year.
Weekend breaks are available all year round.
The hotel is not suitable for disabled visitors; children
and dogs are welcome
Price for dinner, with wine, bed and breakfast for
two – under £100.
Credit cards Access, Visa, Amex and Diners
Club.
Overall mark out of ten 8

Set in 34 acres of lawns, parkland and beautifully kept rose
gardens, Rowley Manor is an extremely attractive Georgian

building in the heart of the Yorkshire Wolds. It provides a perfect haven from many of the stresses of the modern world, combined with the comforts of a well-appointed Country House Hotel in an extremely attractive part of northern England.

Rowley Manor began life in the early seventeenth century as an old rectory for the small church which can still be seen in the grounds today. The busy life of the parish came to an abrupt end later that century when the rector persuaded all his parishioners to join him on the long voyage to Massachusetts, then one of the flourishing new emigration centres of the American colonies. Once there, he and the survivors established the settlement which became known as Rowley Massachusetts. In later years Rowley Manor was to become the home of Philmer Wilson, a senior member of the family which established the Ellerman Wilson Shipping Line.

All the public rooms are furnished in period style, with antiques wherever possible. The main lounge is wood panelled all round and has an elaborate carved fireplace which forms a magnificent frame to the roaring log fire during the colder winter months. Gold-framed oil portraits adorn the walls, and subtle lighting creates a marvellously informal atmosphere in which to sit back and relax with an after-dinner coffee or liqueur.

The dining-room is the largest public room and has a very traditional decor, with period-style furniture and solid polished wooden doors which contrast well with the darker wallpapered walls. Wood panelling frames the fireplaces and, as with the main lounge, a number of original oil paintings finish off the room splendidly. Up to 80 can be served at once and Rowley Manor's dining-room is extremely popular with non-residents in a ratio of approximately three to one. The management recommends at least a week's advance booking.

Rowley Manor specializes in serving fine fresh English cuisine, and Head Chef Leonard Bourne's fine à la carte menu is presented on thick parchment-type paper held together by a red ribbon. There are about fifteen starters to choose from, ranging from the standard selection of fruit juices and seafood cocktails to more elaborate dishes like Courgettes filled with Savoury Mince, and an exquisite plate of Smoked Salmon Cornets filled with Prawns and Crabmeat, served in a subtle Mousseline Sauce.

Half a dozen fish choices follow, and you may prefer a dish of King Prawns served in Garlic Butter, or even a large grilled Halibut Steak covered with a Tomato, Asparagus and White Wine Sauce as a main dish rather than a fish course. Before making up your mind, do at least have a read through the detailed list of main dishes proper. There are generally about 20 main dishes available, including at least half a dozen steaks ranging from a massive 1lb T-bone to a more manageable sirloin cooked in garlic. Other options include traditional English specialities like duckling, venison, honey roast lamb and loin of pork, and there is also a small range of vegetarian dishes available at a very reasonable set price which compare favourably with the meat dishes.

Rowley Manor has sixteen bedrooms, although by the time of publication four luxury courtyard suites should be completed. All but three rooms are double or twin-bedded, and all have private bathroom facilities, colour television, complimentary toiletries and direct-dial telephone. As an added bonus, all the rooms have good views across the surrounding 34 acres of private estate attached to the hotel, and a number have antique four-posters to add that little extra to a special break.

The hotel's only leisure facility is a solarium, although most common sports such as golf and fishing can be arranged locally, and other nearby attractions are numerous. These include the town of Beverley, with its superb old Minster, the Museum of Army Transport, Skidby Windmill, Hull Marine and Maritime Heritage Centre, Spurn Point, the magnificent Humber Bridge just ten minutes' drive away, and the cities of Hull and York within an easy drive.

43

SCALE HILL HOTEL

Loweswater, Cockermouth, Cumbria CA13 9UX
Tel: 090085 232

Nearest town Keswick.
Directions Easiest access is from the M6, junction 40 onto the A66 west. Bypass Keswick. At Braithwaite take B5292 over Whinlatter to Lorton. Join B5289 south to Loweswater.
Open throughout the year, except January and February.
Two ground floor rooms for disabled visitors; children welcome; dogs allowed, but not in public rooms.
Price for dinner, with wine, bed and breakfast for two – under £100.
Credit cards none accepted.
Overall mark out of ten 6.5

Nestling in the Loweswater–Buttermere valley, Scale Hill, the main part of which dates from 1620, originated as a farmhouse, but has been an inn for most of its life. It was well known as a stopping-off place on the route to West Cumberland, and its reputation for comfortable accommodation and good, wholesome food has changed little in the past 350 years.

Encircled by the North Western fells, and in close proximity to Low Fell (1360 ft) and Grassmoor (2791 ft), Scale Hill offers easy access and is an excellent touring base from which one can explore the central Lake District, and also the lesser known but equally beautiful Ennerdale and Wastwater Valleys, Cumbrian Coast, Border country and Roman Wall. As a Country House Hotel, this is one of the least pretentious in this guide. It is not a crystal- and silver-type place, and it must not be compared to the likes of Middlethorpe or Cliveden, but it is included here because it offers a superb setting for a country break in quiet and secluded surroundings, with very good food and wine, and at a very reasonable cost.

The hotel has been in the same family for over 50 years, and it is very much a family concern. Sheila Thompson and daughter, Heather, prepare the food, while Michael and daughter, Hazel, take care of 'front of house'. The family atmosphere pervades the hotel and the friendliness and relaxed pace of life are two of the main reasons why people come back here time after time. There are seventeen comfortable bedrooms, most of which overlook the valley and garden, and all of which have *en suite* bathrooms and double glazing to shelter the occupants from the worst of the winter weather, which can batter this part of the country. There are no televisions, radios or even telephones in the rooms – the owners take the 'get-away-from-it-all' aspect of a stay here very seriously! Two of the double rooms on the ground floor are particularly favoured by the elderly or disabled, as, unusually for a building of this age, there are no steps in the house, apart from the original main staircase. There are four lounges and the dining-room, which enjoys glorious views to Low Fell. Open coal and log fires and the antique furniture in these areas add to the cosy appeal of the house.

The menu is good, traditional English fare, with an accent on local produce and filling 'meat and two veg' dishes for those who have spent their day on the hills. The wine list is comprehensive and very reasonably priced. Among the activities available nearby are golf, at Silloth and Seascale; squash in Keswick; pony trekking within a few miles of the hotel;

161

and fishing in the three lakes in the valley. All the local lakes contain trout, pike and perch, and Congra Moss reservoir, which belongs to the local angling club, is well stocked with trout.

44

SHARROW BAY

Penrith, Cumbria CA10 2LZ
Tel: 08536 301

Nearest town Penrith.

Directions Leave the M6 at junction 40 and follow signs towards Martindale. After Pooley Bridge it is only a few miles along the edge of Ullswater to Sharrow Bay.

A member of the **Relais et Châteaux** consortium.

Awards AA *** (red) graded and two rosettes for food; British Tourist Authority commended; major awards include Egon Ronay's Hotel of the Year 1974 and Restaurant of the Year 1980 (the only British hotel ever to have won both Gold awards); Egon Ronay/Sunday Times Taste of England Award 1983; Consumers' Association Good Hotel Guide César Award 1985; British Academy of Gastronomes Chef Laureate Award 1986; Ackerman Clover Leaf Award 1987.

Open from early March until late November or early December.

Special rates available during March and November for mid-week stays.

The hotel is unsuitable for the disabled; children under fourteen and dogs are not allowed.

Price for dinner, with wine, bed and breakfast for two – over £150.

Credit cards None accepted.
Overall mark out of ten 9

Judging by the number of major awards the Sharrow Bay hotel has won over the last decade or so, it is not difficult to understand why this is one of the best all-round Country House Hotels in England. The main hotel building is basically an early Victorian mansion, built in 1840, but a cottage was known here in the eighteenth century and the house was built on the same site to include part of the original cottage.

Sharrow Bay remained a private residence until 1949 when it was turned into a Country House Hotel. Resident proprietors Francis Coulson and Brian Sack are, this year, entering their 41st season at Sharrow Bay and have come a long way since the bleak post-war years when they took over the house. This hotel was the first of its kind in the UK and, they claim, the definitive Country House Hotel which started the whole movement in this country.

The style of life at Sharrow Bay is unhurried and traditional. There are two beautiful public lounges where afternoon tea, complete with home-made scones, jam, fresh cream, cakes and unlimited tea, is served. Decor and furnishings are a relaxing blend of browns and golds, although to many people's tastes the public rooms and bedrooms alike are a little cluttered, with ornaments and bits and pieces accumulated over four decades in the hotel business. The enormous picture window in the drawing room is a delight, offering an ever-changing panorama across the lake to the Martindale Fells.

Asked to name her favourite restaurant in 1984, romantic novelist Barbara Cartland had no hesitation in calling Sharrow Bay 'one of the most romantic and exciting places in the British Isles. The food defies description . . .' English-style food is served, and at least three weeks' advance booking is recommended for non-residents. Lavish praise is more than deserved for the exquisite five- or six-course table d'hôte menu.

Nearly a dozen starters include a selection of Sharrow speciality soups and a range of more substantial hors d'oeuvres, which includes a delicious Duck Foie Gras served on a bed of dressed salad, and a Terrine of Fresh Salmon and Sole, served with Salmon Caviar and Tomato Vinaigrette. It is worth noting that there is no additional surcharge for the traditionally more expensive options such as smoked salmon or foie gras.

A modest set fish course, followed by a fruit sorbet, precedes the outstanding list of main dishes. Main courses include Fresh Local Salmon, Roast Lancashire Duck, Cumberland Pork Cutlets and Fresh Scallops from the Kyle of Lochalsh, all cooked in a unique style and dressed with sauces richer than you ever thought possible. If you have room for a sweet, the laden sweet trolley is one of the best-known features of the hotel; indeed, Egon Ronay once asked Francis Coulson to present an Old English Regency Syllabub at Maxims in Paris.

Menu specialities do, of course, change from season to season, but whatever you opt for the overall presentation and quality is unrivalled in northern England. Once you've eaten dinner at Sharrow Bay it is not difficult to understand why the Consumers' Association Good Food Guide repeatedly awards the restaurant one of its highest ratings anywhere in England.

Sharrow Bay has a total of 30 bedrooms, including six singles, available in the main hotel building and in several renovated outbuildings in the immediate vicinity. The Edwardian Lodge gatehouse is about 400 yards from the hotel and has three suites and one twin-bedded room. About 100 yards from the hotel lies the aptly named Cottage in the Grounds, a delightful little cottage with one suite, one twin and one small single. For visitors looking for that little bit extra privacy or seclusion, the hotel also has a seventeenth-century cottage, fully furnished and available for only one couple at a time, and also the Bank House, a converted seventeenth-century farmhouse, about a mile from the main hotel. Breakfast and afternoon tea are served here, but lunch and dinner must be taken at the Sharrow Bay.

All bedrooms are furnished to the highest standards, although one or two rooms in the main hotel do not yet have private bathrooms. Television comes as standard, and little racks of antique porcelain and pieces of period furniture give each room a distinctly individual touch. Virtually all the rooms, particularly those in the main building and Bank House, have breathtaking views across Ullswater. Sharrow Bay was given a special award by the AA in 1977 for having the best views of any hotel in the United Kingdom. Whichever part of this marvellous hotel you choose to stay in, advance booking by at least two months is essential.

Nearby attractions include the market town of Penrith seven miles away, the city of Carlisle about 25 miles away, Hadrian's Wall to the east of Carlisle, Wordsworth's cottage eighteen miles away, Beatrix Potter's house where the natural beauty of Cumbria inspired her to write her numerous classic children's tales about Peter Rabbit and his friends, and the Long Meg stone circle near Penrith.

UPLANDS

Haggs Lane, Cartmel, English Lakes LA11 6HD
Tel: 044 854 248

Nearest town Cartmel.
Directions Leave the M6 at junction 36 and follow
the signs to Grange-over-Sands. In Grange go past
the station (on your left), up the hill, and turn right
at the Crown Hotel. Go straight across crossroads
near here into Grange Fell road, past the golf course,
and turn right at T-junction for Cartmel. Uplands is a
little way up this road on the right.
Awards AA *** graded and rosette for food.
Open mid-February until about 2nd January.
Special breaks Mid-week breaks are available
outside the main summer season.
The hotel is unsuitable for disabled visitors; children
under twelve are not allowed; dogs are allowed, but
only in the bedrooms.
Price for dinner, with wine, bed and breakfast for
two – £100–£150.
Credit cards Access and Amex.
Overall mark out of ten 7

Standing in two acres of garden, with magnificent views far
across Morecambe Bay estuary, Uplands almost qualifies as

the smallest hotel featured in this guide. With only four double bedrooms, accommodating a maximum of eight residents at once, the hotel is never crowded or noisy, and consequently resident proprietors Diana and Tom Peter haven't had to work *too* hard to retain an intimately informal atmosphere.

The house was built around the beginning of this century for a British admiral, and as such is a solid, functional building with few architectural points of interest. The present owners altered the building considerably when they bought it in 1984: the staircase was moved, several walls were knocked down to make the dining-room and lounge much bigger, a completely new hall, kitchen and cold room were added, and the house was completely replumbed and rewired.

Shades of pink, grey and blue have been used throughout the ground-floor rooms, and these pale pastel colours contrast charmingly with the numerous Impressionist prints which came from the Metropolitan Museum of Art in New York. The whole effect defies expectations you may have of a Country House Hotel, both in terms of the distinctly modern interior design and the genuinely informal atmosphere which prevails throughout your stay because there are so few residents. But it is a very pleasant place overall and one to which many people return.

The restaurant seats up to 30, most of whom are non-residents, and in keeping with the rest of the ground floor the decor comprises pale grey walls and pink curtains; more pink-framed Impressionist prints enhance the walls. The style of cooking is best described as modern British, and the four-course table d'hôte menu changes nightly. Prospective guests should note that simple bed and breakfast is not available; all tariffs include dinner, bed and full English breakfast.

New speciality starters are constantly being thought up but two typical dishes are Fresh Squid, with the tentacles filled with a rich Stuffing made up of Tomatoes, Garlic, Onion and Fresh Basil, all served with a Chive and Cranberry Sauce. You may prefer instead, though, a more traditional Gravlax – Fillet of Salmon marinated in Hazelnut Oil, Brandy Sugar, Salt and

Dill – all served with mustard and a thick home-made dill mayonnaise.

A soup or fish course follows, which is likely to be anything from Lemon and Mint Soup to Poached Monkfish served with Cucumber and Dill Sauce. There are generally three options on the list of main dishes. Marinated Local Wood Pigeon, dressed with Pear Purée and Lemon Thyme Sauce is an unusual option but you may prefer something more traditional like Roast Norfolk Duck or Roast Sirloin of Lakeland Beef. One of the most original creations from the Uplands kitchen is one which comprises generous Medallions of Fillet Beef and Pork, stuffed with Gruyère and Parma Ham and served with Mushrooms and Marsala Sauce.

Uplands has only four double bedrooms at present, and there are no plans to destroy the intimate atmosphere by adding any more. The existing rooms, however, have impressive views over the surrounding two-acre garden or Morecambe Bay estuary. Each one is individually furnished in a relatively modern style and complete with comfortable accessories like colour television, hairdryer, a generous supply of reading matter and a Travel Scrabble set. Three have private shower and toilet facilities, and one has a full bathroom.

The main attraction of a small Country House Hotel like Uplands in this part of England is the natural beauty of the Lake District all around you. The two nearest villages are appealing for the casual visitor who hasn't come on holiday to indulge in any 'heavy-duty' sightseeing: Cartmel (about a mile away) has an attractive eleventh-century priory, and Grange-over-Sands (about two miles away) is a relatively unspoilt Victorian seaside resort. The town of Kendal is a short drive away, and there are one or two fine old stately homes in the area including Holker Hall, Levens Castle and Sizergh Castle.

WHITWELL HALL

Whitwell-on-the-Hill, York YO6 7JJ
Tel: 065 381 551

Nearest town York.
Directions From York, follow the A64
Scarborough road and the hotel is situated just off
this road after about twelve miles.
A member of the **Historic and Romantik** and
Relais du Silence hotel groups.
Awards AA *** graded; recommended by Ashley
Courtenay, Egon Ronay and Michelin guides.
Open throughout the year.
There are no **special breaks** available, but winter
rates do apply from October to April.
*The hotel is suitable for the disabled; dogs are taken
only in the Coach House and owners are urged to keep
them well away from the proprietors' numerous pets;
children under 18 are not permitted.*
Price for dinner, with wine, bed and breakfast for
two – £100–£150.
Credit cards Access, Visa and Amex.
Overall mark out of ten 8.5

A Country House Hotel of genuine character, Whitwell Hall is an intriguing combination of Tudor and Gothic architectural styles which belie its rather more recent nineteenth-century origins. Originally built in 1835, the magnificent Virginia Creeper-clad mansion is now owned and run as a first-class hotel by a retired naval officer, Lieutenant-Commander Peter Milner, and his wife Sallie.

The house is set in eighteen acres of terraced lawns, rose beds and ageing woodland, and visitors to Whitwell are likely to be struck by the magnificent panoramic views across surrounding Yorkshire and York Minster in the distance before they even enter the wide entrance hall. The hotel is a popular retreat for VIPs, and one of the most famous was the late Richard Burton, who stayed here for three days in the summer of 1982 while filming a few scenes of *Wagner* in York's National Railway Museum. Among the many services the Milners provided was taking telephone messages from his equally famous ex-wife Elizabeth Taylor – and only then after she had proved her identity by repeating her Swiss telephone number!

All the public rooms are large and comfortably furnished, but few nineteenth-century buildings can boast an elegant stone-arched entrance quite as striking as this one. Complete with high vaulted ceiling, warm red carpeting and a large log fire when the weather demands it, the main reception area has all the trademarks of a fine Country House, and the Lt-Commander assures you of an enthusiastic personal welcome when you arrive.

Of the other public rooms, which include a drawing-room and cocktail bar in the Orangery looking on to the swimming pool, the one which really stands out is the Great Hall leading off the reception area. A cantilevered staircase ascends to a long balcony off which the bedrooms lead. The dining-room is equally delightful with its rose-pink walls and patterened carpet creating the perfect setting in which to enjoy the very high standard of cooking. Fresh local produce is used wherever possible and, as you might expect, fine china tableware is used throughout.

New-style table d'hôte menus are available each evening, but the à la carte is much more impressive. Starters, termed 'aperitifs' on the hand-written menu, include Home-Cured Salmon, Fresh Duck Pâté and a very enjoyable Vineyard Salad composed of pieces of chicken and halves of black grapes all tossed in green olive oil and lemon juice and served on a bed of crisp lettuce. The Chef de Cuisine is more than happy to prepare any dish you care to mention, within reason, given enough time.

A typical evening's table d'hôte menu includes a range of more traditional English Country House-style dishes like Roast Rack of Lamb and Prime Cut of Yorkshire Beef. Other specialities from the Whitwell Hall kitchen include Breast of Aylesbury Duckling, sautéd pink and dressed on an Orange and Green Peppercorn Sauce, and a pair of Pigeon Breasts roasted and placed on a Sweet Wine Sauce and garnished with baby vegetables.

Whitwell Hall has 20 bedrooms, each with private bath or shower rooms, and eleven are located in the main building. The remaining nine are situated a short distance away in the Coach House which is ideal for small conferences or a more secluded private holiday. The rooms in the main hall lead off the large balcony, and are distinguished by grand Gothic-style headboards. Antique dressing tables and wardrobes have been placed in all the rooms creating a very comfortable nineteenth-century atmosphere. This is further enhanced by the absence of any direct-dial telephones, television sets or radios, but these facilities are available in your room on request.

The hotel has a number of leisure facilities available, including a heated indoor swimming pool, a sauna, games room, bicycles for residents' use, and outdoor area to play croquet or tennis. Nearby attractions are numerous and include Castle Howard, the city of York, Rievaulx Abbey, the towns of Helmsley, Whitby and Scarborough, and a number of stately properties in the care of the National Trust.

WORDSWORTH

Grasmere, Cumbria LA22 9SW
Tel: 096 65 592

Nearest town Grasmere.
Directions From the south, leave the M6 at
junction 36 and follow A590 dual carriageway
towards Kendal. Take second exit (marked
Windermere – A591) at large roundabout and
follow through until past Rydal. Take first left
(signposted Grasmere) and the hotel is on your
right just after the church.
Awards AA and RAC **** graded.
Special breaks Winter breaks available from 1st
November until 31st March; four-day House Party
at Christmas and three-day House Party at New
Year.
The hotel is suitable for disabled visitors; children are
welcome but dogs are not allowed.
Price for dinner, with wine, bed and breakfast for
two – £100–£150.
Credit cards Access, Visa, Amex and Diners
Club.
Overall mark out of ten 9

Set in the heart of the area of Cumbrian lakeland which so
inspired the poet after whom the hotel is named, the Wordsworth is certainly one of northern England's finest hotels.

Offering a sophisticated class of luxury service and comfort for the businessman and holiday-maker alike, the Wordsworth combines a reputation for fine cuisine with the peace and tranquillity for which this region is so famous.

Originally a stone-built country lodge, the present hotel briefly became home to the Earl of Cadogan in the mid-nineteenth century. It became a hotel as early as 1874, although originally known as The Rothay Hotel, but then, as now, it was a popular staging post on many a traveller's long journey north or south. Through the years a great many distinguished visitors have stayed here, but few have aroused so much interest as former United States President, Woodrow Wilson, nearer the beginning of this century, who was on his way to Carlisle to try and trace his ancestors.

The building had fallen into disuse by the 1970s, and the present owners bought the building in a near derelict state about ten years ago and embarked upon the long, slow task of completely renovating and refurbishing it. In 1981 it opened its doors, renamed as the Wordsworth Hotel, and has been providing year-round comfort and luxury to visitors ever since.

One of the many attractions of the Wordsworth is the refreshing choice of interior decor throughout the hotel. Its relatively recent renovation, combined with the fact that the house has not been lived in as a private residence for well over a century, has thankfully encouraged the proprietors not to work too hard to recreate in reproduction a stately-home atmosphere which many Country House Hotels, blessed with a richer historical pedigree, try to achieve.

There are few pieces of antique furniture, particularly in the bedrooms, and those you will see are tastefully placed and are the real McCoy: the occasional Victorian coffee table, a marvellous old oil painting of Wordsworth above the fireplace in reception, a gold-framed mirror above the fireplace in the lounge and so on. The emphasis really is on unrestrained luxury rather than a deliberate recreation of life as it might have been a hundred years ago at the old Rothay Hotel, and

174

few visitors to the Wordsworth would argue that that aim hasn't been achieved.

The Prelude Restaurant, so named after what is probably William Wordsworth's most celebrated work, really is a delightful room, with a quality of service and cuisine to match. It is bright, cheerful and owing much to its relatively recent renovation which managed to reconstruct much of the nineteenth-century charm which was lost when the building fell into disuse in the 1970s. Tables are laid with fine linen, your meal is served on Wedgwood bone china and your choice of wine from the 100-bottle wine list poured into crystal glassware.

A limited (seasonal) à la carte and a five-course table d'hôte menu, offering a choice of starter and dessert only, are available each evening. Some guests may find the limited choice rather annoying but such is the quality of the Wordsworth that even the most firmly held prejudices about a particular dish can be quickly dispelled.

Both menus have a strongly English emphasis although the style of presentation has been influenced considerably by *nouvelle cuisine*. Head chef Bernard Warne and his deputy were both trained through the Savoy Hotel group, and their enthusiastic young team have come up with a creative and original selection. A typical evening's main course might be a Mignon of Veal topped with a Mushroom Duxelle, glazed and served with a Madeira Sauce; or perhaps Mignonettes of Beef and Pork Fillet on a two-toned Brandy Sauce with sautéed Wild Mushrooms. Served, of course, with a generous selection of lightly cooked fresh vegetables.

There are 35 bedrooms at the Wordsworth, mostly doubles, including two ground-floor rooms which are particularly suitable for disabled or elderly visitors. One or two suites are available by prior arrangement, and the hotel offers an excellent three-day inclusive package for honeymooners which – naturally – includes accommodation in one of the larger doubles with a four-poster bed for that extra romantic touch. All rooms have private bathroom facilities, colour television and direct-dial telephones and are furnished in a modern style.

The Wordsworth has an excellent range of leisure facilities available for residents. In addition to pool and table tennis tables, there is an indoor heated swimming pool, sauna and solarium. All major outdoor recreations such as horse riding, fishing, golf, tennis and water sports can be easily arranged locally. Other nearby attractions include the former homes of Beatrix Potter, poet John Ruskin and William Wordsworth himself, the Lake District National Park visitors' centre, and the towns of Kendal, Penrith and Carlisle.

CENTRAL ENGLAND

48

BROOKHOUSE INN

Brookside, Rolleston-on-Dove, near Burton-on-Trent,
Staffordshire DE13 9AA
Tel: 0283 814188

Nearest town Burton-on-Trent.
Directions From the north, travel via the A38
from Derby towards Rolleston; from the south,
head out of Birmingham, on the same road. The
turn-off for the village of Rolleston is clearly
signposted and the hotel is located in the village.
Awards British Tourist Authority commended;
Ashley Courtenay recommended.
Open from mid-January until Christmas Eve.
Special **weekend breaks** are available throughout
the year from dinner Friday until breakfast
Sunday.
Children under the age of ten are not catered for; dogs
are allowed.
Price for dinner, with wine, bed and breakfast for
two – under £100.
Credit cards Access, Visa, Amex and Diners
Club.
Overall mark out of ten 7

The Brookhouse Inn is hidden in the quiet Staffordshire village
of Rolleston-on-Dove, and offers the luxurious tranquillity

you would expect of a Country House Hotel with the added charm of a typical rural English village. Originally a farmhouse, the hotel was built during the brief joint reign of William and Mary at the end of the seventeenth century. It had an undistinguished history until 1977 when present owners Bill and Deirdre Mellis bought it and recognized the potential which the old red stone building had to be converted into a hotel.

The end result is a relaxed and informal little hotel, not a Country House in the strictest sense because of its village location, but more than fitting the comfort standards associated with Country House Hotels. From the moment you approach the hotel you will be struck by its solid exterior. It was built in the generation which immediately preceded the elaborate Georgian era of English architecture and its symmetrical window pattern, with small frames and brilliant white paintwork, contrasts starkly with the red brickwork.

The hotel's main public room is a large reception lounge, its red and black carpet enhancing the bare brickwork of a couple of the walls. Blue and white china candelabras are crafted in a design similar to old brass lanterns, and give a glimpse of what life might have been like at the Brookhouse Inn in former years. Perhaps the proprietors have tried a little too hard to recreate the period feel in this room as the imposing old fireplace is almost groaning with china plates and antique trinkets.

Whatever your own impressions, the bedrooms at Brookhouse are a delight. Each one is individually furnished in a period with huge overhead wooden beams, swirling curtains and matching counterpanes. Most of the six double bedrooms have huge four-poster beds and are furnished with authentic chairs and dressing tables. The gentle aroma of Victorian-style pot pourri is a pleasing touch.

There are sixteen bedrooms in all, plus one suite, and eight of the rooms are in the main farmhouse building. The remainder are in the carefully renovated old barn. All bedrooms have private bathroom facilities, with a number of little extras like exclusive soaps, talcum, shampoo, foam bath, crystals and even a thoughtful glass of detergent for emergency washing. As an added concession to modern comfort, colour television and telephones are included in all bedrooms.

One of the principle attractions of the Brookhouse Inn is its high standard of cooking. The dining-room promises an atmosphere of homely elegance and evening meals are served on the finest Staffordshire bone china. The room feels rather small, but this lends a sense of intimacy rather than cramped-ness. You sit at antique tables laid with heavy silver plate and cut crystal while chef David Bould and Deirdre Mellis take charge of the cooking. Twice weekly trips to Birmingham ensure that all produce for the Brookhouse table is fresh and of the highest quality. The menu has few surprises at first glance, but you will quickly discover that virtually all main dish choices are enhanced by unique speciality sauces from the Brookhouse kitchen. A few interesting French dishes pop up amid the more standard English Country House-style menu, including Snails on the range of starters and Breasts of French Duck stuffed with Chicken Mousse on the list of main dishes.

Lobster is generally available, prepared in a Cream, Wine and Mustard Sauce, glazed in its shell with cheese, and a good buy at around £15 per head. All main course dishes include vegetables, a sensible addition which, more often than not, comes as an extra few pounds on your bill. Bill Mellis is considered something of a connoisseur of wine and has built up a strong cellar in the space of a decade, including a number of more unusual foreign vintages.

Nearby attractions include the towns of Burton-on-Trent, Stafford, Derby and Stoke-on-Trent together with the city of Birmingham. Golf and fishing can be arranged nearby, and for a relaxing walk you won't need to look further than the Brookhouse's country garden – complete with English brook flowing through.

49

BUCKLAND MANOR

Buckland, near Broadway, Gloucestershire WR12 7LY
Tel: 0386 852626

Nearest Town Broadway.
Directions From Moreton-in-Marsh take the A44
to Broadway, or the B4632 from Stratford-upon-
Avon, head through the village and continue along
the B4632 signposted to Cheltenham. After about
1.5 miles there is a turn-off to Buckland signposted
on the left-hand side of the road.
Awards AA *** (red) graded and rosette; Best
New Hotel in Britain Award in the 1984 AA Motel
and Restaurant Guide; Michelin red M award;
British Tourist Authority commended; highest
rating of any Cotswolds hotel in the 1988 Egon
Ronay guide, a distinction the hotel has had since
1983; 1986 Top English Hotel Award from Andrew
Harper's Hideaway Report.
Open Early February until mid-January.
Special **winter breaks** are available.
*The hotel is suitable for the disabled; children under
twelve are not permitted in the hotel, nor children under
eight in the restaurant; dogs are not allowed.*
Price for dinner, with wine, bed and breakfast for
two – over £150.
Credit cards Access and Visa.
Overall mark out of ten 8.5

Tucked away in the heart of the Cotswolds, Buckland Manor assures you a warm and homely welcome. Settled in several acres of ornamental garden, this small Country House Hotel is ideally located for touring central England, with Shakespeare's Stratford-upon-Avon just seventeen miles in one direction and attractive Regency Cheltenham fourteen miles in the other direction. Its superb setting and de luxe standards make it easy to understand why the hotel has won a string of major awards since opening less than a decade ago.

Few Country House Hotels can trace their origins as far back as Buckland Manor. The first written record of a house on the site of the present hotel stretches back almost one and a half millennia to the seventh century AD, further even than the history of England as a united nation. In those far-off Dark Age times the estate of Buckland was given by Kynred, King of Mercia, to the Abbot of Gloucester. The very fact that those distant origins are known today helps explain the name Buckland: the title to the land, unusually for the Dark Ages, was inscribed in a book and the Old English 'bookland' was corrupted to form the name of the nearby village as it is known today.

The estate remained in the ownership of the church until 1536 when, on the dissolution of the monasteries, the land passed into the private hands of the Gresham family. Two famous sons of this family rose to become Lord Mayors of London. Buckland Estate was sold again in 1802, and has been owned by four private families since then, prior to its purchase in 1981 by Adrienne and Barry Berman who converted it into a luxury Country House Hotel.

A principle aim at Buckland, according to the owners, is 'to pamper and cosset each guest in the tranquillity of the Cotswolds' and certainly no one could fault the staff for being inattentive to the care of their guests. Elegant public rooms are sumptuously furnished with authentic antiques and deep-cushioned sofas and armchairs. Throughout the hotel you will be struck by the old panelled walls, thick-beamed ceilings and narrow-paned windows – no more so than in the superior ground-floor dining-room.

The style of cooking at Buckland Manor is an interesting combination of traditional English Country House and the best of French cuisine. An impressive à la carte menu is available each evening and, since few places are generally available for non-residents, advance booking is strongly recommended. Sautéed Cornish Scallops are a favourite starter, but the top speciality opener is Cassolette d'Escargots à l'Oseille, which consists of braised vineyard snails lightly flavoured with aniseed and served in a cream, peppercorn and fresh sorrel sauce. At around £10 per serving it is more expensive than most of the main courses, but nevertheless a worthy hors d'oeuvre for most main dishes. Fish is well represented on the menu and if you really want to appreciate local salmon at its finest, don't resist the temptation of the chef's Saumon Mi-cuit à la Marinade de Truffes – a lightly cooked escalope of fresh salmon accompanied by a marinade with a gentle flavour of truffle.

Buckland Manor has eleven bedrooms, including a large family suite of two adjoining twin-bedded rooms – which is a rather interesting feature considering this hotel takes the Victorian view that children under the age of twelve are not allowed (and how many parents want their secondary school-stage offspring sharing their room?). Two rooms are really four-poster suite-size doubles and all rooms have their own bathroom facilities, with bathwater drawn straight from the manor's own spring water, just as it has been for centuries. All rooms are individually furnished and it has not been difficult to create a distinct identity for each, considering the hotel is relatively small.

In terms of leisure facilities, Buckland Manor has an outside heated swimming pool, putting green, croquet lawn, tennis court, ornamental gardens, facilities nearby for riding and golf, and acre upon acre of naturally beautiful gardens and paddocks. A thirteenth-century church is next door to the hotel, with a wonderfully ornate ceiling, and other nearby attractions include the towns of Stratford-upon-Avon (with all its numerous places of interest associated with William Shakespeare), Worcester with its famous porcelain works, and countless Cotswold villages with a timeless charm few can fail to appreciate.

50

COTTAGE IN THE WOOD

Holywell Road, Malvern Wells, Worcestershire WR14 4LG
Tel: 06845 3487

Nearest Town Great Malvern.
Directions Leave the M50 junction 1 and follow
signs to Malvern. After going through Upton-on-
Severn follow signs to Malvern Wells which will
bring you to a T-junction with the A449. Turn
right and then first (sharp) left, past the Jet petrol
station.
A member of the **Consort Consortium** of top
hotels.
Awards AA *** graded; English Tourist Board
four Crowns; Egon Ronay recommended.
Open throughout the year except for a week over
Christmas.
Special **winter breaks** from November until April
are available.
Children are welcome but dogs are only permitted in the
Coach House and Beach Cottage; the hotel is suitable for
the disabled.
Price for dinner, with wine, bed and breakfast for
two – £100–£150.
Credit cards Access and Visa.
Overall mark out of ten 6.5

The name 'Cottage in the Wood' is a bit of a misnomer as you'll find a modern-day hotel rather more than a tiny Cotswolds cottage, nestling in acres of secluded forest, which the name implies. The hotel is, in fact, a charming Georgian dower house set in seven acres of private woodland, and guests have the option of accommodation in one of three hotel buildings: the main house has eight bedrooms, the Coach House (about 200 yards from the main hotel building) another eight, and Beech Cottage another four, about 74 yards from the hotel proper.

The hotel was first built and owned by a minor Georgian noble, Duke Gondolphi, and converted into a hotel shortly after the end of the Second World War. In the decades which followed, demand to stay at this tranquil haven increased, and Beech Cottage and the Coach House were also converted into comfortable accommodation.

Wherever you choose to stay at the Cottage, in the main house with its lovely views across 30 miles of Severn Valley, the charming Beech Cottage, or the old Coach House with its smaller but no less intimate rooms, you can be assured of very high standards of comfort. All rooms have private bathroom facilities, colour television, clock radio, tea- and coffee-making facilities, telephone, and are furnished in a very individual style which clearly distinguishes one room from another. Four-posters are available in some rooms. Beech Cottage and Coach House guests have the option of taking breakfast in the main hotel dining room or in their room. The Cottage in the Wood has one main public lounge, a simple but comfortably furnished room in Georgian style. There are no beamed ceilings or antique tables, which is a little disappointing, but you can be assured of a very high standard of personal care and attention from resident proprietors John and Sue Pattin.

The dining-room can seat up to 50 at any one time; dinner is served from 7 p.m. until 8.30 p.m. (last orders). Lantern-style lights create a gently intimate atmosphere and reflect off the Indian prints all around the dining-room walls in a rather intriguing fashion. Chef Graham Flanagan has developed a good reputation for producing English Country House-style cuisine of a very high quality, and you are unlikely to be disappointed by either his à la carte or table d'hôte selections.

Local produce is used as much as possible to create his speciality dishes, and fresh line-caught salmon is a favourite base for starters and main courses alike. One of the best dishes with a local flavour is Hot Baked Crab glazed with Gloucester Cheese, although Marinated Goose Breast in local Cider with Endive and fresh Coriander Salad is an interesting alternative. Soup and fish courses are invariably offered, and the chef will be delighted to cater for a vegetarian diet if requested in advance.

The table d'hôte menu is reasonable, and good value. Main course options include Fillet of Rainbow Trout steamed with Mussel Seasoning and Pink Peppercorns, and Limeswold Stuffed Chicken Breast, dusted with breadcrumbs. Two dishes do stand out from a typical evening's à la carte menu, however, and of the two menus this one can be recommended more enthusiastically: Breast of Guinea Fowl in Dill and Mushroom in a fine pastry and dressed with a rich Watercress Cream is delicious, but still cannot beat the chef's Boned Quail Pot Roast with Chicory, Walnuts, served with a fresh truffle.

The hotel has no leisure facilities of its own available, although the location is a walker's paradise and nearby attractions are numerous. The Wye Valley and Wales are accessible by a short drive, as are the three cathedral cities of Worcester, Hereford and Gloucester and the old town of Tewkesbury with its ancient abbey. The obvious scenic attractions of the Cotswolds are all around you, and an interesting day trip can be made to the Worcester porcelain factory about seven miles away to see how this amazing chinaware is made.

51

THE ELMS

Abberley, near Worcester, Worcestershire WR6 6AT
Tel: 029 921 666

Nearest Town Worcester.
Directions From the M5, turn off at junction 5 for Worcester. Drive through the city and pick up the A443, signposted to Tenbury Wells. The Elms is on the right, twelve miles from Worcester and two miles after passing through Great Witley.
A **Norfolk Capital** Hotel.
Awards AA *** (red) graded and rosette, RAC *** graded and Blue Ribbon; British Tourist Authority commended; Egon Ronay recommended.
Open throughout the year.
Special breaks Weekend breaks available all year; special Christmas programme.
Children are welcome but dogs are not allowed – kennels located nearby and can accommodate dogs by prior arrangement.
Price for dinner, with wine, bed and breakfast for two – £100–£150 (just over £100).
Credit cards Access, Visa, Amex and Diners Club.
Overall mark out of ten 7.5

The Elms Hotel is undoubtedly one of the architectural treasures of Worcestershire, and for years has had the distinction of being the first hotel listed in the AA handbook. A solid old baronial country seat, the house is one of the few outstanding architectural creations from the reign of Queen Anne. The Elms was completed in 1710 and designed by architect Gilbert White, a pupil of Sir Christopher Wren who built St Paul's Cathedral in London. White was also responsible for the imposing design of the Guildhall in Worcester and many features of it and the hotel are similar: the main pediment and, particularly, the amazing moulded cornices in the rooms of both buildings.

The Elms has always been known by that name. Records show that the sweeping carriageway was lined with elm trees for generations. Presumably they were planted here when the house was built, but they have long since gone and today the driveway from the main road up to the front of the house is flanked with lime trees. In 1840 the Country House became part of Abberley Hall Estate and was, for a while, the home of Admiral Malin. In the late 1920s new owners built two new wings on to the hotel, but on the first night of occupancy, after they were completed, a devastating fire completely gutted the house, leaving only the bare shell standing. The then owner, Sir Richard Brooke, had the house completely rebuilt as before – except that a flat roof was added – and he continued to live at the Elms until 1946, when it was finally turned into a luxury hotel.

All the public rooms are bright, spacious and comfortable, largely furnished with antiques and offering majestic views across the surrounding countryside. The Library Bar is particularly distinctive and, like most of the large rooms, still retains its original fireplace and the huge mahogany bookcases, despite the fire in 1927. Fresh flowers are a nice touch in all the public rooms and most of the 27 bedrooms.

There are nine bedrooms in the adjoining Coach House, and all are furnished to very high standards of comfort with colour television, private bathroom facilities and direct-dial telephone as standard. Four-poster bedrooms are generally available. In most of the bedrooms the curtain material is co-ordinated with the wallpaper, a minor detail which you may find appealing or irritating, depending on your individual taste. Have a look at the bedroom illustrated in the hotel brochure and you'll see what I mean!

The hotel has a particularly attractive dining-room, furnished in rich Regency style. Tables are a good distance apart and the sensible limit of 60 persons dining at one time (well below the realistic capacity of this lovely room) means that guests have space to sit back and enjoy a thoroughly relaxing dinner without any feeling of being 'hemmed in' which is so often a complaint even in the best restaurants and hotels. A dark wood antique fireplace, with a huge oil seascape above it, is an effective centrepiece to the whole room.

In keeping with the style throughout the rest of the hotel, the style of food is traditional English, although because the Elms is fortunate in having one of the largest herb gardens in Britain, an interesting French flavour is added to many main dishes. There is no à la carte menu available, perhaps surprising for a hotel of The Elms' reputation, and the table d'hôte menu is basic. One highlight is their Whole Young Chicken grilled and served on a bed of Leeks with a Lime and Vermouth Sauce. A good selection of cheeses is available as an alternative to a choice from the sweet trolley.

A number of leisure facilities are available around the hotel: croquet, tennis and putting within the hotel grounds, and both riding and golf can be easily arranged nearby. Other nearby attractions include the historic city of Worcester, with its famous cathedral, Royal Porcelain factory and Civil War centre; Elgar's birthplace and musuem near Worcester; the Elizabethan moated manor house at Harvington Hall; Hartlebury Castle; and a number of National Trust properties including Croft Castle, Berrington Hall and Hanbury Hall.

52

ETTINGTON PARK

*Alderminster, near Stratford-upon-Avon,
Warwickshire CV37 8BS
Tel: 0789 740740*

Nearest town Stratford-upon-Avon.
Directions Follow the A34 Stratford to Oxford
road and the hotel is five miles along this road.
Awards AA **** graded and rosette for food;
Good Food Guide Newcomer of the Year 1986.
Open throughout the year.
Special **weekend breaks** are available throughout
the year.
*Children under seven are not permitted; dogs are not
allowed.*
Price for dinner, with wine, bed and breakfast for
two – over £150 (approaching £300).
Credit cards Access, Visa, Amex and Diners
Club.
Overall mark out of ten 10

Everything about Ettington Park Hotel typifies the highest
international standards of comfort which the hotel has striven
to achieve since ISIS, the world-wide construction group,
bought this outstanding property in 1983. From the quality of
the complimentary toiletries right down to the depth of the
polish on the intricate hand-carved wooden friezes above the

fireplace in the reception lobby, there can be no question that Ettington Park is one of Britain's finest hotels.

Even the history of the Ettington estate has an impeccable pedigree and puts this hotel at the top of the luxury Country House Hotel bracket. Ettington Park is remarkable in that it is the only property in England still in the same ownership as at the time of the Domesday Book – and it is almost certain that the tenure of the Shirley family was established long before the Norman Conquest of England in 1066. Although the present house dates almost entirely from the nineteenth century, the Gothic-style architecture has clearly been influenced by the legacy of earlier manors on this site. In 1086 the original manor was held by a nobleman known as 'Saswalo' (or Sewallis), and it was his grandson, another Sewallis, who became 'de Shirley' from the village of Derbyshire where he already held lands.

A direct line of descent can be traced from the time of the Conquest to the present Shirley family, who live nearby and take a keen interest in the overall running of the hotel. Fourteen bas-reliefs around the exterior of the hotel record a number of more noteworthy members of the family who all knew the Ettington estate through the ages: Sir Thomas Shirley, a great crusader; Sir Ralph Shirley, who fought bravely alongside Henry V at the Battle of Harfleur; and Sir Robert Shirley, who fought nobly for his king, Charles I, and was imprisoned by Oliver Cromwell during the English Revolution. During the lifetime of William Shakespeare, who lived and worked at nearby Stratford-upon-Avon from 1564 to 1623, Sir Robert Shirley was acquainted with the Underhill family who leased the house for a while at the end of the sixteenth century.

Ettington Park hotel today stands amid 40 acres of grand estate, dominated by an enormous lawn whose rigid stripes are lovingly groomed, and it really is impossible not to be hugely impressed by your first sight of this Gothic house. With its narrow windows and pointed cornices you can understand why the author of at least one guidebook said: 'One could run out of superlatives to describe Ettington Park.'

193

The various public rooms are furnished in the most sumptuous fashion, and the main public lounge is breathtaking, simply because of its scale. Like in a grand Edwardian ballroom, long blue curtains form the perfect accompaniment to the rich white and gold ornate ceiling. Few other hotels could have a grand piano in their main lounge which looks so distinctly 'settled'. Look out for those finely carved wooden fireplaces, complete with inset family crests. Gently pass your hand over their intricate surface and feel the sense of history beneath your fingers. One of the highlights of the hotel is the beautifully panelled dining-room with its 1740 rococo ceiling and glorious views out across the garden.

Head chef Patrick McDonald has a strong team working under him, and has come up with one of the finest Country House menus in Britain. An à la carte menu is available, but most guests seem more than content with the four-course set table d'hôte menu at a fixed price of around £25 per person. House specialities are a blend of the finest English and French cuisine and are really too numerous to mention; suffice to say that no favoured dish requested by a dinner guest has ever been refused. A favourite speciality is the Fillet of Beef with a Wild Mushroom Casserole. Advance booking, particularly at weekends, is essential.

The hotel has a total of 49 individually furnished bedrooms, including nine suites, whose decor can only be described as luxury of the highest grade. Original antiques and fine oil paintings complement spacious private bathroom facilities, colour television and telephone, and provide the perfect setting for that special break.

An integral part of Ettington Park is the quite superb leisure complex, providing a variety of activities which can be as relaxing or as energetic as you choose. In addition to a large heated indoor swimming pool, you can relax in the sauna, whirlpool spa bath or solarium. Virtually all outdoor sports, from tennis to fresh-water fishing, can be arranged easily through the hotel reception.

Nearby attractions include Stratford-upon-Avon and all that

has to offer: Shakespeare's birthplace, Anne Hathaway's cottage, the World of Shakespeare centre, and a superb shopping centre. Warwick Castle and the towns of Oxford and Banbury are within easy reach.

53

THE FEATHERS

Bull Ring, Ludlow, Shropshire SY8 1AA.
Tel: 0584 5261

Nearest town Ludlow.
Directions From Hereford or Shrewsbury, follow
the A49 to Ludlow. The Feathers is located in the
town centre.
A member of the **Select British Hotels** group.
Awards AA *** RAC graded; British Tourist
Authority commended; Egon Ronay
recommended.
Open throughout the year.
The hotel has a lift so is reasonably suited for disabled
guests; children are welcome but dogs are not allowed.
Price for dinner, with wine, bed and breakfast for
two – under £100.
Credit cards Access, Visa, Amex and Diners Club.
Overall mark out of ten 7.5

One of the most famous Elizabethan buildings in England, the
Feathers in Ludlow has been known to travellers since the

time of Shakespeare. Since the early seventeenth century the town of Ludlow has continued to grow up around this inn with the result that today, though the Feathers is not a Country House Hotel in the strictest sense because of its location in the bustling Ludlow town centre, it does possess all the touches traditionally associated with Country House Hotels and the 'olde worlde' charm that many have.

The heart of the hotel is an early seventeenth-century building which was almost certainly built on the site of an earlier edifice. Originally built as a private home, the Feathers first became an inn in 1670 with John Morris as its first landlord. The present King James I room was identified in a 1713 inventory as the most important room available for guests, with furniture then valued at an astonishing £16! The two other main public rooms in the early eighteenth-century inn are now spacious bedrooms: rooms 211 and 212 respectively. Rooms at the rear of the inn were spared the noise of coaches passing on the road outside – and were a little larger to accommodate a table in order that their rather wealthier occupants could enjoy the luxury of dining in their bedroom.

The Feathers has always played a central part in the life of the town, and the first-floor balcony was built in the early nineteenth century for electioneering purposes in the days when, prior to 1874, elections were conducted by a public show of hands by all the wealthy landowners in the area. In 1839 a rather corrupt transaction is recorded where one Feathers guest received £300 in bribes to support a particular candidate.

Even as you first approach the Feathers you cannot fail to be struck by its quite stunning period exterior. Three storeys high, it is a beautiful contrast between dark brown beams and brillian white paintwork. The steep cornices and diamond-paned windows complete the authentic period feel of the building which, you will find, has been equally well maintained inside.

Your first impression is of the warmth created by the contrast between the plush red carpets, which adorn all the public rooms, and the dark beams hung with a variety of copper pots, small barrels and other assorted reminders of the Feathers in earlier centuries. Easily the most attractive room in the hotel is the King James I lounge which is rightly famous for its truly magnificent carved fireplace, showing the king's arms, and acting as a focal point for the whole room. Up above it you can see an elaborately ornamental plaster ceiling, with a red and gold boss also portraying the Royal Arms of James I.

Next door, the decor is only marginally less striking as you enter the Writing Room which has a slightly less elaborate overmantel above the fireplace. If you look above the door in this room you will see the arms of two well-known local families, Fox and Halcuit, who prospered in the Ludlow area in the sixteenth century. The largest public room is the Prince Charles suite, which has been refurbished as a banqueting hall complete with beamed ceiling and, as you might imagine, is a very popular 'society' function suite. By the time of publication, a garden-room and patio should also have been built.

The main dining-room is known as the Richard III restaurant and, with its huge original seventeenth-century fireplace, was once the inn's kitchen. It can seat up to 80, and advance booking for non-residents is strongly recommended during the main May to September season. Food is served in traditional English style and is delicious, but the set menu choice is disappointing, resembling little more than an average bar supper menu. The main à la carte menu is superb, however. Specialities include Poached Strips of Chicken in Kiwi Fruit Sauce, and a rich Stuffed Fillet of Pork with Sherry Sauce. Unusually, there is a choice of at least three vegetarian dishes available at around two-thirds the average £10 per head main course price.

The Feathers has 37 bedrooms, including seven with four-posters, and all are spacious and individually furnished to the highest standards. The elegance of the four-poster bedrooms especially, with their ornate drapes and matching decor, is worth the extra investment. In addition to private bathroom facilities and extras like colour television and telephone, most of the rooms give a reassuring impression of space which is far from obvious from the exterior of the old inn.

Nearby attractions include historic Ludlow itself (a walking and historical guide is provided free to all guests) with its medieval castle and fine old Tudor and Georgian buildings; several National Trust and English Heritage sites nearby; and the river valleys of the Teme, Wye and Severn are all within easy reach.

54

GRAFTON MANOR

Grafton Lane, Bromsgrove, Worcestershire B61 7HA
Tel: 0527 31525

Nearest town Bromsgrove.
Directions The hotel is situated 1.5 miles from
the centre of Bromsgrove, just off the B4091
twelve miles north of Worcester.
A member of the **Pride of Britain** consortium.
Awards AA rosette in *Good Food Guide*; Michelin
red M; Ashley Courtenay recommended.
Open throughout the year.
The hotel is not suitable for the disabled; children under
the age of seven are not permitted and dogs are not
allowed unless kept in kennels outside the hotel
bedrooms and public areas.
Price for dinner, with wine, bed and breakfast for
two – £100–£150.
Credit cards Access, Visa, Amex and Diners
Club.
Overall mark out of ten 7.5

Although the distinguished old Grafton Manor Hotel dates
from 'just' 1567, it is built on the site of a much older manor
house which was for many years home to a cousin of William
the Conqueror. Today Grafton flourishes in more peaceful
times, but remains surrounded by 26 acres of Worcestershire
parkland and garden which haven't changed all that much
over the last few centuries.

Few major events in English history have failed to touch the Grafton estate in some way. Sir Humphrey Stafford was lord of Grafton Manor during the reign of Henry VI, and his loyal friendship to his monarch cost him his life in a violent feud. The estate was inherited by his nephew, another Sir Humphrey, who fought bravely alongside the usurper Richard III at the Battle of Bosworth in 1485. Unlike his sovereign master, Sir Humphrey managed to escape with his life but was brutally executed as a traitor after dismissing a pardon from the new king, Henry VII, and launching a hopeless coup against his government.

The Talbot family inherited the estate after Stafford's disgrace, and probably the best-known member of the family was one John Talbot, who was a reluctant co-conspirator in Guy Fawkes' gunpowder plot to blow up parliament in 1605. He escaped with his life, only to die of natural causes five years later, but several decades earlier he had built a completely new Grafton Manor which forms the basic shell of the present hotel.

The manor was all but destroyed by fire in 1710, a very common occurrence in Country Houses throughout Great Britain, but the entrance hall and adjoining gable in the hotel give you an idea of the proportions of John Talbot's new home. Over the next 40 years the manor was rebuilt to its original form, and some of the rooms were made even grander than those which were lost in the great fire. The main public room, for instance, is still known today as the Great Parlour and had an ornate ceiling and large family coat of arms added when it was rebuilt.

Grafton Manor remained the family seat of the Earls of Shrewsbury until 1934, when is was finally sold. The present proprietors have owned the estate since 1970, but it was a further decade before Grafton Manor finally opened its doors as a luxury hotel.

The dining-room seats 45 and has been furnished in traditional decor, complete with oil paintings and open log fire, which creates a warm atmosphere in more ways than one. The style of food is distinctly modern British, but has been carefully developed by three members of the Morris family (John, Nicola and Simon) who own the hotel.

A four-course table d'hôte menu is offered each evening, although residents must make a specific point of reserving a dinner place as this is not done automatically. The menu opens with a soup and is followed by a choice from at least four or five starters – most restaurants open with a starter and follow with the lighter soup course before the main dish, but this slightly unconventional presentation makes little difference to the overall enjoyment of dinner at Grafton.

Squid Provençal is a commendable option to open with, and two in-house specialities from a typical menu include Supreme of Chicken poached in White Wine and served with a Ginger and Cardamom sauce, or the equally delicious Loin of Pork sautéed in butter and served with a Herb Ratatouille and a Madeira Sauce. A very positive plus is the option of a full vegetarian table d'hôte alternative menu, at the same price (around £21) as the standard menu, instead of the rather tokenistic vegetarian main course offered by so many restaurants.

Grafton Manor is one of the smallest Country House Hotels included in this guide. It has just nine bedrooms, all individually furnished to the highest standards of comfort, featuring an excellent combination of period furniture and the attractive option of an open fire, and private bathroom facilities, colour television and direct-dial telephone. A number of rooms have four-posters with a rather unusual velvet drape hanging from a central point above the bed. Pleasing little extras are the bowl of fruit and bottle of Malvern mineral water left in each bedroom.

Grafton Manor is close to the main motorway network, so nearby attractions are plentiful. Worcester and Birmingham can be reached within 30 minutes by car, and Stratford-upon-Avon, with its theatre and Shakespearean attraction, is just under an hour's drive away. Additional attractions include the Avoncroft Museum of Buildings and the Brierly Crystal factory.

55

THE GREENWAY

Shurdington, Cheltenham, Gloucestershire GL51 5UG
Tel: 0242 862352

Nearest town Cheltenham.
Directions Leave Cheltenham on the A46 Stroud
road, pass through the small village of
Shurdington, and on leaving the village you will
see the entrance Lodge and gates on your left.
A member of the **Pride of Britain** consortium.
Awards AA *** (red) graded and rosette for food;
British Tourist Authority commended; Michelin
three red Turrets, Egon Ronay 79%; one of
Wedgwood's Top Fifty Hotels of the World.
Open throughout the year, except for two weeks
in January.
Special **winter breaks** are available from 1st
November until mid-March.
*The hotel is suitable for the disabled; dogs and children
under seven are not allowed.*
Price for dinner, with wine, bed and breakfast for
two – £100–£150.
Credit cards All major cards.
Overall mark out of ten 8

Surrounded by three acres of ornamental garden, the Greenway enjoys the luxury of being hidden from the hustle and

bustle of daily life and within view of the sweeping Cotswold Hills. In darker centuries, the translation 'green way' meant grove or sheep road and the hotel takes its name from a pre-Roman path which led from the hotel to the hills. The path makes an interesting afternoon's stroll as it eventually leads to Long Barrow, an ancient burial site and the remains of a pre-Iron Age fort dating back 5,000 years.

The land upon which the hotel now stands was originally known as the Little Shurdington Estate, and early records reveal that it belonged to the Lawrence family as early as 1521. The family itself can trace its roots back to the twelfth century, and the records show that one William Lawrence commenced construction work on his new manor house in 1584. The family originated in Lancashire, and it can be reasonably assumed that they were involved with the wool trade, using Gloucester docks, and hence their interest in the Cheltenham area.

By 1616 the Greenway was complete, and in that year it first appears in the Court Manorial Rolls for England. The Lawrence family sold the hotel in 1854, and it went through a succession of different owners before finally being opened as a Country House Hotel in 1947. Ever since then, the emphasis has been on personal, friendly and attentive care for all guests – without being obtrusive. When the hotel is full, a maximum of 38 guests are looked after by a total staff of 40.

All the Greenway's public rooms, including the bright reception area with its proud old grandmother clock, are airy and informal. The main drawing-room has a charming period decor, matching the deep floral-patterned armchairs and fine antique furniture in the room. The warmth and comfort of this room, and indeed the hotel as a whole, is unmistakable.

The hotel's dining-room is actually an elegantly restored conservatory, seating up to 50 guests at once and offering fine views of the gardens and parkland all around. The restaurant is very popular with non-residents, and on average the ratio between residents and non-residents is about half and half.

Advance booking, by at least a week and particularly at weekends, is essential.

The style of cooking is in the modern Country House style and a fixed-price table d'hôte menu is presented each evening by head chef Tony Robson-Burrell. First courses can be a choice of home-made soup – beetroot, or something similar – or a more substantial starter like Monkfish and Wild Mushroom Mousseline, served with a Sorrel Sauce, or even a delicious Wild Rabbit Terrine served with Apple and Blackberry Chutney.

Main dish options are reasonably varied and include venison, veal, beef, chicken and at least two fish dishes. Fillet of Skate, braised in Dry Cider and Chervil, is a more intriguing alternative to the rather traditional Escalope of Salmon – even if it is served on a mouthwatering Julienne of Vegetables in a Sparkling Red Burgundy Sauce. The sweet menu is extensive, and not for those even beginning to contemplate a diet! A popular speciality of the Greenway is their Hot Pear and Hazlenut Cream Puff, served with an Orange Sabayon – delicious – although at least fifteen minutes must be allowed for preparation of this dish.

The Greenway has nineteen bedrooms, all of which are either double or twin-bedded and all with private bathroom facilities, remote-control colour television, direct-dial telephones and, above all, outstanding views of the surrounding garden and countryside. Each one is individually furnished and styled, and a number still have an authentic supporting beam under the ceiling as a gentle reminder of the solid age of the hotel.

A number of special leisure facilities are available to residents at the Greenway; in addition to three acres of lovely garden, there are a croquet lawn and no fewer than four eighteen-hole golf courses within a four-mile radius of the hotel. In addition, tennis, squash and horse riding can all be easily arranged. For something really special, you will have difficulty resisting the appeal of a tour of the Cotswolds in an eight-seater 1934 Rolls Royce. Picnic lunches are served from a traditional hamper strapped to the back of the car and, honestly, if the weather is kind then there are few more idyllic ways of getting a real glimpse of life as it was a couple of generations ago for those fortunate enough to live in a house like the Greenway throughout the year.

56

HAMBLETON HALL

Hambleton, Oakham, Rutland LE15 8TH
Tel: 0572 56991

Nearest town Oakham.
Directions From the south, take the A606
towards Oakham. Approximately one mile before
Oakham look for the (signposted) left turn to
Hambleton village only. About 2.5 miles down this
road is the village itself and the hotel is on the
right at the end of the village.
A member of the **Relais et Châteaux** consortium.
Awards AA *** (red) graded and rosette for food;
AA award for Best Welcome 1985; Michelin three
(red) Turrets; Egon Ronay 82% and award as
Hotel of the Year 1985; Egon Ronay Cellar of the
Year 1986; *Good Hotel Guide* César Award for
comprehensive excellence in the Luxury class
1985; Badoit and *Decanter* magazine Restaurant of
the Year 1987.
Open throughout the year.
Special breaks Winter breaks available
November until April.
The hotel is suitable for disabled guests; children and
dogs accepted by prior arrangement.
Price for dinner, with wine, bed and breakfast,
for two – £100–£150.
Credit cards All major cards accepted.
Overall mark out of ten 9

Tim and Stefa Hart opened Hambleton Hall as a hotel in 1980. When they did so, they had a keen desire to retain the Hambleton style of English country living which had distinguished it in the century or so before, when it was a private residence. The house was built in 1881 by Walter Marshall as a base for his hunting activities with a number of local fox hunts. Marshall never married, is remembered for the excellence of his dinner table and cellar, and the somewhat generous level of female company he kept at Hambleton.

His younger sister, Mrs Eva Astley Paston Cooper, inherited the house after his death and became quite a socialite in her day. Well-known figures such as Noel Coward, Charles Scott Moncreiff and Sir Malcolm Sargent are all known to have visited Hambleton Hall at least once. The house had various owners prior to 1980, and although the interior had undergone few fundamental changes since the last century, the whole countryside around Hambleton Hall changed markedly in 1976 with the creation of Rutland Water. Acres of land were deliberately flooded, creating what is now a rather picturesque man-made reservoir and lake.

One of Hambleton Hall's most attractive rooms is the main dining-room, a bright restaurant decorated by internationally known decorator Nina Campbell and with a seating capacity for up to 50 people. The views far across Rutland Water are wonderful and would almost convince you that the great lake has always been there. The cuisine at Hambleton is extremely popular with residents and non-residents alike, and the proprietors advise that up to a month's notice is generally required for non-residents wishing to dine here on a Saturday evening. For other nights, try to allow at least a week's warning.

Chef Brian Baker's style of cooking has been highlighted by an impressive number of guide books, and it combines some of the charm of *nouvelle cuisine* with a healthy respect for the fundamentals of traditional stocks and sauces where appropriate. Even the printed menu is impressive: an ornate rectangular card, designed by artist Hugh Robson, it looks more like a family tree plan at first glance than a menu. And, as in the best family trees, you can be assured of [...] surprises as you read through it.

A set table d'hôte menu is available each eve[...] appreciate the luxury cuisine offered by Hambleton[...] would be well advised to glance through the à la carte [...] before making up your mind. The most expensive starter is [...] exquisite panfried Foie Gras served with Mango and Corn Salad. Fish courses work out around the same price as the Foie Gras, and include panfried Fillet of Sea Bass, served with a Salad of Baby Leeks, which is a commendable, if at first glance rather unusual, choice.

Main dish options are unlikely to disappoint you, and if you really feel like splashing out on that special occasion, don't hesitate to try the Freshly Poached Lobster, served in its shell with Fresh Basil. It really is a magnificent dish as presented at Hambleton. Whatever your choice, there is an extensive wine list which is pretty well guaranteed to include your favourite bottle. As the proprietors themselves admit, the wine list concentrates on bottles which are excellent to drink rather than a worthy accumulation of fashionable labels with indifferent contents.

The hotel has fifteen bedrooms, all with private facilities, colour television and telephone, and most with great views across Rutland Water and beyond. There is also a lift to all floors.

A helpful booklet, updated annually, is given to all guests and outlines a host of things to do around Hambleton Hall. A number of recreation facilities are available at the hotel, including trout fishing, sailing, riding, tennis, golf and shooting. A rather unusual recreation, fox hunting, is unlikely to be to everyone's taste, but can be arranged for guests keen to try this sport of the English upper classes.

Nearby attractions include Belvois (pronounced 'beaver') Castle, Althorp (home of the Earl and Countess Spencer, father and stepmother of the Princess of Wales), Lincoln, Stamford, Broughton and Burghley.

HAM HALL

Suffolk IP8 3NS
47 387 268

[a few interesting
ing, but to
Hall you
dishes
an]

Nearest town Ipswich.
Directions From Ipswich, Hintlesham Hall is easily located just five miles west, on the main A1071.
A member of the **Relais et Châteaux** consortium.
Awards AA *** graded and rosette; Egon Ronay 80%; 1988 *Good Hotel Guide* César Award.
Open throughout the year.
Special breaks A number of theme breaks – shooting, racing and so on – are available.
The hotel is unsuitable for the disabled; children over ten are allowed, and dogs by special prior arrangement only.
Price for dinner, with wine, bed and breakfast for two – over £150.
Credit cards Access, Visa, Amex and Diners Club.
Overall mark out of ten 9.

Set in eighteen acres of gardens and parkland, it is not difficult to see why Hintlesham Hall is occasionally referred to as the most beautiful Country House in East Anglia. The original house was built in 1578, during the reign of Elizabeth I, but it was substantially altered during the Georgian era at the end of the eighteenth century by Richard Powys, then serving as a principal clerk of the Treasury.

Today the hotel still has a long, straight drive running to the front door. Well-groomed lawns and white-chain-linked posts line the edge of the substantial gardens, and this rather direct approach to the front of the hotel allows visitors to really appreciate the marvellous Georgian façade. The main building is built in the fashion of a single rectangular E-shaped block, with two extended and symmetrical wings protruding past the entrance lobby. One small feature you cannot miss are the fat Georgian chimneys, with their wide tops, which provide an evocative reminder of the days when wood-burning fires were more fashionable than the more messy, but longer-lasting, coal fires.

Your first glimpse of the interior of Hintlesham Hall will be the long, cool entrance hall which acts very much as a 'no-man's land' between the warm interior of the hotel and the outside world. Its smooth hexagonal stone tiles are complemented by marble benches and large wandering pot plants. Inside, the public rooms are no less impressive, and the huge square lounge is clad with honey-coloured pine panelling and filled with comfortable armchairs. A number of antique oil paintings offer a pleasing alternative for you to admire should you ever tire of the views far across the hotel grounds from the lounge windows.

Hintlesham Hall has seventeen bedrooms, all luxuriously furnished, and a number of the suites are reckoned to be among the most comfortable in East Anglia. The Rosette Room, with its rose-pink decor and fine cloth-draped four-poster, is understandably one of the most popular rooms in the hotel. All bedrooms have private facilities, and a range of little extras, like a refrigerated mini-bar and Crabtree and Evelyn toiletries.

The hotel has two restaurants, although the smaller of the two, which can accommodate up to sixteen people at once, is reserved for private functions. The main dining-room is panelled in a similar style to the main lounge and bar areas, and the end result is as relaxing as it is pleasing to the eye. Hintlesham Hall has developed a fine reputation for its cuisine, and it is extremely popular with non-residents who are advised to book well in advance for both lunch and dinner. Lunch is available all week except Sundays.

The style of cooking is modern French and English, with, interestingly, distinct Japanese influences. Local home-produced ingredients are used as far as possible, but the addition of some splendid foreign delicacies works extremely well. A four-course table d'hôte menu is available each evening, with a choice of two main dishes, but the full à la carte menu is extremely difficult to resist. Four courses for two, including wine, will leave you little change out of £80 – and will cost even more if you go for the top-price dishes – but the quality is indisputable. The obvious highlight from the range of hors d'oeuvres is an ounce and a half of Sevruga Caviar, served on ice with Warm Russian Pancakes and Sour Cream. At almost £20 per person it is three times the price of the average starter, but a worthy indulgence if you enjoy this most classic of dishes.

Two recommended specialities from the nine or ten main course options are Breast of Norfolk Guineafowl, served with Smoked Bacon and Green Lentil Ragout, and a very filling composition of Mignons of Veal, Black Truffles and Escalopes of Foie Gras. Whatever main course you decide to choose, it will still work out cheaper than your caviar if you've opted for that luxury as a starter!

One outstanding feature of Hintlesham Hall has to be its wine list, which is easily one of the best of any hotel featured in this guide. Stretching to over twenty closely typed pages, several hundred vintages are available. Virtually all come from Italy, France or Germany, and prices range from a very respectable house white – a light, dry Cler Blanc, Maître de Chais – at around £7 a bottle, right up to a number of bottles in excess of £250. There are some classic red Bordeaux included, offering most vintages right back to 1955, at very reasonable prices.

Nearby attractions include a wide range of walks and strolls within the hotel grounds, facilities for tennis (indoor), horse riding and golf. In addition, you can visit Flatford Mill, best known for its association with the painter Constable, the regional capital Norwich with its ancient cathedral and castle, and the town of Colchester with its nearby oyster farms.

58

HOTEL DE LA BERE

Southam, Cheltenham, Gloucestershire GL52 3NJ
Tel: 0242 37771

Nearest town Cheltenham.
Directions The hotel lies on the B4632 from
Cheltenham to Stratford-upon-Avon, about three
miles out of Cheltenham.
Awards AA *** RAC graded.
Open throughout the year.
Special breaks 'Getaway' two-day half-board
breaks available all year; also half-board weekly
rates.
*A number of rooms in Lodge accommodation in the hotel
grounds are suitable for disabled guests; children are
allowed but dogs are not permitted..*
Price for dinner, with wine, bed and breakfast for
two – under £100.
Credit cards All major cards accepted.
Overall mark out of ten 8.5

For nearly five centuries, a graceful old mansion house has
stood at the foot of Cleeve Hill just a couple of miles north of
the bustling Cheltenham Spa. The precise date of the house's
construction is lost in the mists of time, but it is fairly certain
that it was begun in 1485 by a local nobleman, Thomas

Goodman. His initials can still be seen carved into the original door, now in the outer wall of the Great Hall.

It is known that the mansion was completed in 1501 by Sir John Huddlestone, a knight and favourite of the enigmatic Henry VIII who was destined to start the Tudor dynasty. The fortunes of the family were entwined with those of the Tudors for decades; indeed, Sir John became an in-law of King Henry VIII when his wife's niece, Jane Seymour, became the king's third wife in 1536. The tragic young queen survived barely a year after her wedding, dying suddenly after the birth of her only son, the future King Edward VI of England.

Later, generations of De la Beres retained the favour of their sovereign. Thomas Bagshot de la Bere was a friend of George III, and entertained him at the house in 1788. In the nineteenth century the house passed into the hands of Lord Ellenborough, a distinguished politician and for a time Governor-General of India. He is responsible for adding the rather ugly Norman-style keep and the Indian memorial in the grounds, which once contained some fine carvings but is now, sadly, crumbling away.

Thankfully, the house has had few later alterations and still looks and feels like the welcoming Tudor mansion it was originally built to be. Such modernization as has taken place has not damaged the Tudor charm of the house, and all the main public rooms retain a rich sense of history. Then, as now, the Great Hall is at the heart of the mansion, and its huge oak beams, wood panelling, stone fireplace and – above all – authentic minstrel gallery cannot fail to evoke just a suggestion of the pageantry which made the De la Bere house one of the principle residences in Gloucestershire for centuries. As you might imagine, a huge roaring fire in the chillier winter months quite completes the atmosphere of this charming room.

Wherever you go in the hotel, you will be surrounded by ornate plaster work, open fireplaces and solid oak panelling – priceless authenticity which so many later hotels try to copy. All the public rooms are named after Royal periods in history: the Tudor Room, the Elizabethan Room, the Royalist Room –

and even a Cromwell Room which, as you might expect, is just that little bit different in terms of decor and comfort, but no less welcoming.

The hotel has two restaurants: the formal Beaufort offers a very good traditional English à la carte menu as well as a reasonable fixed-price menu; the second restaurant is a Wheelers of St James fish restaurant. There is little difference in price or quality, and both restaurants offer equally adventurous menus, with a range of tantalizing specialities. Good wine lists accompany both menus, and really your choice of restaurant should be governed by little more than the level of formality you wish to enjoy whilst dining.

The hotel has 46 bedrooms, including five four-posters and all with private bathroom facilities, colour television and all the standard extras you would expect of a three-star Country House Hotel. One or two bedrooms have the supreme luxury of a Jacuzzi as well. The individual style of decor in each room is interesting, and each one is named after an English king or queen who may or may not have stayed at the mansion during his or her lifetime.

Leisure facilities at the Hotel De la Bere are excellent. All guests have honorary membership of the hotel's Sports and Country Club for the duration of their stay. Amenities there include five squash courts, indoor and outdoor tennis, badminton, snooker, an outdoor heated swimming pool, saunas, a solarium and a full gymnasium.

In addition to the hotel's own facilities, nearby attractions include Cheltenham, Shakespeare's Stratford-upon-Avon, Bristol, Oxford and the natural beauty of the surrounding Cotswold Hills.

59

LANGAR HALL

Langar, Nottinghamshire NG13 9HG
Tel: 0949 60559

Nearest town Nottingham.
Directions Langar Hall is located twenty miles
south of Leicester, and is signposted off the main
A46 Leicester to Newark road via Cropwell
Bishop, or else off the A52 Grantham to
Nottingham road.
A member of the **Wolsey Lodges and Country
Homes** group.
Open throughout the year, except weekends in
January and February when the hotel is open by
arrangement only to groups of four or more.
No **special breaks** available, although private
parties can be accommodated.
*The hotel is not suitable for the disabled; children are
allowed but dogs are permitted only by prior
arrangement, unless their owner is staying in the
Parachute Suite.*
Price for dinner, with wine, bed and breakfast for
two – under £100.
Credit cards Access, Visa and Diners Club.
Overall mark out of ten 7

Langar Hall is one of those places which seems to have been forgotten by the outside world. Few other guides, even the normally thorough AA, acknowledge the existence of this little hotel, and for guests who are attracted by a secluded atmosphere this is one of the most positive features of Langar Hall. The hotel is the ideal base for exploring most of the southern English shires, and a comfortable stop for travellers heading from north to south, or vice versa.

The house is unobtrusive, with the emphasis on comfort and privacy rather than pampered luxury, and even the history of the present late Georgian house is rather undistinguished. Yet there is something about Langar Hall which, for many, makes it simply irresistible. It was built in 1830 on the site of a great house, and was for a while home to Admiral Lord Howe who was the hero of the 'Glorious 1st of June' English naval victory in 1794.

All of the public rooms and bedrooms enjoy fine views across ancient parkland and a veritable maze of medieval fish ponds. A sprawling garden around the hotel provides much of the vegetable produce for the dinner table, and also the basis of a number of entertaining short walks of varying length, depending on how much energy you have to spare.

This hotel is different in so many ways that it is rather difficult to describe by the same objective criteria as virtually every other hotel in this guide has been described. Suffice to say that it offers rather more than an informal welcome to guests by catering for a maximum of just six at once who are all treated like personal friends of the resident owner Imogen Skirving. Throughout your stay at Langar Hall you will be able to appreciate her unique combination of the standards of a good hotel with the hospitality of Country House living. As she herself is proud to admit, this enjoyable experience is 'delightfully different'.

In summer, guests use the White Drawing Room, a marvellous old Adams-style parlour with comfortable armchairs and a wide collection of local guide books and up-to-date magazines for guests to browse through or ignore just as they could in their own homes. In winter, the main public room is the library with its welcoming log fire.

Breakfast is served in the Kitchen Dining Room which is more properly known as the Pillared Dining Hall. The walls are a veritable art gallery of nineteenth-century to modern paintings, and if one happens to take your fancy then you can even take it home as they are exhibited for sale.

In the evening, all six guests generally dine together, round an old circular table. This level of intimacy with your fellow residents may or may not be to your liking, although business people away from home often enjoy the company this arrangement offers. Guests can, if they so choose, dine at separate tables and a few non-residents are now permitted. A four-course set meal is provided each evening; there is no choice, but the standard of food is very high and house specialities include Rabbit Terrine, Creamy Chicken Liver Pâté, Rack of Lamb with Sauce Palloise, Sole Veronique and – in season – Asparagus, and early forced Rhubarb with Ginger. Menus are flexible to suit guests, and all fall into the category of 'imaginative' British Country House style.

Langar Hall has just three bedrooms: The Brownlow, with its old four-poster, overlooks the park; the Edwards is a larger double with a solid half-tester-style bed and views across the park and moats; and The Charlotte is a twin-bedded room overlooking the garden. All three have private bathroom facilities, colour television and tea- and coffee-making facilities. In the adjoining Coach House, The Parachute Suite has a double-bedded room with adjoining twin-bed sitting-room and kitchenette, making it ideal for families with children.

Nearby attractions include Belvoir Castle, Belton House, Doddington Hall, Southwell Minster, Newstead Abbey, Sherwood Forest (where Robin Hood once roamed) and the beautiful city of Nottingham. The stately home of the Dukes of Devonshire, Chatsworth, is less than an hour's drive away.

60

LORDS OF THE MANOR

Upper Slaughter, Bourton-on-the-Water, Cheltenham,
Gloucestershire GL54 2JD
Tel: 0451 20243

Nearest town Cheltenham.
Directions The hotel is in the village of Upper
Slaughter, some fifteen miles east of Cheltenham;
it is two miles west of the Fosse Way (A429)
between Stow-on-the-Wold and Bourton-on-the-
Water.
Awards AA *** RAC graded; British Tourist
Authority commended; Egon Ronay
recommended.
Open throughout the year.
Winter breaks are available from the start of
November until the end of March.
The hotel is suitable for the disabled; children are
welcome, and dogs are permitted in the bedrooms only.
Price for dinner, with wine, bed and breakfast for
two – £100–£150.
Credit cards Access, Visa, Amex and Diners
Club.
Overall mark out of ten 7.5

A couple of miles on from Bourton-on-the-Water, unques-
tionably one of rural England's most attractive villages, the

colourfully named Lords of the Manor hotel is a converted country rectory that has lost little of its rustic appeal. The building dates from the seventeenth century, although major structural additions were made in the eighteenth and nineteenth centuries. It is a yellowing, elongated stone house and lies below a small hill invariably planted with wheat during the main arable season.

For two centuries the house was home to the Witts family who were parish rectors for four generations between 1763 and 1913, and were designated Lords of the Manor (hence the hotel's name) from 1852. The present head of the family converted the house into a hotel in 1972, and it is still managed by members of the family.

When you first approach the Manor – as it is more usually called – you are likely to be pleasantly surprised by its setting. It quite dominates the little village of Upper Slaughter and is surrounded by creaking old boughs, leafy country lanes and long meadows – real Laurie Lee stuff! Well-tended gardens enhance the exterior of the Manor and make a delightful splash of colour throughout the busy summer season. A small lake has formed within the hotel grounds, through which the River Eye runs, and trout fishing on this particular stretch is a popular attraction.

Upper Slaughter itself makes an interesting stroll, though the rather sinister name is derived from nothing more harmful than the old Anglo-Saxon word 'sloh' meaning 'a marshy place'. It has a church dating from Norman times, and half a mile upstream on the River Eye (a tributary of the River Thames which eventually reaches London) Milton is reputed to have written his great classic *Paradise Lost*. Virtually no building has taken place anywhere near the Lords since the turn of the century, and with no through traffic allowed, the area is a very peaceful haven from the bustle of everyday city life.

The various public rooms are large and comfortably furnished, although the distinctly old-fashioned atmosphere in the public areas, as opposed to a more welcoming period 'feel', is likely to be gone by the time of publication as a result of a series of major alterations. The old dining-room, created from the merger of a number of smaller rooms, will be reconverted into a small intimate lounge, a new library and a ground-floor bedroom for disabled guests. The new dining-room will be situated where the present kitchen now stands, with access to the landscaped garden through large French windows. A new kitchen building is currently being built.

A extensive à la carte menu is available each evening, and the style of food is best described as modern English with more than a hint of continental influence. The atmosphere in the dining-room is informal and unhurried, and the menu contains a number of interesting surprises. A very rich hors d'oeuvre is the chef's crisp French Salad dressed in a Honey Vinaigrette and accompanied with Oak Smoked Salmon and Venison. From a typical main course selection, two house specialities stand out: Breast of Cornvale Duck, gently cooked and enhanced with quite a strong Game Sauce – and a hint of Beaune de Venise – and a less exotic Cornish Sea Bass, lightly cooked with Vermouth, Basil and finely sliced vegetables.

All fifteen bedrooms have an individual character and are named after the numerous families with whom the Witts have been connected through marriage over the last couple of centuries. In addition to private bathroom facilities, all have one or two pieces of antique furniture and more up-to-date luxuries like colour television and telephones. Two rooms have four-posters and, by the time of publication, an additional six bedrooms and three suites will have been added.

Nearby attractions include the Duke of Marlborough's Blenheim Palace (birthplace of Sir Winston Churchill), the magnificent Warwick Castle, Sudeley Castle (once home of Katherine Parr, one of Henry VIII's six wives), Chastleton House, Broughton Castle and Berkeley Castle, where Edward II was murdered in 1327.

61

MALLORY COURT

Harbury Lane, Tachbrook Mallory, Leamington Spa,
Warwickshire CY33 9QB
Tel: 0926 30214

Nearest town Leamington Spa.
Directions Drive two miles south out of
Leamington Spa, on the A452. Take the left
turning signposted to Harbury and the hotel is
about half a mile away on the right-hand side.
A member of the **Relais et Châteaux**
consortium.
Awards AA *** (red) graded and two rosettes for
food; Egon Ronay recommended; Michelin
recommended – and the only restaurant in the
area with a coveted rosette as well.
Open throughout the year.
Special **winter breaks** are available; rates on
application.
The hotel is unsuitable for disabled visitors; children
under twelve and dogs are not allowed.
Price for dinner, with wine, bed and breakfast for
two – over £150.
Credit cards Access, Visa, Amex and Diners
Club.
Overall mark out of ten 9.5

Mallory Court is an outstanding example of early twentieth-century architecture and, despite being one of the youngest Country House Hotels featured in this guide, it nevertheless promises as warm and luxurious a welcome as any which has been standing for centuries. It embraces many features from earlier periods of building, such as its mellow stonework and leaded windows, and this combines with the space and comfort which are associated with properties belonging to this century.

The house was actually built between 1913 and 1915, and was for many years the family home of Sir John Black, who founded Standard Motors. It remained a family home up until 1977 when the present owners, Jeremy Mort and Allan Holland, bought it. Within a short space of time, the delicate task of upgrading it from a comfortable, but private, family home into a luxury hotel was completed.

Of all the outstanding rooms in the hotel, most agree the huge Pink Lounge is the *pièce de résistance*. The decor speaks for itself, and there really can be few public roms in any hotel more attractive than this grand lounge. It makes no pretences to echo a particular period in history, but, like the rest of the house, offers a combination of the best of several periods, and the overall effect is most pleasing.

The front of the house was the first part to be refurbished and opened as a smart restaurant before the remainder of the hotel was ready to be opened to the public. Even today, the dining-room holds pride of place at Mallory Court. It is a magnificent oak-panelled room, with seating for up to 50 people, and the sensibly arranged tables are not too close together, so offering a level of intimacy and informality which should be the envy of many larger establishments.

Shining silver and crystal glasses rest on pale lemon table-cloths, and the overall impression is one of great elegance. Demand by non-residents to dine here is considerable, so advance booking by at least a week really is essential.

Food is light and innovative, and served in a classical French style. Co-owner Allan Holland is a trained chef and personally supervises the kitchen most evenings. The influence of

French-style *nouvelle cuisine* is considerable: sauces made from cream and stock rather than the usual butter and flour mix are only one example. The extensive table d'hôte menu is one of the most expensive featured in this guide (about £30 for three courses), but be in no doubt that the quality and presentation are outstanding, and after one meal at Mallory Court you will understand why the restaurant deserves the generous accolades it has received over the past twelve years.

Just to give you an idea of the type of choice you can expect at Mallory Court, two of Allan Holland's exquisite starters are: a delicate Warm Mousseline of Lobster filled with White Crab Meat and surrounded with a light Lobster and Dill Sauce; and a Mould of Smoked Salmon enclosing a Smoked Trout Mousse served on a bed of Leeks with a Dill Sauce and garnished with Asparagus.

Main course choices are no less sumptuous. Two easily recommended delights are Breast of Guinea Fowl, roasted with Honey and served with a light Garlic and Cream Sauce flavoured with Brandy and Red Wine, and Thin Fillet of Veal, grilled and garnished with a Julienne of Fresh Ginger, Grapes and Lime Segments served with a Port Wine and Lime Sauce. If you still have room for a dessert, you are likely to have difficulty resisting one such as Hot Coconut Soufflé, flavoured with Malibu and accompanied with a Pineapple Sorbet.

Mallory Court has eight bedrooms, all double or twin rooms, and one luxury suite. The standard of furnishings and comfort in all the individually decorated rooms is extremely high, and all enjoy fine views across the surrounding Warwickshire countryside. As you would expect, all have good-sized private bathroom facilities, colour television, telephone and a complimentary range of toiletries. The Blenheim Room has to have the edge over the others, though, with its king-sized double bed, huge bay windows, balcony and south-facing view across a flourishing rose garden.

Leisure facilities at Mallory Court include ten acres of landscaped gardens to explore, an outdoor heated swimming pool, squash court, all-weather tennis court and a croquet lawn. Golf, riding and fishing are all available nearby. Other attractions in the surrounding area include Warwick Castle, historic Stratford-upon-Avon, Farnborough Hall, Packwood House, and the numerous attractions of easily reached nearby towns such as Tewkesbury, Gloucester, Worcester and Cheltenham.

62

THE MANOR

Lower Slaughter, Gloucestershire GL54 2HP
Tel: 0451 20456

Nearest town Stow-on-the-Wold.

Directions From Evesham follow the A44 (which changes to the A424) to Stow-on-the-Wold. Then follow the A429 turning for the villages of Upper and Lower Slaughter. As you reach Bourton-on-the-Water, the Manor is the big house in front of the stream.

A member of the **Relais du Silence** hotel group.

Awards AA *** graded; English Tourist Board five Crowns.

Open from the start of February until the end of December.

No **special breaks** available.

The hotel is unsuitable for the disabled; children under ten, and dogs, are not allowed.

Price for dinner, with wine, bed and breakfast, for two – £100–£150.

Credit cards Access and Visa.

Overall mark out of ten 8.5

The Manor Hotel is one of only a handful in the UK which is affiliated to the prestigious French group Relais du Silence. Since its foundation in 1969, the group now includes over three hundred hotels throughout Europe and one simple factor unites them: the ability to offer supreme peace and tranquillity in a rural setting combined with some very high standards of comfort. The Manor more than fits that description, standing, as it does, in many acres of private ground and surrounded by mature shady trees and colourful narrow flowerbeds.

A manor house was known on the site of the present hotel as long ago as 1004 AD, and in 1443 it became a convent housing nuns from the order of Syon. The medieval two-storey dovecote that you can still see within the grounds is said to have supplied the nuns with a source of food for decades. The Manor returned to the Crown shortly after 1534 when the order was dissolved as a result of Henry VIII's break with Rome.

In the year James VI of Scotland ascended the British throne as James I, The Manor was granted to Sir George Whitmore, High Sheriff of Gloucestershire, and it remained in the possession of his family for over three centuries, until 1964. Most of the present hotel dates from 1655 when Sir George's son, Richard, had the old house almost completely rebuilt. One Valentine Strong was contracted for the task, as old records show, 'For the sum of £200-0s-0d in lawful English money'. Valentine Strong's son was destined to outstrip even his father's achievements as an architect when he was employed by Sir Christopher Wren in the building of St Paul's Cathedral in London.

Like most Country Houses in Great Britain, The Manor has been altered considerably by successive generations; fashions change, but thankfully few of the main interior fittings have been altered. As you enter the hotel for the first time, you cannot fail to be struck by the attractive old stone fireplace in the main reception area. This dates from 1658, around the time when the entire West Wing was constructed. The ornate ceiling in the drawing-room, the hotel's most appealing public room, is decorated in a pattern incorporating medallions of fruit, flowers, birds and angels, and is contemporary with the seventeenth-century additions to the building.

A further small addition was made to the west of The Manor in 1864, and the present East Wing dates back no further than 1891. A rather fetching feature of the staircase in the hotel is the attractive gazebo window located on the main landing. The view overlooking the gardens to the north is a treat, and this is one of the best vantage points from which to admire the grounds in all their glory.

The restaurant seats up to 30 people and is luxuriously decorated. Traditional English country-style cooking is preferred, and locally grown produce and herbs from the hotel's own gardens are used throughout. A table d'hôte menu is available each evening with a choice of at least five dishes for every course. If you enjoy unusual dishes then you will adore The Manor's own creation of Calves' Sweetbreads and Kidneys lightly sautéed with Wild Mushrooms and bathed in a rich Champagne Sauce. It is a truly magnificent dish of subtle flavours, and even those not normally keen on these ingredients will be impressed.

Main course dishes are strong on local fish and game: Breast of Chicken (which, they point out, was maize-fed) is served with an imaginative parcel of Puff Pastry containing Livers and Shallots; Fan of Salmon and Brill is a favourite fish dish, and comes steamed and served with Baby Leeks in a Vermouth Sauce, already seasoned with Fresh Basil and Julienne of Vegetables. An excellent wine list, bound like a little twenty-page booklet and enriched with a few well-chosen quotes from Walter Scott to Thackery about wine drinking, will accompany your menu. A separate aperitif list is available should you decide on a modest tipple in the library before dining.

The hotel has a total of 21 quite luxurious bedrooms, all with private bathroom facilities and the additional trimmings you would expect in an upper-class Country House Hotel. Guests have the added advantage of a range of good leisure facilities at the Manor, and can enjoy a heated indoor swimming pool, sauna and solarium, outdoor hard tennis court and a croquet lawn.

Nearby attractions include day trips to historic Stratford-upon-Avon, Gloucester, Oxford and Tewkesbury. One of the joys of this part of England is the choice visitors have to explore all the history and culture of large towns like Stratford and Oxford, or else explore the scenic beauty of the surrounding countryside – and all the quaint little villages like Upper and Lower Slaughter, and Bourton-on-the-Water.

63

THE MANOR HOUSE

Castle Combe, Chippenham, Wiltshire SN14 7HR
Tel: 0249 782206

Nearest town Chippenham.
Directions The Manor House lies between the
M4 and A420 just off the B4039, six miles from
Chippenham. If travelling here on the M4, leave at
junction 17 or 18. From junction 17 it is
approximately fifteen minutes' drive along country
lanes.
Awards AA and RAC *** graded.
Open throughout the year.
Winter breaks available.
Children and dogs are both welcome, by prior
arrangement.
Price for dinner, with wine, bed and breakfast for
two – £100–£150.
Credit cards All major cards accepted.
Overall mark out of ten 7.5

Settled amid 26 acres of garden and parkland, the Manor
House of Castle Combe has stood in the green Wiltshire
countryside for over a thousand years. Earliest settlements
have been traced to Roman times, although it is more plausible
that those early visitors chose the site above the valley because

of its great defensive position rather than the undoubted beauty of its surroundings.

The original Manor House was first built in the fourteenth century, when England was in one of its few peaceful phases during the medieval centuries, and the nearby Castle Combe fell into disuse. Most of the original building was destroyed by fire a couple of generations later, and only a grain-drying kiln and granary (which was not discovered until the 1970s) can reasonably be dated to the original fourteenth-century building.

Most of the front of the present building was completely rebuilt in the seventeenth century, although some alterations have been made right up to the present generation. The house's best-known former Lord of the Manor was the long-lived Sir John Falstaff who resided here from 1390 until 1460. A magnificent eighteenth-century Italian frieze, depicting Shakespearian characters, hangs in the public lounge next to the front hall, and it is generally believed that Sir John was the inspiration for Shakespeare's imaginative character, Sir John Falstaff.

Your first sight of the interior of the house will be the wide entrance hall, and the warmth of the welcome you are certain to receive when you arrive will be typical of the friendly, yet unobtrusive, care and attention which you can expect throughout your stay. Still in the entrance hall, look out for the intricately carved oak panelling all around you. The date 1664 is rather confusing as the panelling was not commissioned especially for the Manor House but was 'borrowed' instead from another house nearby.

The main public room is the comfortable public lounge, with the Shakespearian frieze, and a rather odd assortment of deep armchairs and little antique tables for you to rest drinks or magazines on. An open fireplace, with white tiled surround, completes the distinctly period atmosphere of this room.

Easily the grandest room in the Manor House is the long dining-room, with its narrow rectangular windows overlooking the surrounding gardens and parkland. The room was added to the hotel in the 1970s, but nevertheless was constructed in a style in keeping with the rest of the hotel and decorated in an unobstrusive combination of browns and creams. The atmosphere is rather formal, but nevertheless welcoming, and the quality of the food most impressive.

The style of cooking is reasonably traditional, and the staff of twelve chefs aims to bring back some more classical dishes, plate-serving them in a lighter, less formal style. Continental and English specialities are available every evening: summer specialities include Wye Salmon and Devon Lobster, while favourite winter dishes include locally shot Pheasant and a Rich Game Pie. Vegetables are all cooked firm to the bite, sauces made by reducing stocks, and no bechemal or demi-glace is ever used in the kitchen. An impressive wine list is also available.

The Manor House has 33 bedrooms, all individually furnished to a high standard with private bathroom facilities, colour television, direct-dial telephone and a thoughtful baby-listening device.

Leisure facilities are excellent: most outdoor activities – fishing, golf, tennis and so forth – can be arranged locally.

Nearby attractions include an inexhaustible range of walks and strolls through the surrounding grounds where, reputedly, there are anything up to 70 different varieties of trees to be seen; Castle Combe itself makes an interesting visit, and a booklet with details of the castle's history is on sale at reception; the ancient Roman town of Bath is only a short drive away and, a little further on, you can visit Bristol, Stroud or even South Wales quite easily.

64

THE OLD RECTORY

Great Snoring, Fakenham, Norfolk NR21 OHP
Tel: 0328 72 597

Nearest town Walsingham.
Directions From King's Lynn, it is 22 miles on
the A148 to Fakenham. Follow signpost to village
of Great Snoring and The Old Rectory is behind
the church on the Barsham Road.
A member of the **Country Homes** group.
Awards British Tourist Authority commended;
recommended by Michelin and Egon Ronay.
Open throughout the year except 25th and 26th
December.
Special breaks available from November until
March inclusive.
*Not suitable for disabled guests; children not encouraged
and dogs not allowed.*
Price for dinner, with wine, bed and breakfast for
two – under £100.
Credit cards Amex and Diners Club.
Overall mark out of ten 7

The name Great Snoring cannot fail to conjure up in your
mind all sorts of romantic images of a secluded little English

village. It is a tiny place, and your impressions of the area will be confirmed as you first drive through the village's attractive Norfolk setting; indeed, one of the best features about the Old Rectory hotel is its wonderful location for exploring the beautiful countryside all around you.

Today the hotel is rather more than the average country parsonage you would expect to find in this part of the world. It is a former manor house noted for its fine architecture dating back to Tudor times. The early history of the house is lost, but it is thought to date back to around 1500 when it was the family seat of Sir Ralph Shelton. At that time the building was hexagonal – a rather difficult shape to imagine when you look at the present, rather solid, rectangular block. During the Victorian era the house underwent considerable alterations and over-enthusiastic restoration work which completely altered the design of the building.

You can still see traces of the marvellous Tudor workmanship around the outside of the house. On the south-east façade, for example, the stone mullioned windows are bordered with frieze designs in terracotta tiling. Alternate male and female heads are depicted, and it can only be assumed that these represent the original Shelton family who first lived here. The Shelton crest can also be seen on the large oak front door, facing the village church nearby.

Relaxed informality is assured at the Old Rectory, and the combination of this and the peaceful surroundings makes this hotel an ideal option if you're after a complete 'away-from-it-all' break. There are fresh flowers in all the public rooms, and generally in the bedrooms as well. During the summer, these mostly come from the hotel's grounds. There is a one-and-a-half-acre garden for guests to enjoy.

The pleasingly informal atmosphere is made possible by the size of the hotel: it is small, with just seven bedrooms and only a couple of airy public rooms. All seven bedrooms have their own private bathroom facilities, colour television, direct-dial telephone, and are individually decorated to ensure that one stands out from another. The overall result at the Old

Rectory is the feeling that you are staying more as a family visitor than a paying guest.

Probably the nicest feature about the hotel is its dining-room. This is a bright, adaptable room with authentic old oak beams and stone mullioned windows. It is not a restaurant as such, and accordingly is not open to non-residents, but it specializes in serving good English-style food to residents.

Dinner is served between 7 p.m. and 8 p.m. with a choice of appetizers: the home-made soup is the most popular. There is also a choice of dessert and a good selection of cheeses. The menu range is quite simple, and although the food is delicious and presentation impressive, the choice is rather unimaginative.

Only one main course dish at dinner is offered. Local game and fish may feature on the selection of main dishes: the Sole served in a White Wine Sauce, garnished with Grapes, is superb, and other specialities include a rich Escalope of Pork, steeped in a Cider and Cream Sauce; also Stroganoff of locally shot Pheasant. A small wine list of around a couple of dozen bins is available.

Nearby attractions include the towns of Norwich, King's Lynn, Ipswich and Colchester, together with the popular summer holiday resort of Great Yarmouth.

65

RIBER HALL

Matlock, Derbyshire DE4 5JU
Tel: 0629 2795

Nearest town Matlock.
Directions Leave the M1 at junction 28 and
follow the A38/A615 signposted for Matlock. The
hotel is about a mile south-east of the town, just
off the main road at Tansley.
A member of the **Pride of Britain** consortium.
Awards AA *** graded; British Tourist Authority
commended.
Open all year.
Winter breaks are available from mid-October
until mid-April.
*The hotel is unsuitable for the disabled; children under
ten and dogs are not allowed.*
Price for dinner, with wine, bed and breakfast for
two – £100–£150.
Credit cards All major cards accepted.
Overall mark out of ten 9

Few other British Country House Hotels can offer a more
tranquil setting than the edge of the Peak District National
Park – and at the same time offer the accessibility of the M1

just twenty minutes away, as well as a number of large towns within half an hour's drive.

Riber Hall hotel was effectively rescued from a derelict shell in 1970, but its origins lie far back in the fifteenth century when it was built by the Riberghs of Riber. By marriage, the house passed through a couple of generations of Robothams, and then the Wolley family, who lived here for a further seven generations until 1668. The most recent structural addition to the house was undertaken by the last of the Wolleys, in 1661, seven years before Riber Hall passed out of the family's hands for good.

Three centuries followed, and gradually the old house fell into a state of disuse which progressed to near dereliction. Only the huge commitment of current owners Alex and Gill Biggin when they bought the house nearly twenty years ago saved Riber Hall, and the magnificent results of their devotion to the huge task of restoring and refurbishing can be seen today.

Beamed ceilings dominate virtually all rooms inside Riber Hall. The main public room, apart from the dining-room, is a long lounge which has the hotel's most striking ceiling. Deep brushed velvet armchairs complement a number of upright antique chairs placed around the enormous carved fireplace, and the little touches like the grandfather clock in one corner, and the old post horn above the main doorway, make it a place of immense character.

The dining-room is a striking early Georgian-style room, with two huge white cross-beams dominating the ceiling and authentic Jacobean and Adam fireplaces. The decor reflects a different period in the history of Riber Hall, making a rather unusual combination of furnishings, but, nevertheless, creating a very unique and pleasing effect. Dark wood period furniture contrasts well with the light wall decor, and the heavy crystal glass, silver cutlery and fan-folded linen napkins complete the intimate period feel.

The style of cuisine is a combination of French *nouvelle* and classical, and Riber Hall has long been ackowledged as an outstanding restaurant in this part of England. Up to 50 can be seated at once, but advance booking is essential for non-residents. There is a fine à la carte menu working out at around £25 per person, inclusive of service and VAT, and there is a strong emphasis on the best local produce, particularly game. The wine list is detailed and thoughtfully put together, with some very nicely priced younger European vintages available.

Riber Hall has eleven bedrooms, all of which offer exceptionally high standards of comfort. All the rooms have a very individual decor: it could be Tudor red, or a gentle blend of pastel shades, but you are unlikely to be disappointed by the clever interior design displayed throughout the hotel. Most rooms still have a number of old support beams blended into the decor of the room, and one or two have the added period touch of authentic stonework on at least one of the walls. In addition to very smart private bathroom facilities, nine rooms have antique four-poster beds and five have that most favoured luxury, a private Jacuzzi. All the rooms are large, airy and extremely comfortable. Probably the highest compliment that can be paid to any Country House Hotel is that it doesn't 'feel' like a hotel. Riber Hall definitely falls into that category, as you will doubtless discover as soon as you enter one of the bedrooms.

Nearby attractions include a number of outstanding stately homes and castles within half an hour's drive. The best of these is Chatsworth House, family home of the Duke and Duchess of Devonshire, but others include Sudbury Hall, Heddon Hall and Hardwick Hall. The Peak National Park is about fifteen minutes away, and of the surrounding towns and villages the most obvious targets for visitors to the area are Derby and Nottingham.

ROOKERY HALL

Worleston, near Nantwich, Cheshire CW5 6DQ
Tel: 0270 626866

Nearest town Nantwich.

Directions Approaching from the south, on the M6, exit at junction 16 and turn right to follow the A500 Nantwich road. Go over the level crossing and turn right at the roundabout taking the A51 past two sets of traffic lights. Take the next right turn on the B5074 to Worleston and this will take you to Rookery Hall after 1.5 miles.

A member of the **Pride of Britain** consortium.

Awards AA *** (red) graded and rosette for food; RAC *** graded and Blue Ribbon; Egon Ronay and Michelin recommended; 1986 *Sunday Times* Sunday Lunch Restaurant of the Year.

Open throughout the year except for three weeks in January immediately after New Year.

Special **winter breaks** are available from 1st October until 31st March.

The hotel is suitable for disabled guests; children under ten and dogs are not allowed.

Price for dinner, with wine, bed and breakfast for two – over £150.

Credit cards All major cards accepted.
Overall mark out of ten 9.5

If the generous praise heaped on to Rookery Hall by assorted hotel and catering organizations and other independent guide books is anything to go by, this particular hotel has managed to attain one of the best reputations of any Country House Hotel in central England. The hotel is set amid 28 acres of exquisite gardens and wooded parkland, and the care and attention which has so obviously been lavished on these is typical of the high standards you can expect inside the hotel as well. All praise *is* deserved and this is, undoubtedly, one of England's finest Country House Hotels.

Rookery Hall was built by William Hilton Cooke at the end of the eighteenth century. It changed hands in 1867 when Baron Von Schroder, a wealthy banker, bought it, and from then until his death shortly before the outbreak of the First World War he gradually changed the traditional Georgian mansion into the small château which you can see today. The external walls are of fine mellowed sandstone, although little remains of the original building, other than some fine plaster-work inside and the attractive marble chimneypiece which dominates the elegant salon lounge.

Wherever you go inside the hotel, there is a feeling of spaciousness. The main staircase is crafted from the finest English oak and gives a reassuring sense of grandeur as you sweep down to dinner dressed in your finery. The sitting-room is the epitome of elegance and, on a breezy Sunday morning, there can be few more welcoming places to enjoy your morning coffee and a leisurely leaf through the Sunday papers.

But it is the restaurant which really stands out as a public room of great class, and it is one of the finest Victorian dining-rooms in England. The walls are lined with highly polished mahogany and walnut panelling, and this is more than complemented by the sumptuous plastered ceiling. Four painted crests stand out from the ornate raised surface which features nine coronets and a frieze of winged cherubs. From the large windows you get a lovely view of the fountain in the centre of the lawn just in front of the main garden area.

The proprietors describe dining at Rookery Hall as 'entirely twentieth century' with the emphasis on traditional English recipes cooked in a modern and original fashion. Top chef Clive Howe came to the hotel from London's Dorchester Hotel, and his favourite speciality starter is a variation on a Welsh recipe for Cheshire Sausages served with a Gooseberry Sauce. The sausages are actually made from crumbled white Cheshire cheese, mixed with herbs, then rolled in bread-crumbs before being fried.

A worthy recommendation for your main course, from the excellent table d'hôte menu, is succulent Rack of Welsh Lamb served with home-grown Mustard Seed Sauce. Another favourite is the Stew of Duckling in Red Wine, served with Garnishes of Bacon and Onions. Whatever your choice, you have the option of at least half a dozen crisp-cooked vegetables and your meal will be served on the finest Aynsley bone china.

The wine list is more than usually detailed, although rather expensive since Peter Marks appears to have over-stocked on some vintage clarets without paying the same attention to the lesser-priced bottles. House wines are around £12.50 a bottle, and only a handful from the 250 or so listed cost less. For the connoisseur, the 1964 Latour at around £160 is an outstanding choice.

There are eleven bedrooms, all furnished to the very highest standards and offering those pleasing little extras like a bowl of fruit, some quality toiletries and a few freshly baked cookies that cost so little but make the difference between a good hotel and an outstanding hotel.

Croquet, tennis, coarse fishing and an endless number of ways to explore the natural beauty of the surrounding area are all available. Nearby attractions are outlined in a booklet which awaits all guests in their room, but some of the more popular are the city of Chester just twenty miles away (and North Wales just beyond), and the towns of Northwich and Crewe.

67

SECKFORD HALL

Woodbridge, Suffolk IP13 6NU
Tel: 0394 385678

Nearest town Ipswich.
Directions From Ipswich, follow the main A12
north-east – the road is signposted so you can
avoid the centre of town. Seckford Hall is
signposted west of the Woodbridge bypass.
Awards AA *** RAC graded; British Tourist
Authority commended.
Open throughout the year, except Christmas Day.
Special breaks Weekend breaks available all
year, as are half-board mini-holidays for two, three
or four nights.
The hotel is unsuitable for the disabled; children are
welcome, as are 'well behaved' dogs which must remain
on a lead unless in owner's bedroom.
Price for dinner, with wine, bed and breakfast, for
two – £100–£150.
Credit cards All major cards accepted.
Overall mark out of ten 9.5

For over five centuries, Seckford Hall was a private home, and
for a couple of hundred years the ancestral home of the
Seckford family. Its relatively recent transformation into one

of the finest Country House Hotels in central England has ensured that very little of its pedigree history, and all that goes with it in terms of fittings and atmosphere, has been lost.

Little documentary evidence has survived about the house's early years, although it is known that it was built for one Thomas Seckford. It is uncertain precisely when the imposing, ivy-covered Tudor house was finished, although it was definitely sometime between 1541 and 1550. Evidence remains of an even older timber-built house which stood on the present site before then, and this marvellous reminder of medieval English architecture has been built into bedroom number seven, with the authentic Tudor Bar beneath it.

The greatest in a long line of Seckfords was the first Thomas Seckford, who served as Master in Ordinary of the Court of Requests to Her Majesty Queen Elizabeth I. In 1574 he was responsible for commissioning the first detailed set of maps of all the English counties. The finished atlas appeared in 1579 and quickly became the definitive English atlas for generations. It was widely believed that Elizabeth I once held Court at Seckford Hall, although, sadly, written evidence has neither proven nor disproven this popular local belief.

Today Seckford Hall retains many contemporary furnishings and has lost very little of the Tudor splendour that Elizabeth I is likely to have known if she ever did visit the house. Virtually all the gracious public rooms and luxuriously furnished bedrooms have oak-beamed ceilings – and one instinctively knows these are part of the original make-up of the house rather than purely decorative. The house was completely refitted after the Second World War, by which time it had been allowed to slowly deteriorate from its original glory.

Then, as now, the focal point of the whole building is the Great Hall, a marvellous old room surrounded by intricately carved and lovingly restored wood panelling. The old fireplace is not elaborate, but its depth and contrasting white surround are obvious reminders of former days when a huge log-burning fire in this room was the principal source of heating for the entire building. Elegant gold and purple suites have taken the place of the more barren Tudor furnishings which

244

the first Seckfords would have known, and make this most attractive room the finest in the house.

Wherever you go in Seckford Hall you are surrounded by a sense of age and history. Suits of armour stand guard at the end of corridors; sweeping Tudor-style drapes hang in public rooms; and the original stonework has been preserved throughout the interior as far as possible. The furnishings are almost entirely period pieces, some inherited from Windsor Castle. The very chair in which King Edward VII died, on 6th May 1910, is here, although it has been re-upholstered since then.

Apart from the Great Hall, this sense of history is no more strong than in the recently extended restaurant which can seat up to 70. The hotel strives to maintain an atmosphere of quiet dignity, which it does with considerable success, and the very detailed à la carte menu is as absorbing as it is mouthwatering just to read. About sixteen starters are available, including such gems as Trinidad-Style Baked Grapefruit, with Demerara, Cinnamon and Rum; and a delicious salad of large Dublin Bay Prawns.

The house speciality is Lobster, which can be prepared in Termidor-, Broiled-, or Salad-style. A large lobster tank is kept stocked throughout the year, with surprisingly few seasonal price variations. Other specialities are Norfolk Duckling, Oxford Smoked Salmon, and a good range of local game from estates throughout Suffolk.

There are 23 bedrooms, all individually furnished and all with the highest standard of modern comforts: large private bathrooms, remote-control colour Teletext televisions, and tea- and coffee-making facilities. Four rooms have antique four-posters, one of which dates back to 1587, the year when Elizabeth I agreed to the execution of Mary, Queen of Scots, at the not too distant Fotheringay Castle.

Although a heated indoor swimming pool is planned within the next few years, in the meantime you can enjoy the swimming pool, complete with sauna and solarium in Woodbridge. Golf, horse riding, trout fishing, sailing and yacht charter can all be easily arranged locally. Other nearby attractions include beauty spots at Flatford Mill, Dedham and painter John Constable's familiar countryside around Kersey and Lavenham. Around the Suffolk coast you can visit Aldeburgh, Snape with its large concert hall, Minsmere bird sanctuary; and the ports of Felixstowe and Lowestoft are the ideal gateways to mainland Europe.

68

STUDLEY PRIORY

Horton-cum-Studley, near Oxford, Oxfordshire OX9 1AZ
Tel: 086 735 203

Nearest town Oxford.
Directions From Oxford, travel to end of the
Banbury road, taking the third exit (towards
London) along dual carriageway for about 3.5
miles. Follow signs to Horton-cum-Studley, and
stay on the same road until you reach a staggered
junction. Hotel at the top of a hill in the village.
A member of the **Consort Hotels** group of
independent hotels.
Awards AA *** RAC graded; British Tourist
Authority commended; English Tourist Board four
Crowns; Egon Ronay (65%) and Michelin
recommended.
Open throughout the year, except for the first
week in January.
Special breaks Available for any two consecutive
nights between 1st October and 1st May; special
Christmas programme available; Chocoholic
Weekends (for chocolate addicts) available.
The hotel is suitable for the partially disabled as it has
ground-floor rooms; children welcome.

Price for dinner, with wine, bed and breakfast for two – £100–£150.
Credit cards Amex, Mastercard, Visa, Access, Diners.
Overall mark out of ten 8

Situated amid thirteen acres of wooded grounds, Studley Priory is just seven miles from the historic city of Oxford and an hour's drive from the outskirts of London. As its rather unusual name suggests, the hotel was originally a nunnery, founded under the Benedictine order in the twelfth century. On the dissolution of the monasteries during the reign of Henry VIII, the estate was purchased by the Croke family, in whose hands it remained for nearly three and a half centuries.

A private chapel was consecrated in 1639, and the present North Wing added in 1666. Only the most minor structural improvements have taken place since the late seventeenth century and the present owners, the Parke family, purchased the house in 1961 in order to turn it into a Country House Hotel.

Studley Priory's most striking public room is its beautifully proportioned bar. Originally part of the main Elizabethan Withdrawing Room, most of the smooth wood panelling you can see today dates from the later Jacobean period. It is not a large room and is furnished with a rather odd assortment of simple dining-room-style chairs and bar stools which match the colouring of the walls. A large open fire blazes on cooler evenings, and the crackle of the logs is the perfect finishing touch to an utterly convivial atmosphere.

The hotel is a very popular conference venue, and for private dinner parties a fine Tudor Parlour can take up to 36 people. The low-ceilinged oak-panelled room was formerly the library of the original manor house, and this is an understandably more intimate setting than the main dining-room – the Croke Restaurant.

The restaurant offers both English and French cooking in a modern style, but the decor is rather disappointing after the beautiful panelling in most of the Priory's other public areas. Rather fresh-looking beams seem strangely out of place in this part of the hotel, though the overall effect is still pleasing, and the high standard of cuisine ensures all eyes are table-bound not heavenward-raised. A three- or four-course table d'hôte menu is available each evening, with about three or four choices available for each course.

The more adventurous à la carte menu has around six options for each course; the range of hors d'oeuvres has some rather intriguing suggestions including a Chilled Mousse of Pimento and Truffles with Asparagus Coulis – and a garnish of hot duck's liver. Principal dishes include a delicious Breast of Wild Duck baked in a salt-crust pastry with Citrus Sauce and Artichoke Heart, filled with a rich Pistachio Nut and Hollandaise Sauce.

A detailed wine list has over 150 bottles available, and many great wines from the 1950s and '60s have been included. Six vintage ports, including a classic 1950 Dow at £55 a bottle, are also available.

Studley Priory has nineteen bedrooms, including five master doubles and one superb suite known as the Elizabethan Suite. All nineteen have private facilities, including colour television, tea- and coffee-making facilities, and direct-dial telephones, but the very popular Elizabethan Suite is easily the most sumptuous bedroom available. A huge, solid half-tester bed dominates the completely oak-panelled room. The stone mullioned doorway and windows, and the view far across the surrounding countryside, have altered little since Elizabethan times, and advance booking for this superb bedroom is essential. It costs roughly double that of an average twin/double room (around £125 per night for bed and breakfast) but this particular room really does represent a first-class opportunity to sample comfort Elizabethan-style.

Leisure facilities at Studley Priory, and in the immediate area, are reasonable. There is a croquet lawn, a grass tennis court, clay pigeon shooting (by prior arrangement), golf, horse riding, and indoor swimming are all accessible. Other nearby attractions include the historic city of Oxford just seven miles away, the beauty of the surrounding Cotswolds, Blenheim Palace (birthplace of Sir Winston Churchill) and Waddesdon Manor. Even the city of London, with its countless attractions for visitors, is just 55 miles away by fast train or car.

69

WHATLEY MANOR

Easton Grey, Malmesbury, Wiltshire SN16 ORB
Tel: 066 62 2888

Nearest town Malmesbury.
Directions From the M4 leave at junction 16, 17
or 18. Whatley Manor is on the B4040 between
the village of Easton Grey and Malmesbury.
Awards AA *** RAC graded; Egon Ronay and
Michelin recommended.
Open throughout the year.
Special **weekend breaks** are available all year.
The hotel is unsuitable for the disabled; children and
dogs are welcome.
Price for dinner, with wine, bed and breakfast for
two – £100–£150.
Credit cards All major cards are accepted.
Overall mark out of ten 8.5

The first thing that strikes many visitors to Whatley Manor is
its rather interesting geographical location. Lying almost half-
way between Bristol and Swindon, the hotel sits right on the
border between Wiltshire and Gloucestershire, near the town
of Bath and on the fringes of the Cotswolds. It is not difficult
to understand why, for miles around, the area is an officially
designated place of natural beauty.

Set in extensive gardens which run down to the banks of

the River Avon, the original Whatley Manor dated back to the seventeenth century. The architecture of the seventeenth-century mansion did not appeal to a wealthy English sportsman who bought the site in the early 1920s, as he proceeded to almost completely alter the house. Thankfully this was no more than a passing fit of vandalism and, like the phoenix, from the ruins of the first Whatley Manor arose the present Tudor-style buildings with a number of purpose-built public and private rooms which today can be appreciated in all their splendour.

All the hotel's public rooms have been tastefully upgraded to modern-day luxury standards without losing their original identity: the old Saddle Room still has its saddle and polo stick racks, but now includes a billiard table as well. The library still has shelves and shelves of nineteenth- and early twentieth-century tomes (including a long run of *Punch*) but is now an elegant little bar. The most attractive room, though, is the enormous — almost disproportionately large — lounge with its oak-panelled walls, deep armchairs and beautifully arranged bouquets of freshly cut flowers. There can be few more relaxing places in this part of England to enjoy an after-dinner coffee, or relax over the Sundays with absolutely no need whatsoever to rush for anything.

The restaurant has superb views across the gardens, and has been carefully furnished and decorated to create an atmosphere that feels both intimate and relaxed. It is a large room, decorated in soft pastel shades and has about twenty tables. More could be seated, but it is to the hotel's credit that they have not crammed the maximum number of tables and chairs into the room, as it means guests can sit back and enjoy a level of intimacy missing in so many British hotels which wrongly believe they have achieved it.

The style of food is modern English, with strong continental influences, and traces of *nouvelle cuisine* can be detected on the menu. Fresh local produce is used as much as possible, and the proprietor Peter Kendall is quick to point out that his kitchens *do* use lots of buter, cream and alcohol in the preparation of the menu each evening, so forget the diet and indulge!

A three- or four-course table d'hôte menu is available, representing superb value at under £20 per person. The hotel is understandably popular with local non-residents and holiday-makers looking for a good evening out, so advance booking, particularly for weekends during the summer, is essential. Whatever you select, there are just under a hundred wines to choose from, although the range of vintages is a little disappointing considering the amount of thought and presentation which has gone into the main dinner menu. Red Bordeaux are well priced, with the obvious highlight a 1970 Château Cantemerle at £32 a bottle.

Easily the highlight from the half dozen or so starters is a fine Game and Pistachio Terrine: a savoury pâté of venison, local game and pistachio nuts served with a brandy and pink peppercorn dressing. If that fails to appeal, then you may prefer to indulge yourself with some Fresh Quails' Eggs, or a platter of Frogs' Legs before venturing into your main dish. The presentation of all meals at Whatley Manor is superb, and one of the chef's speciality main courses is Chicken and Pork Choysan, served stir fried in sesame oil, with Spring Onions, Chinese Lettuce Leaves, Radish, Pineapple and succulent Waterchestnuts. The end result is finished with honey and rice wine – very oriental!

Whatley Manor has 26 bedrooms, double the number here just six years ago when the present owner took over the hotel. All are furnished to very high standards, with period furniture used throughout. All have their own bathroom facilities, colour television, fresh flowers whenever possible and great views over the surrounding estate.

The hotel has facilities for tennis, croquet, fishing, sauna, solarium, Jacuzzi, table tennis and snooker, in addition to a large heated outdoor swimming pool. Nearby attractions include Bristol, Bath, Cirencester and Cheltenham as well as Longleat stately home and safari park, and the magnificent standing stones at Stonehenge.

WALES

70

BODYSGALLEN HALL

Llandudno, Gwynedd, North Wales LL30 1RS
Tel: 0492 84466

Nearest town Llandudno.
Directions Follow the A55 into north Wales from
Chester through Colwyn Bay and down towards
Conwy as far as the junction with the A470. Take
the A470 north, past Llandudno Junction, and the
turn-off for Bodysgallen Hall will be clearly
marked on your right after a few miles.
A member of the **Prestige Hotels** consortium.
Awards AA *** (red) graded; British Tourist
Authority recommended (1983 Heritage Award
Winner); Civic Trust Award 1984; Europe Nostra
Diploma of Merit 1983; Prince of Wales Award
1983; Queen's Award for Export 1987.
Open throughout the year.
Special breaks Summer breaks from April to
August for three days half-board or longer; Winter
Champagne breaks from mid-October until March
– two days half-board for two.
Children under the age of eight only accepted at the
discretion of the management; dogs are not allowed
except in the Courtyard suites.
Price for dinner, with wine, bed and breakfast for
two – over £150.

Credit cards All major cards accepted.
Overall mark out of ten 9.5

Bodysgallen Hall embodies the spirit of a true British Country House Hotel. It stands on a hill looking down on the grand site of Conwy Castle, and on a clear day you can see as far as the mountains of Snowdonia. The earliest part of the present hotel was built in the thirteenth century, and was once used as a lookout by soldiers serving the English kings of Conwy Castle. Today it is reached by a narrow, winding old stone staircase and is used for little more than admiring the truly outstanding views in all directions.

The idea for the house came soon after Conwy Castle itself was built, when there was a need for a smaller castle to act as a watchtower and guard the southern approach slopes to the main castle. Bodysgallen Hall's history is thereafter lost until the Elizabethan era when the Mostyn family, who owned the house, gained control of more of the immediate area. Richard Mostyn rose to become High Sheriff of Caernarvonshire, but with the marriage of his daughter Margaret to Hugh Wynn the house came into the possession of the much stronger Wynn family.

The main body of the hotel was built in the seventeenth century under the auspices of the Wynns and there are a total of five storeys, including the attic and cellars, dating from this time. Pink sandstone, quarried from a nearby field, has been used throughout the hotel's long history for any building or restoration work. The skilful restoration work which has been undertaken this century on both the house and surrounding gardens has earned a number of major awards for the owners and the architects. All work has been carried out in a way that emphasizes the natural beauty of the house, and both furnishings and paintings have been chosen carefully for all the public rooms and bedrooms alike in order to ensure that a warm and comfortable atmosphere is retained.

The hotel was only opened in 1982, and in the space of a single season firmly established itself as one of Britain's top Country House Hotels – with a pleasing emphasis on special romantic breaks. Advance booking of at least six months is normally essential, particularly if you have a preference for any given room or suite. Even for dinner, if you are a non-resident, a fortnight's notice is generally required.

Bodysgallen House has nineteen supremely comfortable bedrooms, each with its own private bathroom facilities and furnished in elegant Edwardian style. Colour television, direct-dial telephone and trouser press are included as standard. Courtyard suites, just off the main body of the hotel, are available for up to four persons. The larger suites have two or more bedrooms and are furnished to the same high standards as the rest of the hotel.

Two of the finest public rooms in the hotel are the grand entrance hall and the main drawing-room on the first floor. Both have authentic period oak wall panelling, stone mullioned windows, and the drawing-room has a very striking ornate seventeenth-century fireplace, complete with Latin inscription, Delft tiles and the original family's coat of arms up above it. Small touches like the mahogany-cased grandfather clock in the reception area and the original oil paintings all around make a big difference to the general atmosphere of the hotel.

The hotel has two dining-rooms, but most meals are served in the larger of the two which can accommodate 70 people at any one time. The cooking is British Country House style, and the dining-room decor is in keeping with the period feel of the rest of the house. Local produce is used wherever possible, but in striving for the very highest standards of international cuisine chef Martin James does look as far afield as Scotland for some of his steaks and the continent for some of the more exotic herbs.

Welsh lamb, though, has been a traditional speciality of Bodysgallen Hall for centuries and is one of the many treats waiting for you on the impressive table d'hôte menu. Vegetables are usually cooked lightly so that they retain their crispness, though anything can be cooked as you like it to suit your preferences. A couple of recommended specialities from the menu are Strips of Chicken lightly roasted in Scotch

Whisky, and Poached Fillet of Conwy Sea Trout with Tomato, Sea Salt and Parsley. In addition, the hotel has a really outstanding wine list, easily one of the finest of any Country House included in this guide with nearly 300 vintages to choose from.

Nearby attractions include Conwy and Harlech Castles, the towns of Colwyn Bay and Chester, the huge public gardens of Bodnant, Caernarfon Castle and the Snowdonia National Park.

71

GLIFFAES

Crickhowell, Powys, Wales NP8 1RH
Tel: 0874 730371

Nearest town Crickhowell.

Directions From Abergavenny, follow the A40 towards Brecon. Two and a half miles west of Crickhowell, you will see the hotel signposted on your right, turn left and drive a mile to Gliffaes gates.

Awards AA *** graded.

Open from the middle Friday in March until the end of December.

Special breaks Good discounts for full-board stays of a week or longer.

The hotel is unsuitable for disabled visitors; children are welcome but dogs are not allowed in the hotel – outdoor kennels are available.

Price for dinner, with wine, bed and breakfast for two – under £100.

Credit cards Access, Visa, Amex and Diners Club.

Overall mark out of ten 7

Relaxed informality is assured at the Gliffaes Country House Hotel. Lying between the River Usk and the Myarth Hill, it is this position which gives the hotel its rather unusual name: Gliffaes is a rather contorted variation of Gwlydd Faes, meaning literally 'the dewy field' in Welsh. As you will surely see on any chilly morning, the river mists rise with the morning light and become trapped by the hillside so that they fall as heavy dew on the surrounding fields. A twelfth-century chronicler, Giraldus Cambrenis, first recorded a variation on the Gliffaes name, but it was another eight centuries before the present house was built.

The house was the brainchild of a Reverend West, and constructed as a secluded family home between 1883 and 1885. The Reverend had travelled extensively throughout Europe and beyond, and had developed a particular appreciation for the Italian style of architecture, so much so that traces of Italian influence can be perceived in the hotel's intricate stonework today. The campanile at each end of the exterior is a distinctly Venetian touch.

The house has passed through several hands in the twentieth century, and in 1936 new owners Mr and Mrs Ernest Beard first opened their home to paying guests. The standards and facilities have been built up slowly since then and, indeed, maintained and extended by the present owners Nick and Peta Brabner since they acquired outright ownership of the hotel in 1972.

One of the most obvious features of Gliffaes today, as it has been for over a century and a half, is its magnificent gardens. These were planned and laid out by the Reverend West's father in the 1840s, and it was his love and appreciation of rare trees which undoubtedly made the gardens the special place you can enjoy today. W. H. West was a prominent member of the Breconshire Agricultural Society and rose to be High Sheriff of the county for a year in 1833.

Later Victorian residents added a labyrinth of gravel paths, small lawns and tasteful little shrub gardens. The driveway alone stretched over a quarter of a mile, flanked by rhododendrons, and it must have been quite a spectacular sight to drive up in an open carriage at the height of summer when everything was in bloom. An interesting thought is that at one stage fourteen gardeners were in full-time employment just to keep the grounds looking in pristine condition. The gardens today still look splendid, although the current owners reckon just twenty hours work every week throughout the year is enough to keep the 29 acres well maintained.

Most of Gliffaes has succumbed to the modern luxury of central heating, and the public rooms also have the more traditional log fire when the temperature outside requires it. There are nineteen bedrooms in all, all with private bathroom facilities and each offering a charming view of the rolling Welsh countryside all around.

The main public room is a huge ground-floor sitting-room, furnished in a curious symmetrical fashion and opening into the drawing-room; little touches like an old copper pan hanging by the fireplace contribute to the period feel. From the comfortable drawing-room, French windows open into an attractive sun lounge with a delightful terrace for guests to sit back and enjoy the garden during the summer months.

Few pieces of period furniture survive in any of the public rooms, with the emphasis more on modern-day comfort. Nevertheless, the decor is pleasing and it is a supremely comfortable and relaxing hotel. The oak-panelled dining-room can seat up to 65 guests, and it too has a large terrace offering stunning views far across the Brecon countryside and down to the River Usk about 150 feet below. Food is served in traditional Country House style, although continental influences can be detected. The chef clearly prefers to concentrate his energies on quality rather than quantity, with the result that only a limited à la carte choice is available each evening in preference to a full table d'hôte menu.

The range of starters is imaginative, but an obvious speciality is the Gravlax dish composed of Fresh Usk salmon (frequently caught that day) marinated with Dill and served with a Dill and Mustard Sauce. Local salmon features again as a main dish, and an interesting choice would be the Breast of Duckling cooked with Nectarines, Fresh Strawberries and a generous splash of Grand Marnier liqueur.

Nearby attractions are plentiful: for the sportsperson, fishing facilities are superb (the average Usk salmon on this stretch is eleven pounds), there is a hard tennis court with resident professional on hand, and riding, golf, bowls, boating, climbing, caving, bird-watching, gliding and even hang-gliding can all be easily arranged through the hotel reception. Within an easy drive you can visit Newport, Abergavenny and the Welsh capital, Cardiff, with all it has to offer.

72

MAES-Y-NEUADD

Talsarnau, near Harlech, Gwynedd, North Wales LL47 6YA
Tel: 0766 780200

Nearest town Harlech.
Directions Drive north from Harlech on the
B4573. The hotel is about three miles along this
road, between Harlech and the village of
Talsarnau. A large sign directs guests to a winding
lane which goes on for about half a mile.
Associates of the **Welsh Rarebits** group of
independent hotels of distinction.
Awards AA *** graded; Egon Ronay and
Michelin recommended.
Open from early February until just after the New
Year.
Special breaks Winter breaks from October until
April; discounts for half-board stays of two days or
more.
*The hotel is suitable for disabled visitors; children under
seven are accepted only at the management's discretion;
dogs are permitted.*
Price for dinner, with wine, bed and breakfast for
two – under £100.
Credit cards Access and Visa.
Overall mark out of ten 7.5

The rather isolated north Wales location of the Maes-y-Neuadd hotel is one of its more obvious attractions. Pronounced 'Mice-er-nayath', which means 'the hall in the field', the oldest part of the present building was completed around 1350. The first addition to the main structure was completed in 1550, and the final wing added in 1720, meaning that no part of the present hotel is less than two and a half centuries old. The main house and all the surrounding buildings, including the cottage and stable block, are built entirely from Welsh granite and slate.

For over 500 years the house belonged to the Nanney Wynn family, and a few surviving descendants still live nearby. Maes-y-Neuadd is reputed to have been used by Oliver Cromwell's forces during the English Civil War while he was laying siege to Harlech Castle. The house never featured prominently in Welsh history, although a number of the Wynn family rose to senior ranks in the army and government service and this is mentioned frequently in ancient poetry.

The family finally sold the house in 1953 and it was owned for a short spell by the Evans family. Margaret Evans has since written two books, one of which, *The Hall in the Field*, recounts her colourful life as a hotelier at Maes-y-Neuadd. Her second title, *The Wild Sky*, is a biographical novel featuring an interesting member of the Wynn family who flourished in the eighteenth century. The hotel today is owned and run by two families, June and Michael Slatter, and Olive and Malcolm Horsfall.

The main bar offers perhaps the best glimpse of what the inside of the house was really like a couple of centuries ago when it was one of the principle private homes in Gwynedd. Enormous dark oak beams have witnessed centuries of history and now provide a reassuring backdrop to the more traditional dark brown leather Chesterfields and roaring log fire on colder days throughout the autumn and winter. The other public room is a bright, informal lounge with sweeping views across the gardens and far beyond across Tremadoc Bay to the Lleyn Peninsula.

The hotel has fifteen bedrooms; thirteen doubles or twin

rooms, one single and one suite. All the rooms have private bathroom facilities and each has a very individual style of decor. The hotel's colour brochure illustrates one of the premier rooms which is furnished with elegant Georgian-style windows and hanging domer above twin beds. Another of the doubles is a particularly appealing little cottage, adjacent to the hotel and very popular with guests who choose to return to the hotel year after year. The cottage is called 'Bwthyn' and was once a gloomy single-roomed building used to house the itinerant sheep shearers when they came to Maes-y-Neuadd each year before market.

The focal point of the hotel is its restaurant, a gracious room with seating for up to 40 guests at any one time. The style of cooking is modern British, although there are always a number of traditional Welsh dishes on the menu. Decor is Georgian, with a soft green and grey colour-scheme enhanced by light gold silk on the wall panels. This style is in keeping with the period in which this 'younger' part of the house was built.

The main dinner menu is interesting, although hardly adventurous. Starters include Grilled Giant Prawns with a thick Garlic Mayonnaise and a rich Chicken Pâté flavoured with Madeira and Cognac. Main dish in-house specialities include Poached Salmon with Fresh Limes and Pine Kernels (for which a small supplement is payable) and a rather intriguing Supreme of Chicken with Banana. Welsh Lamb is on the menu each evening, as you might expect, and is cooked in a variety of different styles. For vegetarians, a Wholemeal Canelloni with Tomato and Chives is available, and all main courses are accompanied by a selection of fresh vegetables grown locally. A moderately priced wine list is available with a good range of mainly younger European wines to suit most palates.

Nearby attractions are plentiful and include a string of historic castles of which the best known is Harlech. The renowned Royal St David's golf course is just three miles away, and there are a number of gorgeous beaches and quaint little resorts all along the north-west Welsh coast.

73

PALÉ HALL

Llanddrefel, Bala, Gwynedd, North Wales LL23 7PS
Tel: 06783 285

Nearest town Bala.
Directions From north Wales, follow A5104 to
Corwen. At a large T-junction and traffic lights a
sign will indicate Llangollen A494 on your left.
Turn left here over the bridge and immediately
turn right signposted Llandrillo B4401. From here
it is 8.5 miles to Palé gates.
A member of the **Josephine Barr** selected British
hotels group.
Awards AA *** RAC graded; Egon Ronay and
Michelin recommended.
Open throughout the year.
Children are allowed; dogs are only allowed at the
discretion of the management – but not in the bedrooms.
Price for dinner, with wine, bed and breakfast for
two – £100–£150.
Credit cards Access, Visa, Amex and Diners
Club.
Overall mark out of ten 9

Almost everything about Palé Hall represents an elegant
reminder of the late Victorian era when the house flourished

as a private home. The house has only been a hotel for a few years, and resident proprietor Mrs Betty Duffin and her family have worked hard to lovingly restore the old house to something approaching its former glory. She has managed to combine period luxury with discreet personal service making this, now, one of the most comfortable hotels in north Wales.

Palé Hall was built in 1870 by a Scottish gentleman, Henry Robertson, who rose to become one of Britain's principal railway engineers by the end of the last century, and who gave the architects unlimited resources for the construction of the house. He was responsible for laying the North Wales Mineral Railway and for the construction of a number of important bridges, including the iron Kingsland Toll Bridge near Shrewsbury in 1879. He twice served as the Liberal Member of Parliament for Shrewsbury, from 1860 to 1865 and again from 1874 (after the introduction of the secret ballot in British elections) until 1885. Once he'd firmly settled into Palé Hall, he served briefly as MP for Meirionyddshire after 1885, but left the Liberal Party in disgust after falling out with Gladstone over the old Prime Minister's controversial proposals for Irish Home Rule. He died suddenly in March 1888 after suffering a paralysing stroke at Palé Hall, and is buried at nearby Llandderfel.

Robertson's son Henry was knighted by Queen Victoria, and he invited her to Palé Hall as his guest in 1889. She stayed a few nights in a plush suite which is now open to residents, and both an identical half-tester bed, and the very bath which she used during her stay can be enjoyed by residents who have booked early enough to secure the Victoria Suite. Her Majesty, understandably, was said to have been 'enchanted' by Palé Hall and thoroughly enjoyed what was to be her only visit during her long reign. In the present century, the house served as a military hospital during both world wars.

The hotel's main public room, then as now, is a small, but truly magnificent, domed lounge with an intricate hand-painted ceiling, rich with gold leaf and ornate paintwork. With its comfortable blue velvet-covered suite and enormous bay windows offering wide views across the surrounding grounds, this room really is a delight. In order to preserve the delicate decor, there is a strict smoking ban as, indeed, there is in the main dining-room for the same reason. The other public room is the Corwen Bar, an interesting place to relax and enjoy an aperitif before dinner as the bar has been made from a number of old marble fireplaces. This isn't instantly obvious and tends to strike most guests as they sit back in their Roman-style bar chairs and study the room's decor in some detail.

The style of cooking at Palé Hall is traditional British Country House, and seldom more than 10 percent of diners are non-residents. Italian carved dining chairs are upholstered in gold, and huge ornate mirros adorn the walls all around. An impressive à la carte menu is available offering a strong range of fish and local poultry; an interesting starter is the Hot Prawn Soufflé with Mushroom Cream Sauce, garnished with Shrimp Tails. For most guests, though, the table d'hôte menu is more than adequate. One fish dish stands out: Trio of Fish, including salmon, trout and whiting, is served poached in Noilly Prat and coated with Shellfish Sauce. The wine list is reasonable but has no outstanding varieties. House wines are particularly palatable, at around £7 a bottle, but if you prefer something a little more adventurous then few of the vintages reach £20.

The hotel has seventeen bedrooms, all doubles except for one single, and all with private bathroom facilities. Little extras like a bowl of fruit, a jar of peppermints and a glass of sherry to greet you are pleasing. One particular luxury double/suite – the Caernarfon Room – represents superb value at around £125 for two inclusive of dinner, bed and breakfast and a private Jacuzzi included in your room as part of the price.

Leisure facilities at Palé Hall are excellent: within the hotel and surrounding grounds there are a sauna and solarium, Jacuzzi plunge pool (with a constant temperature at a luxurious 100°) exercise equipment, two golf courses and a riding centre. Nearby, fishing can be arranged in the rivers Dee and Tryweryn as well as in Bala Lake; also clay pigeon and game shooting; and even rapid-riding and windsurfing for the young at heart. The hotel advises that both can be a little wet!

Nearby attractions, other than the impressive range of leisure facilities, include Harlech Castle and the surrounding beauty of Snowdonia, Shell Island (Mochras), a man-made island formed in 1819, and the seaside resort town of Barmouth.

74

RUTHIN CASTLE

Ruthin, Clwyd, Wales LL15 2NU
Tel: 08242 2664

Nearest town Ruthin.
Directions From the town of Chester, Ruthin
Castle is located 22 miles south-west of Chester on
the A494 Ruthin to Corwen road, just off the
roundabout in the village of Ruthin.
A member of the **Best Western Hotels**
consortium.
Awards AA *** RAC graded; British Tourist
Authority Services to Tourism Award 1979.
Open throughout the year.
Special breaks Getaway breaks for two days or
longer are available all year.
*The hotel is suitable for disabled visitors; children and
dogs are welcome.*
Price for dinner, with wine, bed and breakfast for
two – £100–£150.
Credit cards Access, Visa, Amex and Diners
Club.
Overall mark out of ten 8

Situated 22 miles south-west of Chester, one of Norman
England's marcher lordships, Ruthin Castle has probably the

finest historical pedigree of any Welsh Country House Hotel. When Reginald de Grey had Ruthin Castle built in 1282 he created not only a magnificent new castle, but also the genesis of an entire community. Officials, retainers, craftsmen, domestic servants and a great many others were brought to Ruthin to maintain and build up de Grey's little empire. For their immediate security a wall was raised round what soon became a small town, and a huge stone gate was erected to make sure only those travellers friendly to the great lord entered the community.

Many features of the original thirteenth-century castle can still be seen today: the early English-style west gate, with grooves for the portcullis; the postern gate with a spiral staircase contained within the 7–9-foot-thick stone walls; and the slanted apertures in the battlements for the bowmen. Parts of the original castle form the shell of the modern-day hotel, but most of the original fortress, which was substantially bigger than the hotel, lies in rather poignant ruin around the main residential building.

The castle endured many attacks down the centuries, particularly during the War of the Roses, but the de Grey family remained in the castle until 1508. It passed briefly into the hands of Henry VIII's bastard son, Henry Fitzroy, but its darkest day came during the English Revolution when both the castle and its Royalist inhabitants were dismantled. Ruthin remained a derelict ruin until the nineteenth century, when much of it was lovingly rebuilt, and a century later – in 1963 – it finally became a luxury Country House Hotel.

With such an outstanding history, guests at Ruthin are thankfully not allowed to forget the heritage which grew up within its four walls. A splendid medieval banquet evening is available, and this is a tremendously entertaining night out which you really shouldn't miss for one night of your stay here. Food is served on large wooden bowls and eaten with the fingers, and accompanied by generous gobletfuls of wine and local mead.

All the public rooms in Ruthin Castle are furnished on a grand scale, and the main reception area is decorated in a traditional style with deer antlers and ancient firearms adorning the walls. Virtually all public rooms have an ornate criss-cross ceiling pattern – a nightmare to decorate but magnificent to admire as you relax in comfortably chairs with an after-dinner liqueur or coffee.

The hotel is one of the largest featured in this book, with 58 spacious and sound-proofed bedrooms, all with private bathroom facilities, colour television and direct-dial telephone. Ruthin Castle is a particularly popular venue for both 'society' weddings and business conferences and seminars. The huge Peacock Room is glass-walled on three sides and allows a terrific amount of natural light to flood in.

The restaurant is an attractive, long dining-room decorated in greens and browns with grand arrays of dried flowers in opposite corners. When full, it can seat up to a 100 people and the ratio of residents to non-residents varies enormously throughout the year. That said, it is seldom necessary to book more than a day or so in advance if you wish to dine as a non-resident. The menu concentrates on British Country House specialities, but there is a strong continental influence in the à la carte menu which represents excellent value at under £20 per person, including a selection from the modest wine list.

A strong range of starters includes a delicious Marinated Frogs' Legs speciality, cooked with different sorts of Mushrooms and served in a Garlic and Oregano Butter. For a more unusual soup, Ruthin offers an impressive Turtle variety topped with a Curry Flavoured Cream. Main course options are equally strong on both poultry and red meat dishes. An outstanding speciality, cooked in front of you, is Steak Diane: this huge, flattened entrecôte steak is sautéed in Butter, Mushrooms and Red Wine and served Brandy-flamed. The sauce is exquisite. For a special luxury dish, few will need to look further than the chef's Futtora Piccata: thin slices of fillet beef, sautéed in butter and served with Mushrooms, Onions and Potatoes.

Nearby attractions include Caernarfon Castle, Conway Castle, the city of Chester, Bodnant Gardens and the splendid National Trust properties of Erddig Hall and Chirk Castle.

LONDON AREA

75

THE BELL INN

Aston Clinton, Buckinghamshire HP22 5HP
Tel: 0296 630252

Nearest town Tring.
Directions The hotel is located just off the main
A41 between Tring and Aylesbury.
A member of the **Relais et Châteaux** consortium.
Awards AA *** graded plus rosette for food; RAC
*** graded; British Tourist Authority commended.
Open throughout the year.
The hotel has a number of rooms suitable for disabled
visitors; children are welcome but dogs only by prior
arrangement.
Price for dinner, with wine, bed and breakfast for
two – over £150.
Credit cards Access and Visa.
Overall mark out of ten 8.5

More than three centuries ago the Duke of Buckingham
recognized the appeal of this attractive site when he is said to
have built the original Bell Inn as part of his large estate. The
flourishing coaching inn quickly became his favourite location
to stop over for rest, refreshment and a change of horses on
his regular journey between his country seat at Stowe and his
large London house. Interestingly, the Duke's London house

became Buckingham Palace, now the official residence of Her Majesty the Queen and a number of senior members of the Royal Family.

Many alterations have been made to the building since the Duke's time but, despite considerable renovation and restoration, the simple red stone façade remains very much as it was in the seventeenth century. The Bell Inn has been owned and run by the Harris family since 1939, the year in which the father of present owner, Michael Harris, left London in order to find a country residence because the Second World War was about to be declared.

Of the various public rooms, the first floor Writing Room is one of the most charming. Sofas and soft chairs are grouped round the fireplace, and this is where many guests prefer to enjoy a pre-dinner drink. The room is furnished in a rich period fashion, with antique furniture and one or two large oil paintings, and is a popular venue for private luncheon or dinner parties. In the old Smoking Room downstairs, look out for two little niches at either side of the fireplace. In earlier times these were used to store wig powder and the heat of the fire kept it dry!

The Bell Inn has 21 delightful bedrooms, six in the main house and fifteen in the cobbled brewery courtyard just round the corner, and all are double or twin rooms which can be used for single accommodation at reduced rates. The Harrises have worked hard to make each of the spacious rooms individual, with antique furniture used wherever possible and with great attention to detail. Private bathroom facilities in all the rooms are made that little bit extra special with the addition of thick fluffy towelling robes and quality bath salts and toiletries. All rooms have colour television, direct-dial telephone and a refrigerated mini-bar. Room 16 is a particularly attractive luxury suite for that special romantic break, with a private front door leading into a little secret garden during the summer months. Or another favourite for romantic weekends is room 50 with its unique and very beautiful painted furniture from Hungary, including a four-poster bed.

Locally at least, the Bell Inn is best known for its restaurant which is certainly one of the most attractive dining-rooms in the London area. Decorated with hand-painted murals depicting the Four Seasons, the dining-room can seat up to 140 people with relative ease. Leather-covered chairs surround the well-spaced-out mahogany tables, and the intimate candlelit atmosphere is so popular with residents and non-residents alike that advance booking by at least a week or two is advisable.

No particular style of cuisine is adhered to, although the influences of *nouvelle cuisine* and *cuisine minceur* are the most obviously identifiable. Traditional dishes like Roast Rib of Beef, or Aylesbury Duckling, are available alongside more adventurous dishes like Sea Bass in Puff Pastry and Choron Sauce or Paupiettes of Sole and Salmon with Chervil Sauce.

The wine list is extensive; indeed, the hotel owns and runs a flourishing retail wine shop near the hotel which offers a twenty-page list and nationwide delivery service. It is a fascinating place, well worth a visit if you're there, with a very comprehensive stock of younger vintages (including an excellent range of red Bordeaux) and some more classic older wines from Europe and further afield.

Nearby attractions include a number of excellent golf courses, the tree-covered slopes of the surrounding Chiltern Hills, countless quaint little villages, Waddesdon Manor, Woburn Abbey, Blenheim Palace (birthplace of Sir Winston Churchill), Windsor Castle, Hatfield House and Luton Hoo. In addition, Oxford and St Albans are well within an hour's drive from here.

76

BRANDSHATCH PLACE

Fawkham, Kent DA3 8NQ
Tel: 0474 872239

Nearest town Longfield.
Directions From the M25, leave at junction 3
(Swanley turn-off) and follow the A20 towards
Brands Hatch. Head for Fawkham Green – the
road goes round the back of the famous racing
circuit – taking the third left turning under the
M20. After about fifty yards you will see the white
fencing and signs for the hotel.
Awards Recommended by Egon Ronay and
Michelin guides.
Open throughout the year.
Special breaks Country House Weekends
available all year round.
*The hotel is not suitable for the disabled; children are
welcome but dogs are not allowed.*
Price for dinner, with wine, bed and breakfast for
two – £100–£150.
Credit cards Access, Visa, Amex and Diners
Club.
Overall mark out of ten 7

Set in twelve acres of garden just a stone's throw from one of
the world's most famous racing tracks, this lovely old Georgian

manor was quickly converted into a modern luxury hotel and became the Brandshatch Place Hotel and Country Club.

The house was originally built in 1806 by the Duke of Norfolk as a country cottage next to one of his farms. It was extended in 1860 by the then owner, and has been considerably extended and modernized by the present owners over the last few years. Little of the original Georgian furnishings survived the renovation. The main lounge is a bright, comfortably furnished public room and, by the time of publication, the elegant library should have been considerably extended for residents' further comfort.

Brandshatch Place is a very popular business and conference centre: the extensive facilities available for seminars are most impressive, particularly the quality of their catering for up to 150 guests at once, and fully justify why such a large proportion of the hotel's brisk trade is made up of business clientele.

The restaurant can seat up to 70 in a quiet and comfortable atmosphere, surrounded by elegant modern wood panelling. Bookings are only needed a day or two in advance except for weekends where three or four days are recommended. Food is served in a pleasing blend of traditional English and *nouvelle cuisine* styles, and a reasonable table d'hôte menu is available each evening.

Starters include a delicious blend of Fresh Scallops, Pink Grapefruit and Jerusalem Artichokes in a Passion Fruit Vinaigrette, and a Terrine of Venison and Hare with Beetroot and Juniper. Main dishes include a Breast of Guineafowl filled with a Mousse of Crêpes and served on a Madeira and Thyme Sauce; or Loin of Veal with Foie Gras, Truffles and Chive sauce. An extensive wine list is available, with a number of wines starting under £10 and the highlight being a 1977 Le Montrachet white burgundy, from the Domaine de la Romanee-Conti, at around £320 a bottle. The hotel has 27 bedrooms in the main house. All rooms are comfortably appointed with plenty of room to relax and move about; the style of decor and furnishings is traditional, allowing for little individuality from room to room. Each bedroom has *en suite* bath or shower rooms, colour television, central heating and direct-dial telephones.

Brandshatch Place has an outstanding leisure complex, known as Frederick's, available for residents' use daily between 10 a.m. and 11 p.m. (10.30 p.m. on Sundays). In addition to three squash courts, a badminton court and all-weather outdoor tennis court there is a fully equipped gymnasium, sauna, Jacuzzi spa bath and heated indoor swimming pool. Two solariums are also available and a licensed bistro restaurant provides an ever-changing menu in an informal atmosphere if your physical exertions have made you peckish.

Other nearby attractions include the famous Brands Hatch racing track, Chartwell (for many years the country home of Sir Winston Churchill), Hever Castle, Leeds Castle, Chiddingstone Castle, and the towns of Tunbridge Wells and Rochester.

77

BURNHAM BEECHES

Grove Road, Burnham, Buckinghamshire SL1 8DP
Tel: 06286 3333

Nearest town Burnham.

Directions From the south (London), leave the
M4 at junction 7. Turn left at the first roundabout
and right at the next set of traffic lights. Follow
this road until you see the hotel sign.

A member of the **Thames Valley Hotels** group.

Open throughout the year.

Special breaks Special activity breaks available
(details on request); Secluded Weekend breaks
during the winter months – also with four-poster
and champagne for an extra charge.

The hotel has a lift and no stairs to reception so may be
suitable for disabled visitors; children and dogs are both
welcome.

Price for dinner, with wine, bed and breakfast for
two – £100–£150.

Credit cards Access, Visa, Amex and Diners
Club.

Overall mark out of ten 6.5

Originally designed and built as a hunting lodge in what was
then part of Windsor Great Park, Burnham Beeches began life
as a popular resting place for royal hunting parties. In 1737

the English poet Thomas Gray visited his uncle, who then owned the building, and was inspired to write his *Elegy in a Country Courtyard*. After a period in the hands of the Clifton-Brown family, the house gradually fell into disrepair and was rescued by the present owners, who turned it into a luxury Country House Hotel in 1965.

Although the boundaries of Windsor Great Park have been pushed back over the years, the hotel today is as secluded and restful as it was two and a half centuries ago when Gray wrote his famous poem. The house is still set in an area of beautiful parkland which borders the Burnham Beeches golf course and the 600-acre forest from which the hotel takes its name.

All the public rooms are furnished in a simple period style and have some interesting pieces on display. The dining-room has recently been refurbished in a subdued decor reminiscent of the era when the house was a bustling private residence. Advance booking is strongly recommended for non-residents.

Meals are prepared in traditional English Country House style. The four- or five-course table d'hôte menu is changed nightly. The presentation and quality of food are good, though the service can lack the personal touch. A typical evening's menu would begin with something light like an Avocado Salad with Pine Nuts and Wine-Steeped Raisins. The fish course might be Poached Salmon with an exquisite Champagne Sauce before the main dish of Saddle of Lamb, with locally grown Garden Herbs and a bouquet of fresh, lightly cooked vegetables. A selection of English farmhouse cheeses is available before your sweet – usually a speciality of the chef, like Strawberries and Cream in a Brandysnap Case – which is rounded off by coffee and *petit fours* in the restaurant or lounge.

The Burnham Beeches Hotel is one of the largest hotels featured in this guide, with 80 bedrooms. Thirty of these were added during a major refurbishment programme in 1987 which also saw the addition of the heated swimming pool and leisure complex. The older rooms have retained much of their original Georgian charm, while the newer ones have been built in a style in keeping with the remainder of the building.

It must be said, though, that the Country House purist would balk at some of the touches, and the modern rooms lack the charm of the originals.

All 80 bedrooms now have *en suite* bathrooms, colour television with in-house video films and direct-dial telephones, although there is little in terms of individuality between most of them because of the sheer size of the hotel. Nearly all have good views across the surrounding gardens and sprawling woodland.

Burnham Beeches has a good range of leisure facilities available for residents. In addition to a hard tennis court, putting green, croquet lawn and fully equipped gymnasium, there is also a heated indoor swimming pool, sauna, solarium and jacuzzi whirlpool. Nearby attractions include Windsor Castle, Savill Gardens, the River Thames, Windsor Safari and Great Park, Eton College, the Royal Mews, Shire Horse Centre and Hampton Court, magnificent stately home built by King Henry VIII in the sixteenth century.

78

CLIVEDEN

Taplow, Berkshire SL6 0JF
Tel: 06286 61837

Nearest town Slough or Maidenhead (both six miles away).

Directions Leave the M4 at junction 7, turn left on to the A4 towards Maidenhead and at the next roundabout turn right where you see the signpost for Burnham. Follow this road for about four miles until you reach a T-junction. The main gates of Cliveden will be in front of you.

A member of the **Prestige Hotels** consortium.

Awards AA ***** graded, Egon Ronay (89%) and Michelin recommended.

Open throughout the year.

The hotel is suitable only for partially disabled guests; children and dogs are welcome.

Price for dinner, with wine, bed and breakfast for two – over £150 (likely to be at least double that).

Credit cards Access, Visa, Amex, Diners Club and Masterchage.

Overall mark out of ten 10

Few can deny that Cliveden is one of the finest hotels in Europe. It certainly qualifies as the finest Country House Hotel in the United Kingdom, and the only stately home in England which has the distinction of being a hotel. Everything about Cliveden is magnificent: the 375 acres of gardens and parkland in which the house is set, the house's long and distinguished history ever since the original building of 1666, the sumptuous bedrooms and public rooms, and, of course, the highest standard of international cuisine.

Cliveden was built by the second Duke of Buckingham, a wealthy courtier, from whose family the Earl of Orkney inherited the house. The Duke of Buckingham was created England's first Field Marshal after the Duke of Marlborough's death, and altered the house and grounds considerably. From 1739 until his death in 1751, George III's father, Frederick, Prince of Wales, lived here before the house passed through a number of hands until the first Duke of Westminster acquired it in 1869. It was he who sold Cliveden to William Waldorf Astor, father-in-law of Cliveden's most famous resident, Nancy Astor, whose husband Waldorf received the house as a wedding present in 1906.

Nancy became Britain's first woman Member of Parliament to take her seat and made numerous improvements to Cliveden (it was she, for example, who called every bedroom after people closely associated with the house): Churchill, Balfour, Rudyard Kipling, Lawrence of Arabia and Bernard Shaw were all regular guests during her stay. Cliveden was eventually given to the National Trust during the Second World War, and in 1984 was entrusted to Blakeney Hotels who completely refurbished the house to its former grandeur and opened it as a grand de luxe hotel in March 1986.

It is easy to run out of superlatives to describe the public rooms at Cliveden. The Great Hall is an enormous room, with ornate wall panelling all around, huge sculpted fireplace and Flemish tapestry wall hangings. Priceless Astor family antiques add immeasurably to the charm of the hotel. The famous Sargent portrait of Nancy Astor, for example, hangs here and is reckoned to be worth at least a million pounds. The Library is a much more intimate, panelled room, with plush period-style armchairs and one or two more family portraits. Arguably the most perfect room in any British hotel in which to relax with the Sundays and just soak up the sense of history all around you.

Nancy Astor's writing-room is now the Boudoir, a marvellous Adam-style morning-room, which is ideal for small private parties or business meetings. An even more outstanding location is the small French Dining-Room, where you will dine, with its rich gold panelling taken from Madame de Pompadour's dining-room in the Château d'Asinières near Paris. The intricate gold leaf in the ceiling pattern is equally magnificent, and a perfect contrast to the reflection of the chandeliers in the huge polished mirrors.

The main dining-room has undoubtedly the finest views of any room at Cliveden, stretching out across the parterre and down towards the River Thames. It can seat 60 in the grandest of Edwardian surroundings, gentle pastel shades making the perfect decor to relax the eye while you are dining. Head chef John Webber prepares a modern-style à la carte menu and fixed-price menus for lunch and dinner, based on classical cuisine, but never losing a strong British influence. A typical starter of Chicken Consommé with Smoked Chicken and Poached Quails' Eggs, or Bavarois of Smoked Salmon, could be followed by Roast Barbary Duck served with Wild Mushroom Essence or a Poached Fillet of Prime Scotch Beef flavoured with Madeira.

Cliveden has 25 bedrooms, each one as enormous and luxurious as the next, with twin or double beds made up with pure linen sheets manufactured to the highest standards. (These are on sale opposite the Footman's Desk at £300 a pair if you fall in love with the luxury.) All of the bedrooms have their own fireplaces, and all have grand private bathrooms with huge bathtubs and specially designed Cliveden bath robes and toiletries as standard, together with a welcoming tray of drinks, in lead crystal decanters. Room rates begin around £150 and go up to £500 for the Royal Suite per night, but the quality of furnishings is simply breathtaking. The Lady Astor Suite, for example, has two enormous family portraits and elegant drapes all around the room's numerous grand windows; the Lord Mountbatten, on the other hand, has a much more 'masculine' feel, with a raised writing table, ornate ceiling and rich wood panelling.

There is an extensive range of leisure facilities available for residents at Cliveden, the most obvious being the sheer enjoyment of 375 acres of magnificent gardens and woodland. This is one of the finest private gardens in Britain and many guests travel up from London by boat on the River Thames, which literally runs through the estate. A handy booklet, prepared by the National Trust, has a number of suggested walks clearly marked on a map of the grounds.

Squash, tennis and fishing are among the most popular facilities, and equipment is available for guests who do not have their own with them. A heated outdoor swimming pool, in the walled garden, is available between 7.30 a.m. and 8 p.m. when weather permits, and riding, boating and golf can all be arranged locally. An exercise room inside the house is ideal for light, unsupervised exercise, and what better way to follow it than with a sauna or Turkish bath in the hotel. There is a wealth of nearby attractions including Windsor Castle, and surrounding safari and parkland, racing at Ascot, Windsor and Newbury, Henley regatta, and the beautiful university cities of Oxford and Cambridge.

79

EASTWELL MANOR

*Eastwell Park, Boughton Aluph, near Ashford,
Kent TN25 4HR
Tel: 0233 35751*

Nearest town Ashford.
Directions From London, leave the M2 at
junction 6. Continue along the A251 and Eastwell
Manor is twelve miles along this road.
Owned by **Norfolk Capital Hotels** and a member
of the **Prestige Hotels** consortium.
Awards AA **** graded and rosette for food;
English Tourist Board five Crowns; British Tourist
Authority commended; Egon Ronay and Michelin
recommended.
Open throughout the year.
Special breaks Mid-week breaks all year round;
special Christmas programme.
*Children are welcome but dogs are not permitted in the
hotel.*
Price for dinner, with wine, bed and breakfast for
two – £100–£150.
Credit cards Access, Visa, Amex, Diners Club
and Masterscharge.
Overall mark out of ten 9.5

Surrounded by 65 acres of undulating parkland in the heart of the north downs of Kent, the present Eastwell Manor dates from no earlier than 1926, although the original manor on this site has a far longer history, dating back to the eleventh century. Eastwell takes its name from a spring known to the Saxon herdsmen of the downs and forests, and prior to the Norman Conquest of 1066 a Saxon nobleman by the name of Frederic held the lordship of the manor from Edward the Confessor.

The manor has had a long and colourful history down the centuries, and this makes fascinating reading in the back of one of the hotel's publicity booklets. In the early sixteenth century, a previous owner of the estate, Sir Thomas Moyle, discovered one of his bricklayers reading Latin and subsequently identified him as Richard Plantagenet, illegitimate son of King Richard III. Sir Thomas took kindly to the disgraced king's son and had a small cottage built for him on the estate where the younger Richard lived peacefully until his death in 1550.

Sir Thomas Finch, who inherited the house in the seventeenth century, distinguished himself by fathering 27 children by his four wives. A couple of centuries later, in 1875, Her Royal Highness Princess Marie Alexandra Victoria (later to become Queen of Romania) was born in the manor. It was demolished after lying untended for a number of years after the First World War, and rebuilt in 1926 by Sir John de Fonblanqua Pennefather, using the original stonework as far as possible, combined with imported architectural accessories to make the 'new' manor even more striking than before.

All the public rooms are designed in a style which is typical of a period much earlier than the 1920s. All have elaborately patterned ceilings and wood panelling, but the main lounge is the *pièce de résistance*. With its soft leather armchairs, enormous carved fireplace and diamond-crossed windows this is a grand room in every sense.

Up to 80 can be seated in two magnificent dark wood-panelled dining-rooms which both offer excellent views across the gardens and surrounding estate. Guests sit back and relax in comfortable leather 'Captain's' chairs as they enjoy a blend of modern cuisine which is influenced considerably by classical French, traditional English and, as the management term it, chef Anthony Blake's 'own interpretation of his culinary art'.

Table d'hôte and à la carte menus are available each evening, and the end result of the combination of styles is an adventurous range of first-class dishes. Speciality starters include a delicious Clear Fish Soup infused with Saffron and garnished with Oysters, Pistachio Nuts and Spring Vegetables, and a Salad of Smoked Trout, Avocado and Fresh Mango all served with a Horseradish Cream.

Main dishes include traditional favourites like Roast Loin of Lamb and Fillet of Scotch Beef together with less common choices such as Fillet of Red Mullet, braised in the oven and served with a Champagne and Parsley Sauce, and a Hot Mousse of Turbot and Brill, wrapped in Leeks and served on a Saffron Butter Sauce. Whatever your choice, the Manor has an extensive wine list with a particularly good range of French wines, together with a few more popular bottles from other countries.

Eastwell Manor has 24 grand bedrooms including three master suites, one de luxe suite, and two standard suites. All rooms are individually styled with period furnishings or quality modern reproductions. Each one has its own private bathroom and the style of some of these 'additional' rooms is extremely attractive. The Edwardian bathroom, for instance, attached to the Countess of Midleton suite has changed little since the turn of the century and comes complete with an enormous mirror, deep bath and marble surround.

A number of sports and leisure facilities are available at Eastwell Manor, or nearby, for residents to enjoy. There is a panelled billiard room adjacent to reception and during the summer months a croquet lawn is set up within the grounds. The hotel has a hard tennis court, but you may prefer to indulge in more relaxing trout fishing which can be arranged locally; both Ashford and Faversham golf courses are within easy reach and both horse riding and squash can be arranged at local centres.

Nearby attractions include the ancient town of Canterbury with its famous cathedral, Dover Castle, Hever Castle, Leeds Castle, Sissinghurst Gardens and the Cinque Ports of Dover and Folkestone. An added attraction of staying in this part of the UK is the relative ease with which it is possible to make day trips across to Calais or Boulogne on the French coast.

80

ELCOT PARK

Near Newbury, Berkshire RG16 8NJ
Tel: 0488 58100

Nearest town Hungerford.
Directions The Elcot Park Hotel is situated just off the main A4 between Newbury (five miles west) and Hungerford (four miles east).
A member of the **Best Western Hotels** consortium.
Awards AA *** graded.
Open throughout the year.
Special breaks Weekend breaks available throughout the year; also special theme weekends including Bridge, Theatre and even Hot Air Ballooning.
The hotel is most suitable for disabled visitors; children and dogs are welcome.
Price for dinner, with wine, bed and breakfast for two – £100–£150.
Credit cards Access, Visa, Amex and Diners Club.
Overall mark out of ten 7.5

One of the primary attractions of Elcot Park has got to be the acres of peaceful woodland in which this former seventeenth-century manor house is set. Although literally a minute's drive off the busy A4, and only a few more from the Berkshire towns of Newbury and Hungerford, Elcot Park occupies a prime location in the magnificent green Kennet Valley.

The hotel was built in 1678 and was formerly the country seat of Lord and Lady Thomas. Today it is still surrounded by a large landscape garden, originally designed by Sir William Paxton (the Royal gardener in 1848), which, even then, made it an idyllic location for house guests to enjoy that perfect 'away-from-it-all' break without the necessity for city-dwellers to stray more than 70 miles from the capital.

Elcot's main public room, other than the restaurant, is the drawing-room, which has now been laid out in the style of an informal lounge. The decor is bright, although there is little in the way of antique furniture, with the outstanding exception of a large art nouveau fireplace which was originally made for the 1900 Paris Exhibition. The Elcot Park is a popular conference hotel, and it has three well-equipped function rooms with all the necessary facilities for just about any kind of business seminar or conference.

The dining-room offers probably the best views of any room in the hotel, stretching far across the green Kennet Valley. Up to 100 can be seated in this impressive high-ceilinged room, with its soft blue and yellow decor and sensibly spaced table arrangement. The style of cuisine is distinctly modern British Country House, although continental influences can be clearly detected.

A la carte and table d'hôte menus are available each evening, offering a range of traditional and more original dishes. Two of the more unusual starters include Avocado Pear, Quails' Eggs and Stilton Cheese all tossed with Walnut Dressing and served warm on a bed of Seasonal Salads, and Exotic Fruits served with the hotel's own variety of Pink Champagne and a Lime Sorbet.

The à la carte includes a choice of around seven main dishes, including more traditional dishes like Prime Fillet of Scottish Beef and Fresh River Salmon. A couple of more interesting specialities are Saddle of Venison matured in Red Wine, panfried and served with two sauces – Pear and Game;

alternatively, there is usually a delicious trio of Fish Mousse-lines, served set in a delicate Chive Sauce.

The hotel has a total of 38 bedrooms, eight of which were added at the end of 1987 and all highly individually designed. Soft pastel shades are predominant and blend well with antique furnishings and modern conveniences such as colour television, direct-dial telephone, hairdryer and a trouser press in each room. A number of the larger doubles have particularly soft and luxurious bed coverings: combined with a four-poster, which features in several bedrooms, the setting is perfect for that special romantic break.

Leisure facilities include golf, croquet, horse riding and, for the more adventurous, the opportunity to try hot-air ballooning under the supervision of a qualified instructor and pilot. This facility is an attraction unique to Elcot Park and is available throughout the year, although obviously depends heavily on the weather. Your fee (around £60 at the time of publication) includes full tuition and is payable only if you get the chance to fly. Other local attractions include Stonehenge, Blenheim Palace, Avebury, Littlecote House, and the cities of Oxford, Winchester and Salisbury.

81

FLITWICK MANOR

Church Road, Flitwick, Bedfordshire MK45 1AE
Tel: 0525 712242

Nearest town Flitwick.
Directions Leave the M1 at junction 12
(travelling from London) and continue along the
A5120 for a few miles. The hotel is signposted
shortly before you reach Flitwick itself.
Awards AA *** graded and rosette for food; RAC
*** graded; British Tourist Authority commended;
recommended by Egon Ronay and Michelin
guides.
Open throughout the year, except Christmas.
Special breaks Very occasional weekend breaks
are available.
The hotel has a number of ground-floor rooms suitable
for the disabled; children are welcome, but dogs are not
allowed.
Price for dinner, with wine, bed and breakfast for
two − £100−£150.
Credit cards Access, Visa, Amex and Diners
Club.
Overall mark out of ten 9

Lying approximately half-way between both Oxford and Cambridge, between the Green Sand Ridge and the Chiltern Hills,

Flitwick Manor is a classic old English Country House Hotel. Since Saxon times there has been a settlement on the high ground where the hotel now stands: the Saxons created the village of 'Fleotwic' – which literally means 'dwelling on the river' – after the Romans left their original village near where the manor stands today.

A manor was known in Flitwick even before Norman times, but the present building dates mainly from the late seventeenth and early eighteenth century. Old records show that in 1674, the then owners, the Rhodes family, were required by law to pay Hearth Tax on ten fireplaces, including the one which you can still see in the hall today. Ann Fisher later inherited the house as part of a marriage settlement with George Hesse and, after his death in 1783, married one George Brooks whose family remained squires in this part of Bedfordshire until 1932.

Today the public rooms are decorated in an informal Regency style, outstanding amongst which is the Brooks Room, with its salmon-coloured napiary, mahogany furniture and a number of elegant family portraits. The Garden-Room was adapted by Sir Albert Richardson RA in the 1930s and has a fascinating collection of sporting trophies for residents to admire should they ever tire of the lovely garden views from this room.

The main dining-room has a fine reputation with residents and non-residents alike, and advance bookings are generally required by at least a week. An imaginative à la carte and a choice of three table d'hôte menus are available nightly with a strong emphasis on fish on all the menus throughout the year. 'Senders' have been recruited in fish markets throughout the UK to select only the finest ingredients for the Flitwick Manor kitchen.

A team of seven young chefs, including resident proprietor Somerset Moore himself, is responsible for the creative and original range of dishes available each evening. One of the table d'hôte menus is devoted to shellfish, the centrepiece of which might be a large selection of fresh shellfish including two varieties of Prawn, Venus Clams, Shrimps, Langoustines and one Oyster. Another menu is devoted to vegetarian dishes and includes a choice of starter and main course. Most of the à la carte specialities are asterisked, and the little note at the foot of the menu indicates that these dishes signify a 'new concept in low calorie eating'. Whether you are calorie counting or not, the range of dishes is outstanding, and the thoughtful preparation and presentation a real delight. Starters include native Helford Oysters, Dressed Crabmeat and a Salad of Smoked Duckling Breast served with Watercress and Exotic Fruits.

Main dish specialities include locally farmed Lamb, Breast of Chicken filled with a Mousse of Forest Mushrooms and Fresh Duck Breast which has been panfried with Peppered Pineapple. Fish dishes, though, are cooked to perfection and one of the favourite choices is a superior plate of shellfish which includes everything you could have as a starter, together with half a lobster. Lobster – served hot or cold from the hotel's own seawater tanks – is also available on its own. Whatever your choice, a wine list with nearly 100 bottles includes most popular French choices, and also features a range of vintage ports sold by the bottle.

Flitwick Manor has fifteen bedrooms, including seven new luxury rooms which opened late in 1987. All fifteen are furnished in a relaxing period style with antique furnishings used wherever possible. In addition to *en suite* bathrooms with a generous selection of quality toiletries, each room has a veritable plethora of additional comforts, including a remote-control colour television, an 'honesty' tray, iced water, a bowl of fresh fruit, a selection of hardback books and games, and a direct-dial telephone. The two best rooms in the hotel are the Four Poster Suite, with its antique bed and private sauna, and the Garden Suite which has a spa bath and sitting-room.

Nearby attractions are numerous: the charming little Georgian village of Woburn, with its famous abbey, is just five miles away, and stately homes of note within a short drive include Luton Hoo and the two Rothschild bequests of Ascott and Waddesdon. Sulgrave Manor was home for many years to George Washington's ancestors, and you can come more up to date historically by visiting Althorp, the family seat of the Princess of Wales' father, Earl Spencer. Towns within easy reach include Oxford and Cambridge – Flitwick Manor lies half-way between the two famous university centres – and both Stratford-upon-Avon and Windsor.

82

GRAVETYE MANOR

Near East Grinstead, West Sussex RH19 4LJ
Tel: 0342 810567

Nearest town East Grinstead.
Directions From London, take the A22 (the
Eastbourne road). About seven miles past
Godstone, you will reach a crossroads where you
turn right on to the B2028 for Turner's Hill.
A member of the **Relais et Châteaux** consortium.
Awards AA *** (red) and rosette for food; RAC
Blue Ribbon; British Tourist Authority commended;
Egon Ronay (80%) and Michelin recommended;
Egon Ronay Hotel of the Year 1978.
Open throughout the year.
No **special breaks** available other than a
Christmas programme, which is always popular.
The hotel is unsuitable for disabled visitors; the hotel
welcome 'babes in arms' and children aged seven or
over; dogs are not allowed.
Price for dinner, with wine, bed and breakfast for
two – over £150.
Credit cards None accepted.
Overall mark out of ten 9.5

An internationally famous hotel which has a deserved reputation as one of Britain's finest Country House Hotels, Gravetye Manor offers exceptionally high standards of comfort and cuisine. In 1978 it won the prestigious Hotel of the Year Award from Egon Ronay, who described it then as 'an outstanding exemplification of Country-House hospitality in a beautiful setting, combined with dedicated, professional hotel-keeping'. Few could argue that its standards have moved in any direction but upwards since then.

Gravetye Manor was originally built in 1598 by Richard Infield for his new bride Katharine Compton. You can still see their initials carved in stone above the main entrance from the Formal Garden and their wood-carved portraits hang in the master bedroom. The manor's most distinguished owner was William Robinson, one of the greatest gardeners of all time, who bought the manor and the one thousand acres in which it still stands in 1884. He realized many great ambitions for the gardens around the house before his death in 1935, and today the gardens are among the most famous Victorian-style formal gardens in England.

The style of all the public rooms is distinctly late Victorian, and much of the wood panelling throughout the hotel was added by William Robinson at the end of the last century from wood on the estate. The sitting-room has wood panelling all around and a sumptuous ornate plaster ceiling which you cannot help but gaze at in amazement as you wonder precisely how it was constructed.

The restaurant, particularly, is a magnificent old room, with a capacity for 50 guests. The combination of solid wood panelling and candlelight creates just the right level of informality which a hotel of this class deserves. Chef Leigh Stone-Herbert describes the style of cuisine as 'electric', but with particular influence from French *haute cuisine* and the best of traditional English cooking.

À la carte and a table d'hôte menus are available each evening, both of which are presented to diners in an attractive glossy card menu folder decorated with tasteful sketches of the house and grounds. A number of starters are also suitable as light main courses. These include Salmon, fresh from the hotel's own smoke-house, Creamed Eggs served with Mussels and Saffron, and an intriguing Middle Eastern speciality – Steamed Lamb's Brains, served in a Light Puff Pastry Slice with a Sorrel Sauce.

Main dishes are all accompanied by a bouquet of vegetables to complement the type of meat or fish chosen. There is a strong selection of fish dishes available, including Steamed Salmon, Roast Fillet of Angler Fish and an interesting dish made up of Boneless Fillets of Mullet and Bream poached in a Fish Bouillon, all served perfumed with herbs. Meat dishes include Roast Fillet of Veal and Pot Roasted Breast of Duck. Gravetye Manor has a superb wine list, one of the finest in England, with over 350 vintages on offer.

The hotel has fourteen bedrooms, including two singles; each one is named after an English tree. All are furnished in a mood of quiet comfort with antique furniture and high-quality soft furnishings throughout. All are bright and spacious, and doubles are available in a choice of three sizes. Each bedroom comes complete with private bathroom facilities, colour television, direct-dial telephone, bathrobes, and a range of hardback books and quality complimentary toiletries, in keeping with the overall luxury standards of the hotel.

Leisure facilities at Gravetye are deliberately limited so that guests may have the opportunity to relax and enjoy the peace and quiet without too many distractions. Horse riding and golf can be arranged locally, though, as can fly-fishing for brown and rainbow trout on the hotel's three-acre loch between May and September. Clock golf and croquet are available on the hotel's large lawn. Nearby attractions include Hever Castle, Chartwell (the former country home of Sir Winston Churchill) and the Glyndebourne Festival Opera.

83

HORSTED PLACE

Little Horsted, Uckfield, East Sussex TN22 5TS
Tel: 0825 75581

Nearest town Uckfield.
Directions Horsted place lies 42 miles from
London and sixteen miles from Brighton. It sits
just off the A26 Uckfield to Lewes road, about a
mile from Uckfield.
A member of the **Pride of Britain** consortium.
Awards AA *** (red) graded; Michelin four Red
Turrets; Egon Ronay 77%.
Open throughout the year.
A special **Winter rate** is available from November
until Mid-March.
The hotel is suitable for disabled visitors; dogs, and
children under seven, are not allowed.
Price for dinner, with wine, bed and breakfast for
two – over £150.
Credit cards All major cards accepted.
Overall mark out of ten 9

Opened only in June 1986 as a luxury hotel, Horsted Place
has the distinction of being one of the most recently trans-

formed Country Houses which is already one of the country's best and therefore featured in this guide. It has only been a few years since the old Victorian house was one of the principle private residences in this part of southern England, regularly playing host to Her Majesty the Queen and many other senior members of the Royal Family.

Horsted was built in 1850 by George Myers for a wealthy London dyer called Francis Barchard. The main influence in the design of the house came from Augustus Pugin, who is probably best known for his work on the House of Lords. The house was eventually bought by Lord Rupert Nevill in 1965. Lord Rupert was for many years Private Secretary to Prince Philip, and became a good friend to the Queen, hence both Her Majesty and Prince Philip, and a number of other senior members of the Royal Family, visited Horsted Place as guests of Lord and Lady Nevill.

One of the most striking features of the hotel is the main staircase, hand-carved in solid English oak, to Pugin's design. A section of the staircase was exhibited in the Medieval Court of the Great Exhibition of 1851 – and the original Victorian packing slip for the delivery of the staircase to Lewes station is still on display in the hotel.

All the public rooms at Horsted are very comfortably furnished and have been carefully designed in a style typical of the Victorian era, when the house reached its zenith as a private residence. The main lounge is a bright room, with its colourful armchairs, two solid stone fireplaces and illuminated oil paintings all around. The little friezes above the doors are a nice touch, typical of the flamboyance of early Victorian craftsmanship.

The centrepiece of Pugin's interior design, however, is the main dining-room with its original ceiling. The style of decor is traditional, but this is complemented by modern porcelain tableware, crisp linen tablecloths and silver cutlery. Cuisine is in the modern British Country House style, and head chef Keith Mitchell has a number of distinguished culinary awards to his credit, which were gained before he came to Horsted Place.

A four-course table d'hôte menu is offered each evening, with at least three options for each course although the chef's recommendation for a perfectly balanced meal is always indicated. A typical dinner could open with a Warm Salad of Local Quail, followed perhaps by a Ragout of Seafood or a dish of succulent Mussels, before a main course of Prime Scottish Beef or Dover Sole. The choice of sweets is rather limited, although a speciality is a light Sponge Roulade filled with Cinnamon Buttercream and served with a Lemon and Saffron Sauce.

Horsted Place has a total of seventeen bedrooms, all of them suites, with the exception of three extremely comfortable double rooms. Each one has a private bathroom, with bath and shower, and is furnished to 'North American luxury' standards. In addition to remote-control colour television, direct-dial telephone and magnificent views across the gardens or Sussex Downs, each suite is individually decorated and comes with its own separate sitting area.

The hotel has a good range of leisure facilities available for residents, including a heated indoor swimming pool, an all-weather tennis court, a croquet lawn and 23 acres of private garden. In addition, other activities such as shooting, golf and fishing can be easily arranged.

Other nearby attractions include the coastal towns of Brighton and Eastbourne, Royal Tunbridge Wells, countless places of historical interest along the coast, and the possibility of day trips to France.

84

KENNEL HOLT

Cranbrook, Kent TN17 2PT
Tel: 0580 712032

Nearest town Cranbrook.

Directions The hotel is situated one and a half miles north-west of Cranbrook, on the main A262 Cranbrook to Goudhurst road. It is signposted a mile past the A229/A262 junction.

Awards AA ** (red) graded; RAC ** graded and Blue Ribbon; British Tourist Authority commended; recommended by Michelin and Egon Ronay guides.

Open from April until the end of October.

No **special breaks** are available.

The hotel is not suitable for disabled visitors; children are welcome, but at the proprietor's discretion if under six years of age; dogs allowed by prior arrangement.

Price for dinner, with wine, bed and breakfast for two – £100–£150.

Credit cards None accepted from residents, but non-resident diners may pay by Access, Visa, Amex or Diners Club if they wish.

Overall mark out of ten 7.5

An outstanding example of a pedigree Elizabethan Country House, Kennel Holt was built in 1560 and positively exudes period charm. A well-kept gravel driveway leads up to the house with its five magnificent brick chimneys which dominate the roofline of the hotel.

Thee wide stacks, with their even wider tops, built in the days when wood-burning fires were much more common than coal or any of the modern options, are typically Tudor.

Kennel Holt has been considerably renovated since Elizabethan times, and modern comforts have been added to existing period fittings to create a pleasingly informal atmosphere. There are two large sitting-rooms, both with thick-beamed ceilings and open fires. The Oak Room and Library is the more appealing of the two, with its soft furnishings and good range of reading material for guests to enjoy.

The front drawing-room has a larger fireplace and leads off the main entrance and hall. It is rather more open than the Oak Room, but is, nevertheless, a delightfully relaxing room and the perfect place to sit back with an after-dinner coffee or liqueur and watch the sunset during the long summer evenings.

The alcove restaurant is a relatively small room, with a capacity for only 25 diners of whom a maximum of eight are non-residents. The room is charmingly intimate and boasts an original fireplace. Probably the best feature about Kennel Holt, however, is its wonderful menu which the proprietor's wife Ruth Cliff has developed to near perfection over the years. Ruth has impeccable qualifications to take charge of the kitchen, having been a teacher at a resident Cordon Bleu cookery school for a number of years.

A five-course table d'hôte menu is offered each evening, and the starters, soup and desserts change from day to day. The three main courses change at least weekly. Typical starters include Avocado with Tomato Ice, Smoked Haddock Gratin, or Danish Tartlets. A soup course (no choice) precedes the main dish, and two selections are usually highlighted as the dishes of the day. Favourite specialities include New Forest Pork with Nuts, Poached Sole stuffed with Scampi or Supreme of Duck Montmorency. In season, fresh vegetables are provided straight from the hotel garden, and there is a very respectable wine list available for such a relatively small hotel.

There are nine bedrooms furnished in a modern style, including seven doubles with a private bathroom or shower, plus a further small double and one single, which also have their own facilities. A number of the doubles are on the small side, but all are comfortably furnished with a colour television (usually portable), hair dryers and radio alarm clocks. One of the doubles has a four-poster bed and most of the rooms have excellent views across the duck pond and surrounding five-acre garden.

Within easy driving distance of Kennel Holt are at least 50 distinguished historic houses, castles and gardens. Sissinghurst is a famous Tudor estate literally just down the road, and Scotney Castle is a fourteenth-century moated castle about five miles away. Other attractions include the gardens at Great Comp and Great Dexter, Hever Castle (once the home of Anne Boleyn), Chartwell, Batemans (where Rudyard Kipling used to live) and Leeds Castle. In addition, there are the ports of Dover, Folkestone, Ramsgate and Sheerness with their day-trip ferry excursion possibilities, and the historic towns of Canterbury, Hastings and Royal Tunbridge Wells.

85

THE MANSION HOUSE AT GRIM's DYKE

Old Redding, Harrow Weald, Middlesex HA3 6SH
Tel: 01–954 4227

Nearest town Stanmore (though really on the outer fringes of London itself).

Directions From London's West End, follow the A5 or A41 on to the A410 through Stanmore. Turn right at the roundabout and cross into Old Redding at the traffic lights.

The hotel is owned by **Select Country Hotels** and is a member of the **Best Western Hotels** consortium.

Open throughout the year.

Special breaks Weekend breaks available all year (different rates in summer and winter); English Evening Weekends (three nights half-board plus entertainment for around £120).

The hotel has twenty ground-floor rooms so may be suitable for the disabled; children and dogs are welcome.

Price for dinner, with wine, bed and breakfast for two – £100–£150 mid-week; under £100 at weekends.

Credit cards All major cards plus EnRoute (Air Canada) and Airplus (major airlines).

Overall mark out of ten 8.5

Less than ten miles from London's West End, the Mansion House at Grim's Dyke is set in over 100 acres of woodland and was once the secluded former home of dramatist W. S. Gilbert who was, for many years, partner to Sir Arthur Sullivan. For those wishing to enjoy the luxury of a Country House Hotel, and at the same time remain close to the capital, the Mansion House is a perfect choice. Even without a car, the hotel is accessible via a short taxi journey from Underground stations Stanmore or Harrow-on-the-Hill, coming direct from the city centre.

The house was originally built in 1875 by Norman Shaw for the Victorian artist Frederick Goodall. W. S. Gilbert and his wife bought the house, which was then known as Grim's Dyke on Harrow Weald, in 1890 and lived here until the end of their lives. In July 1907 William Gilbert left the house for the twelve-mile drive to Buckingham Palace, where he was knighted by King Edward VII, and thus made his entry into the history books as the first British playwright to be so honoured.

During his lifetime, W. S. Gilbert took an active interest in the development of his substantial garden. One of his main projects was the creation of a small lake, which he personally helped dig in 1900, and it was in the lake that he eventually suffered a fatal heart attack while trying to save the life of one of his favourite students who had fallen in.

All the public rooms can accurately claim to offer 'warm luxury and furnishings, in keeping with the relaxing mood which Sir William Gilbert would have appreciated'. The oak-panelled drawing-room has a particularly attractive recessed stone fireplace and doubles as one of the three intimate dining-rooms for that special private dinner or function.

The hotel's most impressive public room is the Music Room Restaurant, with its enormous marble fireplace. As the room's name implies, this was for many years Sir William Gilbert's music room and was refurbished in August 1987 in traditional Edwardian shades of peach, pale green and cream. Up to a 100 can be seated. The restaurant, with its fine cuisine, is extremely popular with non-residents, so advance booking of between a week and a month is essential, depending on the season.

Chef Michael Brooke offers a unique choice of classic British dishes in traditional Country House style. Local produce is used wherever possible for à la carte and table d'hôte menus, and the à la carte offers an interesting range of imaginative dishes. Hors d'oeuvres include a delicious Terrine of Lobster and Pike, served with an Avocado-Yoghurt Sauce, and a duet of Smoked Goose and Comice Pears cooked in fine Sauternes.

Main dishes include a number of fish choices, such as steamed wild River Tay Salmon and Supreme of Sea Trout with Fresh Scallops. Breast of Chicken filled with Dublin Bay Prawns and a Lobster Cream offers an intriguing contrast of tastes, but the top dish generally available is a rich helping of Grilled Venison, marinated in Ginger Wine, Juniper and Burgundy.

There are 48 bedrooms at the Mansion House, including three luxury rooms. Forty are in the Garden Lodge. All the rooms in the main house are decorated in classic English styles, and the soft colours contrast well with the dark wood period furniture. The Gilbert Suite and Gold Room offer the added romanticism of a four-poster bed. All rooms have private bathrooms, complete with quality bath oils, large towels and cut flowers to add that extra fresh touch.

The hotel has an original Victorian croquet lawn for guests to enjoy, and most other leisure facilities are available close by. Grim's Dyke golf course is adjacent and fishing, squash and even flying lessons can all be enjoyed within a mile. Gilbert and Sullivan evenings of music and song are organized throughout the year. An inclusive charge (under £25 per person) includes a three-course dinner with coffee and entertainment. Other nearby attractions, including the obvious appeal of the city of London itself, are the Stuart house of Moor Park golf club, Aldenham Country Park, Harrow village with its famous Elizabethan school, the Roman town of St Albans, and the beautiful Chiltern Hills only a short drive away.

86

OAKLEY COURT

Windsor Road, near Windsor, Berkshire SL4 5UR
Tel: 0628 74171

Nearest town Windsor.
Directions From the M4, leave at junction 6 and
follow the A332 towards Windsor. Turn on to the
A308 towards Maidenhead and the hotel is located
on the right-hand side.
Owned by **Norfolk Capital Hotels** and a member
of the **Prestige Hotels** consortium.
Awards AA *** graded and rosette for food;
British Tourist Authority commended; Egon
Ronay's highest recommended hotel in Berkshire.
Open throughout the year.
Special breaks Weekend rates, winter breaks
and Easter breaks are available.
The hotel is unsuitable for disabled visitors; children are
not discouraged but dogs are not allowed.
Price for dinner, with wine, bed and breakfast for
two – £100–£150.
Credit cards All major cards accepted.
Overall mark out of ten 9

It is likely that you will feel a certain familiarity with Oakley
Court the first time you set eyes on its semi-Gothic, semi-
château stonework. Between 1955 and 1969 it was one of the

principle locations for Southern Pictures and about 200 feature films were made in and around the property including most of the classic *St Trinian's* series. Tommy Steele's famous *Half a Sixpence* was filmed here, as were many of the Hammer Horror Dracula productions. In 1981 the old house was opened as a luxury hotel after a major programme of refurbishment.

Rather surprisingly, very little is known about the early history of Oakley Court, despite its fame through so many films. It was originally built in 1859 for Sir Richard Hall Say, and legend has it that it was built in the style of a French château to comfort his homesick French wife. The building passed through a number of hands, and it is believed that the English headquarters for the French resistance were based here during the Second World War. If this is the case, it is pretty certain that President De Gaulle stayed in one of the Mansion bedrooms.

Oakley Court is another of the largest Country House Hotels featured in this guide, with a total of 91 bedrooms. It is inevitable that hotels of this size have a reputation for impersonality, but the staff and management at Oakley Court are friendly and informal, and they work hard to provide as personal a service as possible to all guests.

Wherever feasible, the public rooms were restored to their original Victorian splendour during the £5 million renovation programme. Most of the furnishings are highly ornate and had to be hand finished. The dark wood staircase leading off from the reception, and the carved fireplace in the drawing-room, have been painstakingly polished back to the authentic shine. Take a moment to admire the rich plastering in the drawing-room, all of which is original.

The Oakleaf restaurant is one of the most delightful rooms in the hotel, and very popular with non-residents. Up to 120 can be seated but, even so, advance booking by at least a week is essential. The food is prepared by one of England's leading chefs, Murdo MacSween, who holds the rare qualification of Master Chef of Great Britain. To describe his cuisine as a combination of English and French styles would be something

312

of an understatement, but it will give you some idea of the type of dishes to expect.

A set-price six-course Gourmet Menu (around £35–£40 per person at the time of publication), together with a table d'hôte and an à la carte menu, are available each evening. Specialities change from season to season, but a typical selection of starters would include a unique Paupiette of Sole Stuffed with Seaweed and a Mousse of Saffron, served with Spinach and a White Wine Sauce, or a Terrine of Pheasant, Partridge and Foie Gras served with Redcurrants in Port Jelly.

Main dishes include Fillets of Monkfish, braised in Sauternes, Dill and Saffron sauce, and served in a pastry case. A more original favourite of Murdo MacSween is an exquisite dish made up of a pair of Quails stuffed with a Mousse of Tarragon, wrapped in Greek pastry and baked, served with a light Orange Sauce.

The total of 91 bedrooms includes seven lovingly restored suites in the main house, and four rooms with antique fourposter beds. Most of the rooms, though, are housed in the Riverside and Garden Wings which were added to the main building between 1979 and 1981. All rooms are comfortably furnished with private bathrooms, colour television, direct-dial telephone and period furniture wherever possible.

The hotel stands in 35 acres of beautifully maintained gardens on the banks of the River Thames, surrounded by woodland and green fields. Leisure facilities include a ninehole golf course, an area for pitch and putt, a croquet lawn and the opportunity for private fishing. Inside the hotel there is a full-sized billiards table which dates back over 300 years.

Major sporting centres, including Sunningdale and Wentworth for golf, Windsor and Ascot for horse racing, Marlow and Henley for boating and Twickenham for rugby are within a short drive. Other nearby attractions include Windsor Castle, Eton College, the towns of Windsor and Maidenhead, Medmenham Abbey, and Marlow, where you can visit Albion House, the former home of the poet Shelley and the place where his wife Mary wrote her classic horror story *Frankenstein*.

87

PENNYHILL PARK

Bagshot, Surrey GU19 5ET
Tel: 0276 71774

Nearest town Camberley.
Directions Leave the M3 at junction 3 (sign-posted Bracknell, Camberley, Guildford) and follow signs for Bagshot. Continue until you reach a T-junction at the end of the village and turn left on to the A30 and then right into Church Road. (with the Hero public house on the corner). The hotel is up on the left at the end of this road.
A member of the **Prestige Hotels** consortium.
Awards AA **** graded.
Open throughout the year.
Special breaks Good value weekend rates available, inclusive of half-board accommodation, complimentary chocolates, champagne and flowers in your room on arrival.
The hotel has a few rooms suitable for the disabled; children and dogs are welcome.
Price for dinner, with wine, bed and breakfast for two – £100–£150.
Credit cards Access, Visa, Amex, Diners Club, Mastercharge and Carte Blanche.
Overall mark out of ten 8

Pennyhill Park is a magnificent early Victorian country mansion which was built in an area of prime parkland once owned by King James VI and I, and his ill-fated son, Charles I. Both monarchs used to enjoy hunting around this part of southern England a couple of centuries before the present house was built. The house was originally designed by a distinguished Canadian who was best known, prior to then, for building the first bridges across the St Lawrence River in 1849. Today the stonework has matured into stately elegance with dense shrubbery slowly covering it from top to bottom.

Pennyhill Park remained a private residence until relatively recently. Today a large staff works hard to retain much of the attentive charm of a bygone era, and all the public rooms are spacious and comfortably furnished. Authentic period furniture has been retained where possible and numerous oil paintings adorn the walls in all the public rooms.

The hotel has a very popular restaurant, the Latymer Room, which is Tudor-styled with authentic Victorian beams. All the chairs are high-backed cane and tapestry-styled and the tables and chairs are arranged in a banquet fashion around the perimeter of the room. Traditional English and French cuisine is the speciality of the chef, although there is always an emphasis on fresh seasonal produce whenever it is available. Local products are almost always used, and there are usually at least one or two dishes available for vegetarians.

There is a more informal restaurant available in the beautifully restored Orangery. Built in 1891, this delightful building now houses the hotel's country club, containing most of the leisure facilities available for residents. The restaurant offers a more relaxing alternative to the main dining-room overlooking the swimming pool and tennis courts. The Orangery decor is altogether brighter, although very modern, and most food is served buffet style.

Pennyhill Park has 48 bedrooms, of which a dozen are ideal for families as they have two double beds. A number of the rooms are a little on the small side, but all have private bathroom facilities, colour television, radio and telephone. Most have good views across the surrounding parkland which gives the hotel its name, and all have retained many of the original antique furnishings.

The hotel has a range of leisure facilities for residents to enjoy, including an outdoor heated swimming pool, sauna, three hard tennis courts, a nine-hole golf course, a private trout lake covering just over three acres, horse riding stables, clay pigeon shooting and 120 acres of private parkland and immaculate gardens. Nearby attractions include Royal Ascot, Windsor Castle, Saville Gardens, the ancient city of Winchester, Eton College, Sandhurst Military Academy, Sutton Place, Berkshire Vinery and Henry VIII's magnificent palace Hampton Court.

88

SELSDON PARK

Sanderstead, South Croydon, Surrey CR2 8YA
Tel: 01– 657 8811

Nearest town Croydon.

Directions Leave the M25 (London ring road) at
junction 6. Follow A22 until junction with B270.
Take first left after joining B270 to Sanderstead up
Tithepit Shaw Lane. Turn left at the end, on to
B269 Limpsfield road to the first roundabout. Take
the third exit right towards Selsdon on A2022 and
you will see the hotel entrance on the right after
half a mile or so.

The hotel is a member of the **Best Western
Hotels** consortium.

Awards AA and RAC **** graded; English Tourist
Board five Crowns; Egon Ronay and Ashley
Courtenay recommended.

Open throughout the year.

Special breaks Weekend and winter breaks are
available, together with Christmas breaks.

*The hotel is not suitable for the disabled; children and
dogs are welcome.*

Price for dinner, with wine, bed and breakfast for two – £100 to £150.
Credit cards Access, Visa, Amex, Diners Club and EnRoute.
Overall mark out of ten 9.5

With 175 bedrooms and one of the finest leisure complexes of any hotel in Britain, Selsdon Park is the largest hotel featured in this guide. It can also claim the honour of being the biggest proprietor-owned hotel in the country. With the added advantage of being situated just thirteen miles out of Central London, it is extremely popular with businessmen and holiday-makers alike who want to stay within easy reach of the capital.

The hotel is an enormous stately old building, and everything about Selsdon Park is organized on a grand scale. Your first sight of it, after you sweep up the long drive, will be its magnificent ivy-clad exterior which has watched over the Selsdon Park estate in one form or another for the best part of twelve centuries. A manor house was recorded on the site of the present hotel as far back as 891 AD which was owned by a Saxon nobleman, Earl Aelfred, who had received an earldom after the Battle of Thanet. When Aelfred and his family lived here, the mansion probably covered no more than the area the indoor swimming pool covers today!

Over the centuries, of course, Selsdon Park passed through many hands and changed size and form many times. The Domesday Book, completed in 1086, records a substantially larger estate than that which Aelfred would have known. Many crusading lords stayed at Selsdon during the Middle Ages and by 1540 the manor was granted to Sir John Gresham, a close friend and adviser to Henry VIII. He became a great servant to Elizabeth I, and the Virgin Queen is known to have visited Selsdon, and hunted in its grounds, on a number of occasions. In 1924 the estate was bought by Allan Sanderson, father of the present owner, who turned it into a hotel soon afterwards.

Although most of the present building dates from no earlier

than the seventeenth century, and it has taken many major alterations since that period to turn it into the present luxury hotel, the public areas retain a marvellous sense of informality and unpretentious quality. Solid old beams still line many of the corridors and rich wood panelling adorns many of the walls. Everyone from the reception staff to the ebullient proprietor, Basil Sanderson, makes an effort to be genuinely courteous to all guests, whether they are non-residents making a first visit for dinner, or millionaires staying a month in the best suite.

The main restaurant is an enormous room, well lit by natural sunlight during the summer evenings and decorated with modern furnishings which blend well with the restful blue, grey and cream decor. Up to 275 can be seated at once, but advance booking is still essential for non-residents. An à la carte and table d'hôte menu is available each evening: both are extensive and the style of cuisine is broadly based and international.

The standard of service is exemplary; a small desk-style buffet area in the centre of the restaurant provides an extensive array of impressive hors d'oeuvres to open your meal. A typical four-course table d'hôte menu would start with a choice of three or four starters which might include Saumon Fumé or a delicious Terrine de Légumes Cressonaire. A speciality soup or light fish course precedes the main course, which is likely to include a fish dish like Paupiette de Plie Bonne Femme (a fillet of plaice filled with prawn mousse and coated with a white wine and mushroom sauce), or one of the chef's more adventurous favourites like Jardinière de Boeuf et Veau Orientale (strips of beef and veal, sautéed with bean-shoots, peppers, onion, pineapple, spring onion and almonds, and served up with a sweet and sour sauce).

All Selsdon Park's 175 bedrooms are extremely well furnished, and come complete with remote-control colour television, direct-dial telephone, spacious private bathroom facilities and a range of complimentary toiletries. The management has successfully created a blend of 'homely' fabrics and colours, and most rooms have the additional advantage of good views (particularly to the front of the hotel) across the surrounding gardens and golf course.

Selsdon Park has a magnificent tropical leisure complex which residents can enjoy completely free of charge (with a few minor exceptions such as sun beds). Most indoor sports can be enjoyed, and the complex forms part of the main hotel building which means there is no need for a chilly dash in the open air to reach it as is the case with so many hotels. Facilities include a heated swimming pool, Jacuzzi, sauna, steam room, squash courts, mini-gym, and even a dry beach where you can relax with a drink after your swim. Outdoors, there are an eighteen-hole championship golf course, a second heated swimming pool during the summer, floodlit tennis courts, croquet, riding, putting and a children's play area.

Nearby attractions include Hever and Leeds Castle, Chartwell (formerly home to Sir Winston and Lady Churchill), Penshurst and Polesdon Lacey. The scenic and historical attractions of Kent, Surrey and Sussex are within easy reach, and Brighton is under an hour's drive away. For golf enthusiasts, Sunningdale and Wentworth are just two of the many great golf courses nearby.

89

TANYARD

Wierton Hill, Boughton Monchelsea, near Maidstone,
Kent ME17 4JT
Tel: 0622 44705

Nearest town Maidstone.
Directions From Maidstone, follow the A274 for
a mile or so towards Tenterden. Turn right at
junction with B2163 (at the Plough Pub) and then
left towards Wierton Place Country Club just
before the Cock public house.
Awards AA National Winners Trophy 1987
(awarded to small hotels, inns and guest houses).
Open from March until December.
No **special breaks** are available.
The hotel is not suitable for the disabled; children under
six, and dogs, are not allowed.
Price for dinner, with wine, bed and breakfast for
two – under £100.
Credit cards Access, Visa, Amex and Diners
Club.
Overall mark out of ten 7.5

Tanyard is one of the most interesting hotels in the London
area, and probably the one which, from the outside, looks

least like a hotel of any in this section. Its early history is uncertain, but it is known to have started life as a Yeoman's house, was then a medieval farmhouse, and ultimately a tannery for many generations.

The hotel is thought to date from around the mid-fourteenth century, and has been lovingly restored to as near its original splendour as possible. The public rooms have been renovated considerably: the kitchen and dining-room are the oldest parts of the house, having been built around 1350, and the lounge and hall area were a later extension, thought to have been added around 1470.

Magnificent old beams are everywhere, both inside and out; indeed, the ancient beams which have been built into the exterior stonework are one of the first features which strike visitors to Tanyard. The public lounge, leading in off the main hall area, is small and comfortable, its dark leather suite the perfect match for the beamed ceiling and antique furnishings which are typical of all the rooms in the hotel.

The dining-room has a massive open fire – its size typical of the days when small tree trunks were thrown on the central fire which had to heat the whole house. Fourteen can be seated at any one time, and unfortunately this number precludes non-residents from dining. Only residents, and their guests, can enjoy the delicious home cooking which proprietor Jan Davies offers throughout the season. Even then, advance booking by at least two months is essential for those wishing to stay at Tanyard.

Dinner is served promptly at eight each evening, and can be as formal or informal as you wish. The style of cuisine is as typically English as you are likely to find in the London area – undoubtedly Jan Davies is influenced by the very age and history of her surroundings and, above all, by the number of repeat bookings she receives from visitors who have been impressed by her homely style and wise choice of menu from evening to evening.

A set menu is offered each evening, with no variations available. A typical evening's dinner would open with something like Avocado, Crab Claw and Grapefruit Salad served in a Ginger Mayonnaise, followed by a main course of fresh Scottish Salmon with a Hollandaise Sauce and a selection of vegetables. The only alternative for any course is the option of one of a number of home-made ice-creams instead of the set sweet. A selection of English cheeses follows before coffee in the lounge, or at your table, as you wish.

The hotel has five delightful and quite individual bedrooms, all of which have private bathroom facilities, telephones, tea- and coffee-making facilities and colour television. Each one has been furnished in elegant period style, although there is an interesting combination of brightly coloured bed coverings and easy chairs in a number of bedrooms. For that special break, the entire second floor of the old house has been turned into a single large suite. With two bedrooms, a sitting-room and a bathroom, this enchanting suite is ideal for up to four people looking for the perfect 'away-from-it-all' holiday in this part of England.

Tanyard has nothing to offer in the way of leisure facilities other than simple peace and quiet. Some popular activities, such as golf, fishing and a range of indoor sports, are available in the Maidstone area. The hotel is ideally placed for exploring Kent and East Sussex, and nearby attractions include Leeds Castle, Sissinghurst Castle, Bodiam Castle and the historic town of Canterbury with its ancient cathedral. The Channel ports of Dover and Folkestone are only a short drive away, offering plenty of opportunity for day trips to the French coast.

90

TYLNEY HALL

Rotherwick, near Basingstoke, Hampshire RG27 9AJ
Tel: 0256 72 4881

Nearest town Basingstoke.
Directions Leave the M3 at junction 5, taking the
A287 towards Basingstoke. Go straight ahead at
the junction with the A30, turn left at the next
T-junction, then right at crossroads signposted
Rotherwick. The hotel is about half a mile on the
left from here.
A member of the **Prestige Hotels** consortium.
Awards AA B.L. and RAC **** and Merit Awards
H.C.R. graded; Egon Ronay 81%; E.T.B. five
Crowns.
Open throughout the year.
Special **weekend breaks** are available throughout
the year.
The hotel can cater for disabled visitors; children are
welcome but dogs are not allowed.
Price for dinner, with wine, bed and breakfast for
two – £100–£150.
Credit cards All major cards accepted.
Overall mark out of ten 9

The magnificent Georgian-style façade of Tylney Hall dominates the 66 acres of private park and woodland in which the
house is set, and without a doubt this is one of the most

impressive buildings anywhere in Hampshire. Although it has only been open as a hotel since Autumn 1985, Tylney Hall has quickly established itself as one of the best hotels in this part of England, offering a class of comfort and service so typical of an earlier era when the house was in its prime as a private residence.

A mansion has been known on the Tylney estate since 1561, although it was not until the start of the eighteenth century that the first Tylney Hall was built by one Frederick Tylney. The family line died with him in 1725 as he failed to produce a male heir, and the original Hall passed into the hands of the fifth Earl of Mornington. He subsequently demolished the house because, it is believed, he was not allowed to fell timber from the surrounding rich woodland so long as the house stood! Lionel Phillips purchased the estate in 1898 and rebuilt the house in the present style.

The interior of the house boasts English oak panelling throughout, and your first sight of this will be the elegant entrance hall, with its sweeping staircase and solid oak pillars. The other public rooms are no less impressive, and the panelled library bar is the perfect place to relax with a pre-dinner drink. There are two public lounges: the Grey Lounge, which is not wood panelled, but has an equally traditional grey decor and an ornate white and gold plaster frieze all round the edges of the ceiling; the Italianate Lounge which has a more spectacular ceiling of intricately carved oak, inlaid with gold leaf, which originally came from the Grimation Palace in Florence.

The restaurant seats 80, about half of whom are generally non-residents, and the room has views of the Dutch garden and outdoor swimming pool. It is dominated by a large glass-domed ceiling which in summer allows the natural daylight to flood in. The remainder of the ceiling is styled with ornate plasterwork and the walls are adorned with hand-tooled Spanish leather panelling.

Chef Stephen Hine trained at the Dorchester in London and offers a table d'hôte and an à la carte menu each evening, based heavily on traditional English styles, although influenced by *cuisine moderne*. There is an excellent range of dishes available each evening: usually at least three choices for each course on the table d'hôte menu and substantially more on the à la carte. Starters include a delicious Salad of Lobster and Mango bound together in a Sherry Dressing and garnished with Asparagus, and a Cocktail of Assorted Seasonal Melon, sprinkled with a Mint Liqueur and served in a coconut shell.

Main dish specialities range from three small Fillets of Panfried Lamb, Beef and Veal served with three different accompanying sauces, to Fillet of Turbot filled with a Scallop Mousse and steamed before being served with a Brandy and Lobster Sauce. One other fish dish worth looking out for is an intriguing portion of Scampi, sealed in butter, which has been flamed with Pernod and casseroled in a Vegetable Butter Sauce.

Tylney Hall has a total of 91 bedrooms, including seven large suites. All are individually styled and furnished to the highest standards of comfort, complete with private bathroom facilities and colour television. All the rooms are a good size, but the suites are particularly large, and each room has at least one or two pieces of antique furniture (a dressing table, wardrobe, fireplace, etc) as a reminder of the days when Tylney Hall was a private residence. A number of the suites also have antique four-posters and private Jacuzzis to add that little extra comfort to your stay.

The hotel has a number of leisure facilities available for residents including a heated outdoor swimming pool, two hard tennis courts, croquet lawn, archery, and there is an eighteen-hole golf course adjacent to the estate. By the time of publication a heated indoor swimming pool and health studio should be in use. Nearby attractions include Stratfield House (former home of the Duke of Wellington), Windsor Castle, Winchester Cathedral, Stonehenge, and the cities of Southampton and Oxford within an hour's drive, in opposite directions, from Tylney Hall.

91

WHITEHALL

Church End, Broxted, Essex CM6 2BZ
Tel: 0279 850603

Nearest town Bishop's Stortford.
Directions Leave the M11 at junction 8 and
follow the B1051 towards the village of Broxted.
The hotel is at the 'church end' of the village.
A member of the **Pride of Britain** consortium.
Awards AA rosette; Egon Ronay and Michelin
guide recommended.
Open throughout the year – although the
restaurant is closed to non-residents in January.
Special **winter breaks** are available from
November until March.
*The hotel is suitable for the disabled; children and dogs
are not allowed.*
Price for dinner, with wine, bed and breakfast for
two – £100–£150.
Credit cards Access, Visa and Amex.
Overall mark out of ten 8

Sitting on a hillside overlooking the beautiful countryside of
north-west Essex, Whitehall is one of the oldest properties in

this part of England which is still occupied. The village of Broxted is recorded in the Domesday Book, and the earliest known reference to the present manor was in 1151 when Alured de Bendaville is known to have given it to the hospital of St John of Jerusalem. The gift was endorsed by King John early in the thirteenth century, confirming that the Order could establish a preceptory in Essex.

By 1541, the manor house was granted by Henry VIII to George Harper, a shadowy historical figure about whom very little is known. Within two years, Harper had conveyed the house to Sir Thomas Audley, then Lord Chancellor of England, and after a number of owners it was eventually occupied by the famous Edwardian hostess the Countess of Warwick around the turn of the century. Current proprietors Gerry and Marie Keane have run Whitehall as a hotel since Spring 1985.

The hotel today has retained an 'old' feel about it. Little has changed structurally in the last few centuries, and it would not be unkind to suggest that parts of the building have been adapted less well than others to the demands of a luxury hotel. The old window frames, for example, have been in place for generations – in some cases for centuries – and do look a little odd with straight new curtain rails concealing their crooked shape. The main public area is the warm reception hall, complete with roaring log fire and delightfully informal atmosphere.

The restaurant is a converted ale house, and has an authentic beamed ceiling (where no two beams are exactly the same shape, size or colour), enormous brick fireplace with exposed chimney and good views across the garden. Like the rest of the hotel, the restaurant is decorated in soft pastel colours. Advance booking is recommended for non-residents, but seldom more than a couple of days is necessary unless you plan to visit on a Saturday evening or public holiday. Food is served in traditional English Country House style, although distinct continental influences can be detected. An impressive three-course table d'hôte menu (plus coffee and *petits fours*) is offered each evening at around £25 per head inclusive of VAT and service. Alternatively, a six-course 'Menu Surprise' is available, and this is made up of light and delicate foods which are sure to create a meal of subtle flavours and imaginative presentation.

There are usually at least half a dozen choices available for each course on the main menu, and you may care to open your meal with a popular starter like Home-Cured Salmon, or else experiment with something a little different such as a Mélange of Calves Liver and Mange Tout, served on a bed of French Leaves in a Raspberry and Walnut Oil Dressing.

Main courses are less adventurous and have two characteristics: good-quality raw ingredients and subtle sauces. Two favourite dishes are Salmon Mille Feulle with Saffron Sauce, and Noisette of Lamb in a Sorrel Sauce. To finish off, you can choose from an extensive cheese board or range of sweets which includes Meringue Cones filled with Honey Ice-Cream on a Chocolate Sauce. Whatever your choice, an extensive wine list is available, with a number of good clarets, to complement your meal.

Whitehall has ten bedrooms, including six new ones which were opened in Autumn 1987. Each room has a definite character of its own, and has been decorated in a choice of soft pastel shades. On the whole, the rooms are furnished in a modern style, although original fireplaces (not in use) and dark wood panelling have been retained wherever possible. Each one has private bathroom facilities, colour television, direct-dial telephone and additional accessories like a hair dryer and trouser press to make your stay here as trouble-free as possible.

Among the leisure facilities at Whitehall which residents can enjoy are a tennis court, a heated outdoor swimming pool and a large walled garden. Nearby attractions include the natural beauty of Constable country, in Dedham Vale to the east; the historic city of Cambridge; the quaint villages of Thaxted and Finchingfield; and the popular old market town of Saffron Walden.

SOUTHERN ENGLAND

92

ALSTON HALL

*Battisborough Cross, Holbeton, near Plymouth,
Devon PL8 1HN
Tel: 075 530 259*

Nearest town Plymouth.
Directions The hotel is situated off the main
A379 Plymouth to Kingsbridge road. Proceeding
towards Kingsbridge, take the Holbeton road for
about three miles and the hotel is signposted on
your right.
Awards AA and RAC *** graded; British Tourist
Authority commended; Egon Ronay, Ashley
Courtenay and Michelin recommended.
Open throughout the year.
Special breaks Limited weekend and winter
breaks may be available.
*The hotel is unsuitable for the disabled; children are
only accepted by prior arrangement and dogs are not
allowed.*
Price for dinner, with wine, bed and breakfast for
two − £100−£150.
Credit cards Access, Visa, Amex and Diners Club.
Overall mark out of ten 7.5

Set in an area of outstanding natural beauty, Alston Hall is
surrounded by four and a half acres of private park and

woodland. It is a typically grand Edwardian Country House, having been built in 1906 by the vicar of Holbeton as his private residence, and remaining so until the 1960s when it was converted into a small luxury hotel. A considerable amount of work has gone into the house since the 1960s in order to up-grade the building to the demanding standards of a quality Country Hotel and, if the popularity of Alston Hall is anything to judge by, these efforts have more than paid off.

The exterior of the hotel is as solid as it is impressive. Constructed from brick and dressed granite, the steeply sloping red clay tile roof contrasts well with the stone mullions and dense Virginia creeper which is slowly covering the walls. You could be forgiven for thinking the exterior of the building is older than it looks because of its semi-Tudor style roof and wide stone chimneys.

A rich oak theme prevails throughout the public area of Alston Hall, and nowhere is this more striking than in the Great Hall which greets you as you first enter the building. This high-ceilinged room is completely panelled and has a distinctive Minstrel Gallery all around the first-floor level. The Great Hall, with its red leather chairs and wide fireplace, doubles as an additional lounge when the hotel is busy.

The oak theme is continued in the bar, although only the bar area itself is totally panelled. Here you can relax with a pre-dinner drink and appreciate some fine views across Dartmoor. The main lounge is purpose-built and serves as a ballroom for weddings, private parties and other functions.

Up to 40 can normally be seated in the comfortable dining-room which is open to non-residents. The atmosphere is quiet and informal, and food is a blend of traditional English and modern French styles. A varied table d'hôte menu is offered each evening, together with a reasonable wine list with a good range of younger European bottles to complement your meal.

Starters include rather unusual combinations like Scrambled Egg and Smoked Salmon, and Grilled Avocado and Stilton Cheese. For your main dish, specialities include Chicken Cagliari (a delicious combination of strips of chicken with prawns in a white wine sauce), Saltimbocca à la Romana (veal

334

wrapped in ham and served in a white wine sauce), or grilled Lemon Sole Meunière.

The hotel has ten bedrooms, all double or twin rooms and all with private bathrooms and showers *en suite*. All have been individually decorated and furnished in a bright modern style with remote-control colour Teletext television, radio and direct-dial telephone. Most of the rooms have large windows offering good views across the gardens and Dartmoor.

Alston Hall has a number of leisure facilities available for residents, including a heated outdoor swimming pool, two all-weather tennis courts and a croquet lawn. Other sports like golf and fishing can be arranged locally. There are a considerable number of local castles and abbeys in the area around Alston Hall, and the port towns of Plymouth, Dartmouth and Salcombe are popular with visitors to the area. When the weather permits, Dartmoor and numerous beaches along the southern coast can be visited.

93

BAILIFFSCOURT

Climping, Littlehampton, West Sussex BN17 5RW
Tel: 0903 723511

Nearest town Littlehampton.
Directions Leave the M25 at junction 9 and
follow the A29 as far as the junction with the
A284. Follow the A284 to the roundabout below
Arundel linking Chichester and Brighton by the
A27. Take the route marked Ford and Climping
and turn right at the T-junction up the A259
Littlehampton to Bognor road. The hotel is a few
hundred yards down the first left turning.
Awards AA *** graded.
Open throughout the year.
Special rates are offered mid-week all year
round.
The hotel is not suitable for the disabled; children under
twelve are discouraged but dogs are 'encouraged to bring
their owners'. Baskets and food can be provided.
Price for dinner, with wine, bed and breakfast for
two – over £150.
Credit cards All major cards accepted.
Overall mark out of ten 9

Few visitors to Bailiffscourt can argue that it is not one of the most fascinating and intriguing properties in southern England. It is built to resemble a sprawling medieval manor house whose Gothic-style windows you can just see glinting through the trees from the nearby main road. Its solid stonework epitomizes the sombre dignity of the Middle Ages.

Ironically, though, Bailiffscourt is the youngest hotel featured in this guide, since it was completed in 1933 – at a fabulous cost – to satisfy a caprice of the late Lord Moyne. The final bill was never revealed, but even in the 1930s it must have cost around £1 million to create this unique house. Architecturally correct down to the smallest detail, both inside and out, the management freely admits that Bailiffscourt would have been an utterly shameless fake were it not for the fact that the house had been built almost entirely from genuine bits and pieces taken from old houses the length and breadth of Britain. The full story of Bailiffscourt, which has been a hotel since 1948, is fascinating, and it is not hard to understand why one leading architect, quoted in *Harper's Bazaar* in 1969, said: 'One fake like this is all right because, as the only one of its kind, it is a unique piece of art. But heaven help us if we have any more.'

Inside the house the attention to detail is amazing. In the Music Room there is an outstanding moulded oak ceiling which came from a fifteenth-century rectory in Somerset. In this room alone there are also two sixteenth-century fireplaces. Throughout the public rooms there are examples of intricate needlework, and tapestry wall hangings, dating back several centuries.

The main restaurant is a delightfully grand room, with a slightly arched oak ceiling and a seating capacity of 65. Medieval drapes, high-backed Jacobean-style chairs and flickering candles quite complete the romantic atmosphere. The chef describes his style of cuisine as 'modern classical' – a description as typically paradoxical as the rest of this wonderful hotel. A most impressive table d'hôte and an à la carte menu are available each evening.

Opening specialities include a rich Game Terrine studded

337

with Fresh Truffle and Pistachio Nuts, placed on a rosette of salad leaves and served with Cumberland Sauce, and a Pastry Pillow filled with Creamed Spinach and Fresh Asparagus Tips, accompanied by a Raspberry Butter Sauce. Main course options include a strong selection of local meat and game. For two persons, an interesting suggestion is best end of English Lamb Baked in a Salt Crust, presented and accompanied by a golden Mint Hollandaise Sauce with a light Rosemary Jus. Another option might be a selection of fresh market Fish, poached in Dry White Wine and Shallots and placed on a Scallop and Noilly Prat Sauce. All main dishes are served with a selection of fresh market vegetables and potatoes.

As you might expect, all eighteen bedrooms (plus two separate cottages nearby) are superbly furnished in the same mock-medieval style as the rest of the hotel. Each bedroom is completely different from the one before it: most have solid oak beams running across the ceiling, and a delightfully spacious feel to them. Eight have four-poster beds, nine have open log fires, and you will be struggling to find a more romantic setting anywhere in this part of England in which to enjoy these particular 'extras'. All bedrooms have their own bathroom facilities, colour television and direct-dial telephone.

One or two leisure facilities, including a sauna, and an (unheated) outdoor swimming pool, are available for residents to enjoy. In addition, there is a 'tee to green' golf practice area on the rear lawns, a croquet lawn (with the necessary equipment available) and a hard tennis court. Clay target shooting can be arranged if guests wish. Nearby attractions include the magnificent Arundel Castle (stately home of the Duke of Norfolk); Chichester, with its famous theatre; Portsmouth, with its many naval attractions including the Mary Rose museum; and the coastal towns of Southampton, Brighton and Eastbourne.

94

BEAUPORT PARK

Battle Road, Hastings, Sussex TN38 8EA
Tel: 0424 51222

Nearest town Hastings.
Directions The hotel is situated just off the
A2100, approximately half-way between (and
three miles from both) Hastings and Battle.
Awards AA and RAC *** graded; English Tourist
Board four Crowns.
Open throughout the year.
Special **bargain breaks** are available all year
round for a minimum of two nights half-board.
The house is not suitable for disabled visitors; children
are welcome, and dogs are allowed.
Price for dinner, with wine, bed and breakfast for
two – under £100.
Credit cards Access, Visa, Amex and Diners Club.
Overall mark out of ten 8

Situated at the western end of a ridge of hills which shelter
Hastings from the north and east, the Beauport Park hotel

enjoys a commanding position with magnificent views in all directions. This site appealed to General Sir James Murray (1721–94), who built Beauport Park between 1763 and 1766, and eventually built up his estate to almost 2,000 acres of prime Sussex countryside. General Murray was one of England's most distinguished soldiers during the latter half of the eighteenth century, having first achieved distinction as a Brigadier General under General Wolfe at Quebec: indeed, Beauport Park is named after the village of Beauport near Quebec. He served for some time as Governor of Minorca at the end of a long spell during which the island was under British rule.

Among the many distinguished visitors to Beauport Park while it was a private residence in the two centuries which followed was Queen Victoria's eldest daughter, Princess Victoria. She was staying at nearby St Leonards-on-Sea in 1868, and came to take afternoon tea with the then owners, the Brassey family. She subsequently wrote to Queen Victoria that she 'liked being here immensely at the house of the Brasseys with the wonderful gardens and especially the trees'.

Although the original mansion was accidentally burnt down in 1923, the main structure survived and it was rebuilt soon after (with the exception of one wing). Inside the public rooms have been decorated and furnished in comfortable Georgian style. The main public lounge has full-length drapes, a polished marble fireplace and soft armchairs.

Both the cocktail bar and the large restaurant overlook the Italian sunken gardens, and the chef has an excellent reputation for traditional English Country House-style cuisine. Both a daily table d'hôte, and a regular à la carte menu, are available, and the hotel specializes in flambé dishes cooked at your table. A la carte starters include popular openers like Avocado with Prawns, and Smoked Salmon with Cucumber and Dill Salad, together with more continental favourites like Marinated Mussels and Burgundy Style Snails cooked in Garlic Butter.

Delicious fish dishes range from Coquille St Jacques Singapore to Rolled Fillets of Sole, poached and served with a

Lobster Sauce and Truffles. Two of the more popular house specialities are Brochette Royale, a dish for two persons comprising choice pieces of veal, beef and lamb, cooked on a sword with mushrooms and peppers. This is flamed in front of you and served with rice pilaff. Alternatively, you may prefer Salmon en Croute: medallions of salmon with spinach and egg, cooked in a pastry case and served with lobster sauce.

The hotel has 23 bedrooms, all decorated in a modern style with quality reproduction furnishings and *en suite* bathrooms. Additional comforts like remote-control colour television, direct-dial telephones and tea- and coffee-making facilities come as standard. The Honeymoon Suite has a four-poster bed, and both the large suites have private Jacuzzis for that extra luxury.

The hotel is situated in 33 acres of private wood and parkland, which includes some of Britain's rarest trees, with well-kept formal gardens at the rear of the hotel. Other leisure facilities available for residents include a heated outdoor swimming pool, a croquet lawn, putting green and an all-weather tennis court. There is an eighteen-hole golf course adjacent to the hotel, and both squash and riding can be enjoyed locally.

Other nearby attractions include the Cinque Ports of Hastings and Rye; many famous castles including Bodiam and Pevensey; the former home of Rudyard Kipling, Batemans; Sir Winston Churchill's country residence at Chartwell; and, of course, the site of probably the most famous battle in history, the Battle of Hastings, which took place three miles from the present hotel in October 1066.

95

BISHOPSTROW HOUSE

Bishopstrow, Warminster, Wiltshire BA12 9HH
Tel: 0985 212312

Nearest town Warminster.
Directions Bishopstrow House is located two miles south-east of Warminster on the A36 – the main road between Bath and Salisbury.
A member of the **Relais et Châteaux** consortium.
Awards AA *** (red) graded, Egon Ronay 86%; Michelin recommended.
Open throughout the year.
Winter breaks are available for any two days, half-board, between October and March.
The hotel has five ground-floor rooms so is suitable for disabled visitors; children under three years of age are not allowed; dogs only by prior arrangement.
Price for dinner, with wine, bed and breakfast for two – over £150.
Credit cards Access, Visa, Amex and Diners Club.
Overall mark out of ten 9.5

Bishopstrow House is an extremely attractive Regency mansion, deceptively larger inside than its ivy-clad façade leads you to think. It is set in 25 acres of private woodland and garden which includes its own river frontage down to the River Wylye. The house has a fairly undistinguished history, having been built by John Pinch of Bath in 1817 and converted into a luxury Country House Hotel this century.

All the public rooms have been furnished in lavish style. The grand entrance hall, with its wide staircase and antique chairs, leads into the drawing-room. This bright lounge has enormous curved bay windows offering good views across the garden, and beautiful arrangements of fresh flowers silhouetted against the sunlight.

The hotel has two dining-rooms, including one which overlooks the indoor swimming pool. The main restaurant seats 60 and has a very traditional decor which verges on the formal. Original oil paintings and quality ornamental chinaware merely add to this atmosphere which, nevertheless, enhances the very high standards of cuisine, in terms of both quality and presentation, which you can expect from head chef Nigel Davis.

The style of cooking is light and imaginative, using local produce wherever possible. Starters include Fresh Cornish Crab set on a light Tomato Mousse with a Cucumber and Dill Salad, and Ballotine of local Duck served with a homemade Apple and Sage Jelly. Main dishes range from Calves' Liver gently cooked with Avocado and Madeira to a delicious Rosette of Veal cooked in Pink Peppercorns and a Cream Sauce. The separate dessert menu is more adventurous than the choice of main dishes and generally includes a selection of treats such as Meringue Crown filled with a light Raspberry Mousse and Champagne Marquise, or perhaps Carmelized Puff Pastry filled with Oranges and coated in a Cream Vanilla Sauce.

The wine list is as long as it is comprehensive – and is definitely one for the connoisseur. Quality vintages include an outstanding selection of classic French wines, although the very drinkable house white or red at around £9 a bottle may be to more people's liking than the Château Petrus Pomerol 1947 at over £500 a bottle!

There are 26 bedrooms available, including eight luxurious suites and one single. Each room is decorated in a lavish blend of soft colours and rich cloth – golds, pinks, yellows and so on – with the occasional piece of antique furniture. A number of newer rooms are situated in a recently converted stable block. All rooms are extremely well appointed and spacious, and come complete with colour television, private bathrooms (and a selection of complimentary toiletries), and direct-dial telephone. One has a round bed, and the addition of a bowl of fruit and fresh flowers adds a personal touch to each bedroom. A number of rooms are fitted with their own safes, and several of the suites are fitted with private Jacuzzis.

Bishopstrow House has a range of leisure facilities to offer residents including both a very attractive heated indoor swimming pool, complete with white marble surround, and a heated outdoor pool. Both indoor and outdoor tennis courts, together with a sauna and solarium, and the opportunity to enjoy private fishing rights on the River Wylye are available. In addition, there is a golf course two miles away and facilities for horse riding about four miles away.

Other nearby attractions include the stately home of the Marquis of Bath, Longleat House, complete with its famous safari park; Stourhead House and gardens; Wilton House; Stonehenge; Avebury; and the historic cities of Bath and Salisbury.

96

BUCKLAND-TOUT-SAINTS

Goveton, Kingsbridge, Devon TQ7 2DS
Tel: 0548 3055

Nearest town Kingsbridge.
Directions Bypassing Exeter, head for the A381
signposted Kingsbridge. Pass through villages of
Herbertonford, Halwell and the Mounts. After 1.5
miles turn left opposite sign for hotel and continue
along single-track road for a mile into Goveton
village. Turn right up a steep hill, with a church on
your right, and the second drive on the right is for
the hotel.
A member of the **Prestige Hotels** consortium.
Awards AA and RAC *** graded; British Tourist
Authority commended; Egon Ronay recommended.
Open throughout the year, apart from two weeks
after New Year.
Special breaks Winter breaks between 1st
November and 31st March; special Christmas
programme available; Lazy Summer breaks in July
and August; November Wine Weekends.
The hotel is not suitable for the disabled or children
under twelve; dogs are not allowed.

Price for dinner, with wine, bed and breakfast for two – over £150.
Credit cards Access, Visa, Amex, Diners Club, Carte Blanche and Connect.
Overall mark out of ten 8.5

The estate on which the Buckland-Tout-Saints hotel has been built has a history which can be charted back to the era before the Norman Conquest of 1066. It was known then simply as 'Bochland' – literally meaning 'by the book' – which meant the land was free of any feudal service to a lord. The Tout-Saints family, after whom the hotel is named, are reckoned to have taken over the estate sometime during the reign of Richard I at the end of the twelfth century. They built the first manor on this site, although the only trace of it now is the stone-flagged floor which is still visible in the basement storerooms of the present hotel.

The building as it now stands was conceived and built by Sir John Southcote at the end of the seventeenth century after he, as a prominent English Catholic, returned from a spell of religious exile in France once the Catholic James II was on the British throne. The architectural style was relatively uncommon in this part of England, but such features as ovolo mouldings for the lower ground-floor windows, and casement rather than sash windows, were already common in eastern England and France where Sir John had already lived.

Many of the public areas of the hotel reflect the grandeur of the late seventeenth and early eighteenth centuries. The wood panelling and ceiling plasterwork in the writing-room are among the best examples of the style adapted by Sir John between 1685 and 1693. The main lounge has been altered considerably since then, although the twentieth-century panelling and plasterwork resembles what the original room was said to look like. Look out for the small writing-room with its very attractive late eighteenth-century Adam-style mahogany door.

The dining-room dates from the Queen Anne era, with the

original Russian pine panelling still intact. An ornate plaster ceiling has not survived but this does not detract from the intimate period feel which the rich panelling creates. The style of cuisine is distinctly modern British, using best-quality food, carefully reduced sauces and imaginative presentation.

An impressive three- or four-course fixed price menu is available each evening, presented in a large folder with a detailed explanation of the type of food served, the style of presentation and the variety of raw foodstuffs used in the preparation of your meal. Typical starters include Sautéed Scallops in a Mild Curry Sauce; a Terrine of Brill, Crab and Watercress with Avocado Sauce; and a Puff Pastry of Calves' Liver, Grapes and Mushrooms.

Main dishes change with the seasons, but generally include most traditional British dishes from Scotch Sirloin Steak, with a Red Wine Sauce and Peperonata, to Best End of English Lamb with Herb Sauce and Courgette Rimbale. One or two more original fish dishes are normally available as well as main courses, and those featured might include Turbot à la Duglère served with Cream, Herbs and Tomatoes, or perhaps Steamed Fillet of Brill with a Hazelnut Mousseline.

Buckland-Tout-Saints has twelve bedrooms, including two large first-floor suites. The Buckland Room has a magnificent hand-carved four-poster which has been made from solid mahogany to match the other antique furnishings in the room. The larger, superior rooms – two doubles and two twins – are also on the first floor while the remainder, with their Provençe-style shuttered windows, are on the second floor of the hotel. All have private bathrooms, colour television, direct-dial telephones, hairdryer, trouser press and good views across the hotel's grounds and surrounding countryside.

The hotel does not actively market any special activities or facilities for residents because, the owners say, they prefer to specialize in offering peace and tranquillity combined with informal but attentive service. Golf, sea and fresh-water fishing, tennis and squash can all be arranged locally, and during the summer months there is a croquet lawn laid out on the lawn. Nearby attractions include the natural beauty of the surrounding Devon countryside, a number of National Trust properties, the towns of Exeter and Plymouth, and the coastal resort of Torquay.

97

CALCOT MANOR

Near Tetbury, Gloucestershire GL8 8YJ
Tel: 066 689 355

Nearest town Tetbury.
Directions From the M5, leave at junction 13
(signposted Stroud) and follow signs for the A46,
turning south towards Bath. Turn left at the
crossroads off the A4135 and Calcot Manor is on
the left-hand side after this turning.
A member of the **Pride of Britain** consortium.
Awards AA *** (red) graded and rosette;
Michelin recommended and star for restaurant;
Egon Ronay 75%; 1986 *Hotel and Caterer*
Newcomer of the Year award.
Open throughout the year.
Special breaks Mid-week breaks and weekend
breaks available between 1st November and 31st
March.
*The hotel has one ground-floor suite suitable for disabled
visitors; children under twelve and dogs are not allowed.*
Price for dinner, with wine, bed and breakfast for
two – £100–£150.
Credit cards Access, Visa, Amex and Diners
Club.
Overall mark out of ten 8

Best described as a fifteenth-century manor house, Calcot Manor was originally a large Cotswold manor, complete with a working farm for centuries, before current owners Brian and Barbara Ball, together with their son Richard, bought it in October 1983. The farm was sold separately, but four acres of garden and woodland have been retained with the house, along with a courtyard of old stables and an attractive tithe barn which is reckoned to date back as far as the fourteenth century. Calcot was once part of the estate of Kingswood Abbey, which was founded by the Cistercians in 1158.

All the public rooms have been completely renovated and restored back to the style typical of the splendour of an earlier era. The house is lavishly furnished with antique family furniture, and the 'peaches and cream' decor of the drawing-room is particularly appealing. The Ball family take pride in running the hotel in as informal and professional a manner as possible; staff are never obtrusive but always available to attend to the requirements of residents.

The main restaurant seats up to 40 and has appealing French windows which lead out on to a garden terrace where you can enjoy a relaxing pre-dinner drink during the milder summer evenings. A combination of square and circular tables complements the green, apricot and grey decor.

Chef Ramon Farthing offers a most impressive three- (or four- including cheese) course table d'hôte menu which embraces the best of modern British cooking. The menu displays a keen speciality in fish dishes, although if fish is not your main preference you are unlikely to be disappointed by the other choices available. Starters include a delicious Hot Tartlet of Fresh Crab and Mushrooms on a Cognac and Cream Sauce, and a light Pigeon Mousse served warm on a bed of Crisp Salad Leaves and Grapes accompanied by a Red Wine and Butter Sauce.

Main dishes include slices of Fresh Seatrout placed on a bed of Braised Onion with Tarragon, served with a delicate Wild Mushroom Sauce; Sea Bass served as a fillet wrapped in Cabbage, with a Sauce of Chives which have been delicately flavoured with Caviar; and a Roasted Loin of Rabbit garnished with Celeriac, cooked in Garlic, Cream and Chives, and served on a Madeira Sauce. All dishes are accompanied by a selection of locally grown vegetables.

The hotel has thirteen bedrooms, including three new ones opened in August 1987. Each has a private bathroom and a unique character in keeping with the style of this marvellous old house. All the bedrooms reflect a particular part of the surrounding region: the Chiltern Room, for example, has hedgerow-patterned wallpaper with matching fabrics and the bathroom tiles have an intricate bramble design on them. All bedrooms have colour television and direct-dial telephone, and the master bedroom has a magnificent canopied and draped four-poster, and is one of three rooms with a private Jacuzzi.

The hotel is situated in the south Cotswolds and is surrounded by beautiful countryside. The main leisure facility, other than walking in the natural beauty all around you, is a heated outdoor swimming pool which is open from May until September. There is a croquet lawn in the grounds, and both tennis and horse riding can be arranged nearby. Other local attractions include Sir Peter Scott's Wildfowl Trust at Slimbridge, Westonbirt Arboretum ten minutes away by car, Blenheim Palace, Stonehenge, Berkeley Castle, Sudeley Castle and the towns of Oxford and Bath within 30 minutes' drive.

98

CAREYS MANOR

Brockenhurst, New Forest, Hampshire SO42 7RH
Tel: 0590 23551

Nearest town Brockenhurst.
Directions Leave the M27 at junction 1 and follow the signs to Brockenhurst. The hotel is eight miles from the motorway exit.
A member of the **New Forest Hotels and Restaurants Association**.
Awards AA and RAC *** graded; English Tourist Board four Crowns; Ashley Courtenay and Egon Ronay recommended; also recommended by a number of European organizations.
Open throughout the year.
Mid-week breaks available all year round.
The hotel is suitable for the disabled; children and dogs are welcome.
Price for dinner, with wine, bed and breakfast for two – under £100.
Credit cards Access, Visa, Amex and Diners Club.
Overall mark out of ten 7

Careys Manor was originally built as a hunting lodge in the seventeenth century and frequently used by King Charles II.

The hotel is named after a local forester, John Carey, to whom the original lodge was given by Charles II for services rendered. In 1888 the building was considerably extended, and it has operated as a Country House Hotel since the 1930s.

Careys Manor is a particularly popular conference venue, and most of the spacious public rooms are large enough to easily accommodate business meetings, or major social functions, such as wedding and anniversary parties. A new conference suite was completed in 1987 and adjoins the main restaurant. The style of furnishing in the public areas varies from the traditional (such as the wood-panelled reception area) to the modern. The main lounge, unfortunately, reveals little of the age of the building, with its polished wooden floor and generous assortment of easy chairs. Nevertheless, the overall effect is relaxing.

The restaurant has recently been refurbished and is decorated in a rich, soft pink and green colour-scheme. It can seat up to eighty. The style of food is a combination of modern British and French cuisine. A three- or a four-course table d'hôte, or an à la carte menu, is available each evening and popular appetizers include a Selection of Seafood in a Lemon Mayonnaise, Avocado and Prawn Salad with Tomato Vinaigrette, and a plate of Chilled Melon with a Ginger Wine Sauce.

From the selection of main dishes, which has a particularly strong range of charcoal-grilled steaks, specialities include Grilled Salmon with Lime Butter, or a Kebab of Scallops and Scampi served on a bed of Rice. There is an extensive selection of over 150 wines and port available, but many diners prefer to look no further than the (French) house wines at around £7 a bottle to accompany their meal.

Careys Manor has 80 bedrooms, nearly a third of which were added as part of a major refurbishment programme in 1987. All are comfortably furnished, with private bathrooms, colour television, telephone and facilities for tea- and coffee-making, although there is little sense of individuality between many of the rooms. The Garden Wing, linked to the main building by a covered walkway, has the most modern-style rooms in the hotel, in terms of decor and furnishings, but these bedrooms have the pleasant advantage of opening directly on to the lawns, or possessing a private balcony which overlooks the five acres of landscaped gardens.

The hotel has an excellent health and leisure complex, the Carat Club, which guests can enjoy on payment of a small daily charge. The centrepiece is an indoor heated ozone swimming pool and Jacuzzi (for which there is no charge) which has a 'jetstream' underwater current system installed for the benefit of serious swimmers. In addition, there is a supervised gymnasium, sauna, Turkish Room, impulse shower and treatment room for massage and beauty treatment. There are no less than eight golf courses within a fifteen-mile radius of the hotel, and numerous local riding stables have facilities available for residents to enjoy should they so desire.

Nearby attractions include the National Motor Museum at Beaulieu, Broadlands (former home of Earl Mountbatten of Burma), Exbury Gardens, Marwell Zoological Park near Winchester, the New Forest Butterfly Farm, the Royal Naval Museum at Southsea and two of England's most famous historical ships, HMS *Victory* and the *Mary Rose*, which are on display at Portsmouth.

99

THE CASTLE

Castle Green, Taunton, Somerset TA1 1NF
Tel: 0823 72671

Nearest town Taunton.
Directions The hotel is in the centre of Taunton, in Somerset, which is easily accessible by the M4 and M5 motorways.
A founder member of the **Prestige Hotels** consortium.
Awards AA **** (red); three (red) Michelin houses and star for cuisine; RAC Blue Ribbon 1987; Egon Ronay recommended (and star); 1987 *Good Hotel Guide* César Award as Best Town Hotel in Britain.
Open throughout the year.
Special breaks Wine Tasting Weekends; Musical Weekends; Fine Wine and Musical Weekends; West Country Breaks; Christmas and New Year programme; Mid-week Breaks.
The hotel is suitable for the disabled; children are welcome, as are 'well-behaved' dogs in bedrooms only.
Price for dinner, with wine, bed and breakfast for two – over £150.
Credit cards All major credit cards accepted.
Overall mark out of ten 9

When the 1987 Consumers' Association *Good Hotel Guide* awarded the Castle Hotel their prestigious César award as the Best Town Hotel in Britain, they recognized a hotel of outstanding merit within its given class. Already it is one of only three hotels in the country to have four AA red stars *and* a coveted Michelin star, and if the continental process of upgrading the bedrooms continues then it can surely only be a matter of time before the Castle picks up its elusive fifth star.

Although it is not in the country, the Castle offers all the charms and comforts of the best Country House Hotel, and it so resembles a fine Country House Hotel that it is included here without apology. The story of the Castle reads like an historical essay, since its earliest origins can be traced as far back as 710 AD. The first castle was burnt down in 722, and a more solid stone successor pulled down by the Danes in 1001. By 1066 a third castle had been built, and although it was fought over and besieged many times, it remained intact until the seventeenth century when part of it was dismantled. Those ruins can still be seen today as a beautiful Norman Garden, but the surviving part of the building became a hotel, providing ever more elaborate facilities for weary travellers. Over the centuries, the guest list has included Queen Victoria, Kings Edward VII and Edward VIII (as Prince of Wales), the Duke of Wellington, Benjamin Disraeli, and Her Majesty Queen Elizabeth the Queen Mother.

Today dense green wisteria covers the Castle's imposing façade. If you have the opportunity to visit in spring then do so, as only then can you fully appreciate the flourishing shrubbery (which is at least 150 years old itself) in all its colourful glory. Inside, the hotel is furnished to the highest standards of luxury and comfort; fresh flowers are everywhere and the quality of the rich period furnishings is virtually inrivalled in town hotels throughout the country. The Castle has had more than three centuries as a hotel to build up such a fine collection, and an all-round reputation for high standards. One of the most appealing rooms is the Moat Room, designed as a private dining-room with its elegant chandeliers and net drapes, and now extremely popular as a venue for small top-level board or senior management meetings.

In the dining-room, the style of cuisine is modern British, but not slavishly so, and the food really is superb. Service is attentive and unobstrusive, and a typical meal for two from the à la carte menu, with a moderate wine, should cost no more than around £60. Head chef Gary Rhodes has prepared an imaginative selection, and starters vary from Brixham Scallops, delicately poached in a Saffron Stock with Diced Mussels and Tomato and served with a Julienne of Garlic and Ginger, to an exquisite dish of Oak-smoked Chicken warmed in Butter, and served with a plate of Corn Salad, Caramelized Oranges and Toasted Brioche.

Main dishes are as elaborate as they are original. Fish choices include a Sea Bass Mousseline garnished with Asparagus Tips, wrapped in Salmon on a light Lemon and Chervil Butter Sauce, although you may prefer a more traditional English speciality such as Roast Best End of Lamb, with a Fresh Mint and Green Peppercorn Crust, served on a Lamb Sauce with Poached Currants; or perhaps Fillet of Beef in a sauce of its own juices and the essence of Girolles. In addition, there is an excellent wine list with over 500 bottles available, including over 100 clarets (with all the Premiers Crus represented) and most of the great French vintages since 1924.

There are 35 luxurious bedrooms at the Castle, ranging considerably in size and price from a small single (at around £50 per night) right up to the enormous Bow Suite which will cost you £240 for two persons per night. The hotel offers no 'ordinary' rooms, since every one has its own individual style of decor and furnishing, and is completely different from the one before. Themes vary from Mahogany to Walnut, and even Painted Bamboo, but all rooms have antique furnishings wherever possible, one or two pieces of fine china in recessed wall shelving, and the additional enhancement of a relaxing landscape. All rooms come with private bathroom facilities (the Bow Suite has two – the additional one is for your guests!), colour television and telephone, and freshly cut flowers to greet you.

The Castle has little available in the way of leisure facilities for residents, preferring instead to concentrate on offering an impeccable personal service, and peace and quiet in luxury surroundings. Most popular sports, however, can be arranged locally and this includes golf, fishing, tennis and horse riding.

Nearby attractions are numerous, and the Castle Hotel is ideally situated for discovering the beauty and heritage of this corner of England. The hotel produces its own pictorial tourist map identifying the main attractions for residents to explore, but some of the more famous places to visit are Avebury Manor, Longleat House and Safari Park, Malmesbury House, the castles of Berkeley, Longford, Old Sarum and Taunton itself, the cathedrals of Bath, Bristol, Exeter, Wells and Salisbury, and the historic cities of Bath, Bristol, Glastonbury and Wells.

100

CHEDINGTON COURT

Chedington, Beaminster, Dorset DT8 3HY
Tel: 093589 265

Nearest town Beaminster.
Directions Follow the A30 (or from London, the M3, M303 and A356) to Crewkerne. From there, continue down the A356 and the hotel is 4.5 miles in the Dorchester direction, just off the A356 at Wynyards Gap.
A member of the **Historic and Romantik Hotel** and the **Relais du Silence** hotel groups.
Awards British Tourist Authority commended; Egon Ronay and Michelin recommended.
Open throughout the year except for a few days over Christmas and a month from mid-January.
Special rates available for stays of two nights half-board or longer.
The hotel is not suitable for disabled visitors; children are allowed; dogs are not allowed in the hotel, but can be accommodated in the boiler room if necessary.
Price for dinner, with wine, bed and breakfast for two – under £100 (or just over).
Credit cards Not encouraged, but Visa and (reluctantly) Amex are accepted.
Overall mark out of ten 7.5

Chedington Court must be one of the most peaceful hotels featured in this guide. It is located in ten acres of mature private park and woodland in the heart of Dorset, and would be the ideal choice for a complete 'away-from-it-all' break, or even a honeymoon. Proprietors Philip and Hilary Chapman are members of the Relais du Silence group of hotels, an organization of privately-owned hotels dedicated to offering their guests absolute peace and quiet.

The house itself is a beautifully romantic old building, although on a stormy winter's night it would be the perfect venue for a horror movie with all its turrets, towers and leaded windows. Chedington Court was built by William Trevelyan Cox in 1840 on the site of a much older house which is known to date back many centuries. By the end of the nineteenth century, the estate comprised over 1500 acres of surrounding countryside but this was destined to be broken up in 1949. The present owners bought the house in 1981, and are constantly making improvements in order to maintain the high standards of hospitality which have been a feature of Chedington Court ever since they first opened it as a hotel.

Inside, Chedington Court has a heavily traditional atmosphere, though perhaps the Relais du Silence aspect is taken a little too seriously as the place is sometimes so quiet one feels the noise of eating dinner is excessive! That said, it is a perfect place for a truly peaceful weekend. There is no public or cocktail bar but drinks can be served in either of two large lounges. Furnishings tend to be solid and antique and, interestingly, some of them came from the state rooms of perhaps the greatest of all ocean-going liners, the *Queen Mary*. One of the bedrooms is named after the old ship as it contains a suite which was obtained after she was decommissioned as a sea-going vessel in the early 1970s.

Chedington Court's dining-room is as small as it is intimate. Only 26 can be seated at any one time, which makes dinner for non-residents a rare privilege when the hotel has its capacity twenty residents dining at once. It is a lovely old room, with its thick curtains, traditional Country House furniture and a daily four-course menu with a two-option choice of starter and a set fish and main course. Guests dine off fine Wedgwood crockery with silver-plated cutlery, and candle-burning table lamps specially imported from Denmark complete the atmosphere, that is only occasionally broken by softly playing classical music in the background.

Hilary specializes in traditional English cuisine, although the influence of French cooking is unmistakable. The food is beautifully cooked and presented and the standards very high. A typical evening's dinner will open with a starter like Celeriac, Cucumber, Radish and Watercress Salad with herbs, or Carrot Soup with Coriander. A light fish course such as Gratin of Scallops with a Saffron Sauce, or Steamed Salmon Trout with Caper Sauce precedes your main dish.

Main courses rely heavily on traditional English meats, although vegetarian preferences and special dietary requirements can be catered for on request, provided that the kitchen is given some advance warning. Favourite meals include Fillet of Beef in Pastry, Roast Dorset Duckling with Limes, and Rack of English Spring Lamb cooked in an assortment of locally grown herbs.

The hotel has ten large bedrooms, all doubles or twins, which can also be used for single occupancy on payment of a £10 supplement per night. All have private bath or shower-rooms (complete with gold-plated taps, no less, and a range of complimentary toiletries), and are mostly named after plants or local regions – Rhododendron, Hollyhock, Dorset, Devon and so forth. The 'Four Poster' room speaks for itself, with a magnificent old antique bed and good views across the garden.

One of its most distinctive features are the ten acres of magnificent ground which surround the house. These are exceptionally well looked after, and within their walls include a number of tombstones in the original churchyard. The fine specimen trees and plants are labelled and cared for by a staff of full-time gardeners. A walk before dinner in the grounds here is an experience worth driving a long way for. Other leisure facilities are croquet or putting on the sizeable lawns.

Nearby attractions include a wealth of famous sites and historic buildings. Among the better known are Pilsdon Pen,

Forde Abbey, Clapton Court, East Lambrook Manor, Barrington Court, Montacute House and Sherborne Castle (and Sherborne's 'old' castle as well). Other attractions include Thomas Hardy's cottage, Abbotsbury Gardens and Swannery, and the towns of Dorchester, Yeovil, Taunton and Shaftesbury.

101

CHEWTON GLEN

New Milton, Hampshire BH25 6QS
Tel: 04252 5341

Nearest town New Milton.
Directions Follow the A337 through Highcliffe
and fork left shortly after the 30 mph speed limit
sign at the Walkford junction. Take the first right
turning into Chewton Farm Road, and you will see
the entrance to the hotel drive on your right.
A member of the **Relais et Châteaux** and of
Britain's **Prestige hotels** consortia.
Awards AA **** (red) graded and two rosettes;
Egon Ronay 87%; Michelin four (red) turrets and
rosette for food; English Tourist Board five Gold
Crowns (the only hotel outside London with the
maximum award); British Tourist Authority
commended; 1976 Egon Ronay Hotel of the Year
Award; 1985 *Executive Travel* magazine Best Time
Off Hotel award.
Open throughout the year.
Winter breaks are available between 1st
November and 31st March.
The hotel is unsuitable for the disabled; children under
seven and dogs are not allowed.
Price for dinner, with wine, bed and breakfast for
two – over £150.
Credit cards Access, Visa, Amex, Diners Club
and Carte Blanche.
Overall mark out of ten 10

If it could not claim the honour outright, Chewton Glen would certainly come very close to being named as southern England's finest hotel. With an outstanding reputation for first-class personal service, an enviable country setting which is within a few minutes' drive of major road and rail links to the rest of the UK, and some of the highest standards of comfort and cuisine in the country, Chewton Glen epitomizes everything a good Country House Hotel should be.

The hamlet of Chewton can trace its origins back to at least the days of the Normans, but the present Chewton Glen manor dates back to 1730s. This was the heyday of the new classical Palladian architectural style, and a watercolour completed about a century later (one of the earliest contemporary illustrations of the house) shows a stuccoed Georgian building with a symmetrical west façade and high proportions typical of the short-lived Palladian style.

Many changes have taken place since the eighteenth century: rainwater pipes on the west side of the house bear the date 1904, a new curved central section was added to the front of the house in the 1830s, and in the last 30 years a new east wing has been added. The most famous former resident at Chewton Glen is Captain Frederick Marryat, who built up a popular reputation as a writer and illustrator after his *Code of Signals for the Merchant Service* was published in 1817. He made a famous drawing of Napoleon on his deathbed in 1821 (two versions of which are on display at the National Maritime Museum in London) and later wrote a series of novels which quickly became classics of their type. His last book, *The Children of the New Forest* (written here in 1846), remains in print today.

The public rooms at Chewton Glen have been lavishly furnished with a stately grace that enhances the elegant exterior and well-tended 30 acres of private gardens and parkland. The Oak Room has polished wood panelling all round and, like the Sun Lounge, offers magnificent views across the estate. The carefully thought-out blend of deeply upholstered chairs, fine antiques and gentle floral patterns on the curtains and armchairs enhances the feeling of space and timelessness which few luxury hotels manage to achieve with such perfection.

Head chef Pierre Chevillard joined Chewton Glen in 1979 from the world-famous Troisgros restaurant in Roanne. Each evening he and his kitchen staff create a splendid selection of à la carte specialities, in a modern French style, which are served in the relaxing surroundings of the coral pink and green Marryat Restaurant. Seating capacity is 90, and non-residents are encouraged to book at least a week in advance, although it is worth pointing out that a full four-course dinner for two, with a moderate wine, will leave little change from £100.

Speciality openers include Quail stuffed with Foie Gras and Pistachio Nuts, garnished with a Port and Pink Pepper Jelly, and a delicious combination of Snails, Button Onions, Mushrooms and Bacon cooked in a Red Wine Sauce and served on a Garlic Crouton. Main dishes range from Dorset Veal Fillet and local Scallops served on a bed of Noodles with a Saffron Sauce, to Breast of Chicken stuffed with Stilton Cheese and Chicken Mousse, served with a Warm Walnut Vinaigrette. The hotel offers an excellent wine list, with a sensible range of moderate wines under £10 a bottle right up to classic vintages such as a 1952 Lafite Rothschild at nearly £200.

All 33 bedrooms, including a number in the carefully restored Coach House, are large doubles or twins, and there are a further eleven extremely well-appointed suites. Each one is named after characters in the works of Captain Marryat – Lady Baker, Mr Midshipman Easy *et al*. A personalized welcome note and complimentary sherry greet you on arrival, and it is these little touches (along with the carafe of iced water, fresh flowers and quality Roger et Gallet bathroom toiletries) that help make Chewton Glen that bit extra special. All rooms have private bathrooms, deep pile carpets and the occasional piece of antique furnishing to create a comfortable combination of modern luxury and the timeless charm of an earlier age.

Among the range of leisure facilities available at Chewton Glen are a nine-hole golf course during the summer months, an outdoor heated swimming pool, an all-weather tennis court, a croquet lawn and a snooker room. Within a short drive, you can also enjoy clay pigeon shooting, fishing, sailing, squash and horse riding.

A handy booklet is given to all guests on arrival detailing many of the sites and things to do in the surrounding area. Among the better-known attractions are Beaulieu Abbey and Palace House; Broadlands (former home of the late Earl Mountbatten of Burma); the birthplace of Thomas Hardy; Longleat House and Safari Park; Wilton House; Exbury Gardens; Winchester and Salisbury Cathedrals; HMS *Victory* and the *Mary Rose* Museum at Portsmouth; Stonehenge; and the towns of Portsmouth, Southampton, Salisbury and Bournemouth.

102

THE CLOSE

Long Street, Tetbury, Gloucestershire GL8 8AQ
Tel: 0666 52272

Nearest town Tetbury.
Directions The Close is situated in the town of
Tetbury, on the A433 between Cirencester and
Bath. If travelling on the M4, leave at junction 17
and follow Cirencester signs.
A member of the **Romantik Hotels** group.
Awards AA and RAC *** graded; British Tourist
Authority commended; English Tourist Board four
Crowns.
Open throughout the year.
Special breaks Champagne Close weekend
breaks (half-board with champagne, chocolates
and flowers) for £120 per person; mini-breaks and
reduced mid-week rates available.
*The hotel is unsuitable for disabled visitors; children
under ten are not encouraged and dogs are not allowed.*
Price for dinner, with wine, bed and breakfast for
two – £100–£150.
Credit cards All major cards accepted.
Overall mark out of ten 7

The Close was built in 1596 and began life as the home of a
wealthy wool merchant. It was extended considerably in 1756,

and at that time the open courtyard was covered with an attractive Georgian domed ceiling which you can still see today. The house remained a private residence until 1960 when it was converted into a modest town hotel. It changed hands again in November 1986 and, under the shrewd general managership of David Broadhead, looks set to become one of the most up-market hotels in this part of southern England within a couple of years.

The hotel has retained its warm interior, although the emphasis is much more on comfort than any attempt to recreate a specific period atmosphere. One of the most attractive public rooms is the Garden Room, which looks directly on to the garden and can accommodate up to 25 guests. As you might expect, this room is particularly popular for informal private functions or business meetings requiring that little bit extra comfort and privacy.

The hotal has two dining-rooms, both originally designed by Robert Adam, although only one retains the original Adam fireplace. Both overlook the walled garden and lily pond. The style of cooking is modern English, and a varied four-course table d'hôte menu, plus coffee, is offered each evening for around £20 per person. The restaurant is popular with non-residents and advance booking by at least two weeks is strongly recommended.

Starters include a number of original dishes, such as Kebab of Monkfish, Turbot and Mussels on a Sauce of Red Peppers, and a Cold Sausage of Duck Livers dressed with Pink Peppercorns. A soup (which might be something like Cream of Vegetable with Coriander) or light appetizers, such as a Vegetable Mousse with a small Salad, precedes the main dish.

Main course specialities concentrate on a number of traditional favourites, such as lightly Poached Scotch Salmon in a Watercress Sauce, and circlets of Scotch Fillet with Spring Onions on a Tarragon Sauce. One of several more interesting favourites is Poached Breast of Chicken, filled with Wild Rice and dressed with a rich Honey Sauce; alternatively, you may prefer Roast Loin of Veal with the taste of a Lime Sauce permeating throughout – and the end result served with shelled Pistachio Nuts.

By the time of publication, the hotel will have twenty bedrooms, each with *en suite* bathrooms, tea- and coffee-making facilities, direct-dial telephone, trouser press and colour television. One or two still have authentic ceiling beams and three have four-posters available for those special romantic breaks. The quality of the views vary from the superb to the mediocre, and the best rooms overlook the quiet cloistered garden.

The hotel has no leisure facilities available at the moment, other than a croquet lawn which is in use during the summer months. Most popular indoor and outdoor sports are available locally, including fishing, golf, tennis and horse riding, and for the sightseer the area is rich in historical sites. Nearby attractions include the historic city of Bath, with its magnificent blend of Regency elegance and Roman antiquities, and the small town of Winchcombe that was once the capital of Anglo-Saxon Mercia. Chedworth still has the remains of a Roman villa, reckoned to be the best in Britain, and south Wales is only a short drive away.

103

COMBE HOUSE

Gittisham, near Honiton, Devon EX14 0AD
Tel: 0404 2756

Nearest town Honiton.
Directions Combe House is situated off the A30
about a mile south-west of Honiton. The hotel
drive is in the village of Gittisham.
A founder member of the **Pride of Britain**
consortium.
Awards AA ** (red) and rosette for food; British
Tourist Authority commended; Egon Ronay and
Michelin recommended.
Open from the last Friday in February until
around the middle of January.
Winter breaks are available from 1st November
until the end of March.
*The hotel is not suitable for the disabled; children and
dogs are welcome.*
Price for dinner, with wine, bed and breakfast for
two – £100–£150.
Credit cards Access, Visa, Amex and Diners Club.
Overall mark out of ten 8.5

Dating back to Elizabethan times, Combe House is an attractive
old mansion house in the heart of rural Devon. The Putt

family held the estate for 232 years, doing much to create the structure of the house and the splendid gardens as they now appear. One family member, Nicholas Putt, was an active Royalist during the period of the English Revolution, and died on his way to London after being carried off by Cromwell's soldiers.

Although the house was ransacked and partly destroyed by fire during Cromwell's time, it has gradually been rebuilt to its former glory and, since 1970, it has been owned and run by John and Thérèse Boswell. Many of the antique furnishings and rare prints which adorn the interior of the house came from Auchinleck House in Ayrshire, the ancestral home of biographer James Boswell. These have undoubtedly added to the period charm of the hotel, and there are few more attractive main halls in any Country House in southern England than that which awaits you at Combe. With its dark wood fireplace, ornate plaster ceiling and family oil portraits adorning the walls all around, you can almost imagine one of the house's fiery old Royalist ancestors sweeping through to join you. All the public rooms have ornate ceilings, but the main lounge area is known as the Panelled Drawing Room and, as its name implies, has plush wood panelling all round. The walls of this charming room are hung with portraits of eighteenth-century ancestors, and the sun streams through the large windows from early morning. The room is finished off by a magnificent rococo marbled fireplace, with a roaring fire when the winter weather so demands.

There are two dining-rooms, each with fine carved pine doorcases; one has been completely muralled by Thérèse Boswell; the other has a magnificent Chippendale-carved overmantel and ceiling ornamentation decorated with the fable of the fox and the crow. Both dining-rooms can seat approximately 25 to 30 guests, depending on the seating plan, and reservations, although recommended at least a couple of days in advance, are not always necessary for non-residents.

Thérèse Boswell supervises the kitchen where Chef de Cuisine Susan Richardson prepares a detailed and varied à la carte menu each evening which has a strong emphasis on the best of British traditional Country House-style cooking. Openers range from an unusual 'Covent Garden' Terrine composed of layers of tiny vegetables and a Chicken Mousse, sliced cold and served on a Tomato Vinaigrette, to a light dish of pieces of Fresh Salmon Marinated in a variety of Herbs and Cream before being served in a round and presented with a finely sliced Cucumber Salad.

For those having difficulty choosing from the eight or nine fish and meat dishes offered as main courses, one particular speciality usually available, and which is worth considering, is made up from a Medallion of Scottish Fillet Steak, a Medallion of Veal and a Chicken Breast. The whole dish is served with a colourful trio of red, yellow and green pepper sauces. Other favourites include a Brace of Quail, cooked in an exquisite Sauce of Red Wine and Cognac, and served with Mushrooms and Button Onions.

Combe House has twelve bedrooms, including one large suite, and all have private bathrooms. All rooms are a good size, with very distinctive individual decor and good views across the estate. Each one is named after a Combe House ancestor (although the favourite is probably the stately Tommy Wax Room) and has a colour television set, direct-dial telephone and a host of antique furnishings which have been personally collected by proprietors John and Thérèse Boswell over the last couple of decades. All bedrooms have one or two little extras, such as a heated towel rail in the bathroom and a vase of cut flowers to bring that extra freshness to your bedroom.

The main leisure facility offered at Combe House is a delightful one-and-a-half-mile stretch of the River Otter, which is ideal for relaxing walks or indulging in a sport of brown or rainbow trout fishing. There is an eighteen-hole golf course at nearby Honiton (three miles away) and riding can be arranged at a local riding school. Nearby attractions include Dartmoor, Exmoor, Dartmouth, the city of Exeter with its cathedral and famous maritime museum, Bicton Park and Gardens, Lyme Regis and the other coastal towns of Sidmouth, Budleigh Salterton, Exmouth.

104

FIFEHEAD MANOR

Middle Wallop, Stockbridge, Hampshire SO20 8EG
Tel: 0264 781565

Nearest town Andover.
Directions Take the A303 to Andover and the
hotel is seven miles from here. From the town,
you should follow the A343 and the hotel is just
after the village of Middle Wallop.
Awards AA ** and RAC *** graded; British
Tourist Authority commended; Egon Ronay
recommended.
Open throughout the year, apart from two weeks
over Christmas and the New Year.
Weekend breaks available from November until
around Easter.
*The hotel is suitable for the disabled; children and dogs
are allowed.*
Price for dinner, with wine, bed and breakfast for
two – £100–£150.
Credit cards Access, Visa, Amex and Diners Club.
Overall mark out of ten 7

The origins of Fifehead Manor date back as far as the eleventh
century, making it one of the oldest buildings in this part of

Hampshire, although only the foundations remain of the original Norman house. One of the earliest residents is reputed to have been the Saxon Earl Godwin, whose beautiful wife, Lady Godiva, has now passed into legend because of her famous naked ride through Coventry on horseback.

For a while the house served as a nunnery, and America's first president, George Washington, is known to have been a direct descendant of a fifteenth-century 'Lord of the Manor of Wallop Fifehead', as the holder of the estate was then known. During the era of Catholic persecution in the early years of the reign of Queen Elizabeth I, many a fleeing priest is believed to have hidden on a narrow ledge inside the huge chimney stack.

By 1982 only the manor house itself, and just over three acres of garden and woodland, remained from the original eleventh-century estate of 600 acres, although the current owner still retains the right to be called Lord of the Manor. Despite its long history, much of the interior of the hotel is surprisingly modern. The main lounge area is comfortably furnished, and the overall impression of the public areas is relaxing.

The most interesting room in the hotel is the main dining-room. Judging by its size and scale in proportion to the rest of the original manor, this was almost certainly the main hall in medieval times. You can still see the remains of the minstrels' gallery dating back to the Middle Ages and, in the evening when this charming room is lit by candlelight, it is the perfect setting for a romantic dinner with old glass and silverware on display around you.

Curiously, the size of print on the à la carte menu is the largest of any hotel I've ever visited, and, although many of the dishes have been cooked in a continental style, the menu has deliberately not been translated into French so that the management no longer needs to worry about 'puzzled looks appearing on our customers' faces'. A sensible enough policy as the detailed selection includes a good range of traditional and more original dishes.

A table d'hôte menu is available as well as the à la carte,

and with refreshing honesty the management also admits the table d'hôte contains either local ingredients that have been spotted that day, or is being used to 'push a slow-moving item on the "carte"'. Starters include freshly Boiled Devon Crab in a Tomato Mayonnaise, dressed with Pink Grapefruit and Avocado, or an unusual mixture of Ham, Parsley and Garlic layered in a terrine, set in the meat jelly on a pool of Mustard Sauce.

Main dishes are rather more traditional, ranging from Steamed Fillet of Brill to a Baked Chicken Breast flavoured with Wild Mushrooms, Meat Glaze, Pears and Cream. Two more original options are a speciality Hampshire Game Pie made from marinated local game and beef, cooked in Port, Red Wine and Juniper Berries, and Roast Duck Breast in a rich Orange, Soy and Ginger Sauce. All main courses are served with vegetables or side salad. The food, it must be said, is of the highest quality and beautifully presented.

There are a total of fifteen bedrooms in an assortment of sizes. All are simply furnished: those in the older part of the house are smaller and have a rather more traditional decor, whereas those in the younger extension are much more modern. All have private bathrooms, although those adjoining the smallest bedrooms are verging on the cramped. Colour television and direct-dial telephones come as standard in all rooms.

The manor's only leisure facility is the beautiful three-and-a-half acre garden, complete with a croquet lawn during the summer months. Fishing on the Rivers Test and Itchen and horse riding can be easily arranged through local instructors. For antique collectors, the nearby village of Stockbridge has at least a dozen antique shops with goods to suit most pockets and tastes. Other attractions within a short driving distance are Marwell Zoo, Longleat House and Safari Park, Beaulieu Palace, the cathedrals of Winchester and Salisbury, and the famous standing stones at Stonehenge, about fifteen minutes away by car.

105

FOX'S EARTH

Lewtrenchard Manor, Lewdown, Okehampton,
Devon EX20 4PN
Tel: 056 683 256

Nearest town Tavistock.
Directions Follow the A30 west from Exeter as far as Lewdown village. Head south for one mile towards Tavistock, on the Lewtrenchard and Chillton road, and you will see the hotel signposted just before the church on the left.
A member of the **Pride of Britain** consortium.
Awards AA rosette; recommended by Michelin and Egon Ronay guides.
Open mid-February until just after New Year.
Special breaks Holiday Weekend and mid-week winter breaks are available.
The hotel is not suitable for the disabled; children under twelve, and dogs, are not allowed.
Price for dinner, with wine, bed and breakfast for two – £100–£150.
Credit cards Access, Visa and Amex.
Overall mark out of ten 8.5

Set in a little valley just off the north-west corner of Dartmoor, Fox's Earth, Lewtrenchard Manor, is a secluded Country

House Hotel which dates back to 1620. It was home for many years to the Baring-Gould family, and the most famous former occupant is probably the Reverend Sabine Baring-Gould who is best remembered for writing one of the greatest hymns of all time, 'Onward Christian Soldiers'. Two friendly family ghosts are reported to make the occasional check on their former home, but no complaints have been reported so far!

All of the public rooms and bedrooms have a number of pieces of antique furniture, and rich oil portraits adorn the walls. These are family pieces, built up over the last couple of centuries by the Baring-Gould family and acquired by present owners Mary Ellen Keys and Greg Shriver when they took over the hotel in 1986. The main lounge is a sumptuous old room, with one of the finest dark wood carved fireplaces in southern England, delicate stained glass windows and an ornate plaster ceiling.

The house is better known locally as Lewtrenchard Manor, but Fox's Earth was added with the interesting little runner which appears along the foot of the brochure, summing up the luxury facilities offered by the hotel, as 'where the smart fox goes when the hounds are getting too close'.

Dark wood panelling is a feature throughout the hotel, and nowhere is this more striking than in the main dining-room. The hotel has two dining-rooms, both relatively small with a total seating capacity of 35, and one enjoys particularly good views across the courtyard. Head chef David Shepherd trained at the Inn on the Park hotel in London and the Greenways, Cheltenham, and offers a table d'hôte Menu Gastronomique or Menu Gourmand each evening. Home-grown herbs, fresh Devon cream and the best local produce will feature prominently in the preparation of your meal.

The Menu Gastronomique offers a limited element of choice among the four courses, but the five-course Menu Gourmand is restricted to a rich pre-set range of specialities, opening with something like a Puff Pastry filled with Fresh Scallops, Chicken Livers, Mussels and Courgettes in a Herb and Garlic Dressing, followed by a Tresse of Fresh Fish, then a Fruit Sorbet before your main dish, which could be anything from Fillet of Veal in a Chablis Sauce, to Wild Salmon.

Fox's Earth has a total of nine bedrooms, with another three suites being planned in space which is available across the leafy courtyard. Each room is quite unique, with good views through the old leaded windows. All rooms are furnished traditionally with a host of antiques, and little extras such as a Victorian wash basin and jug as a charming reminder of the days before *en suite* bathrooms were standard. Most of the bedrooms have polished wood panelling covering at least part of the walls in keeping with the style throughout the rest of the hotel. In addition, all rooms have colour television and direct-dial telephone.

The hotel has a two-acre stocked trout lake within its grounds, and four miles of private fishing rights on the nearby River Lew, so this is a haven for keen fresh-water fishers. The other main leisure pursuit on offer is the opportunity to rough shoot on the thousand-acre estate, although nearby driven shoots are occasionally organized. Horse riding can also be arranged if you wish. Golf can be enjoyed at the famous St Mellion golf course which top professional Jack Nicklaus designed. Nearby attractions include the many historical places of interest throughout Devon and the beautiful Cornwall coast, plus the Dartmoor National Park about fifteen minutes' drive away, Lydford Gorge, and the city of Plymouth.

106

GIDLEIGH PARK

Chagford, Devon TQ13 8HH
Tel: 06473 2367/9

Nearest town Chagford.

Directions Find the centre of Chagford, facing Webbers store with Lloyds Bank on your right, turn right into Mill Street. After about 150 yards, fork right and go downhill to factory crossroad. Go straight across into Holy Street and follow the lane for 1.5 miles to the end.

A member of the **Relais et Châteaux** consortium.

Awards AA *** (red) and rosette; British Tourist Authority commended; Michelin three (red) turrets and rosette for restaurant; Egon Ronay 81% and star for restaurant; Egon Ronay Wine Cellar of the Year Award 1984; Consumers' Association Country House Hotel of the Year Award 1987.

Open throughout the year.

Special breaks Winter rates and Walking Weeks available.

The hotel is not suitable for the disabled; children 'are treated as adults, charged as adults and expected to behave as adults'; dogs are allowed in bedrooms.

Price for dinner, with wine, bed and breakfast for two – over £150 (up to £250 more likely).

Credit cards (In order of preference) Access,
Visa, Diners Club and Amex.
Overall mark out of ten 9

Gidleigh Park is one of the half-dozen most expensive Country House Hotels in Britain and sits in an exceptionally beautiful part of the Devon countryside. It is located near the hamlet of Gidleigh, so named after King Harold's mother Gydda who settled here in the eleventh century. The foundations of her Saxon longhouse can still be seen near the thirteenth-century church. Gidleigh Park is considerably younger, having been built originally as a country retreat by the Australian shipping magnate C. H. C. MacIlwraith, although it is known that a manor house has stood on this site since the sixteenth century.

American proprietors Kay and Paul Henderson have run Gidleigh Park since 1978 with the avowed aim that it should function along the lines of a private home rather than a luxury hotel. The hotel is extremely comfortable and, although inside and out the old mansion is a delight, it could hardly be described as ostentatious. The staff are predominantly young, and their enthusiastic personal service is one of the many attractions of Gidleigh Park.

Apart from the main entrance hall and the bar loggia, the main public room is the large sitting-room where a welcoming log fire generally burns on all but the mildest of summer evenings. It is a supreme luxury to throw off your walking boots at the main door and relax in here for a while after an afternoon's stroll across the moor, knowing that the most arduous task which still awaits you is a long bath before dressing for dinner.

Paul Henderson has had a secret desire to offer the best English breakfast of any Country House Hotel in Britain and, as one sharp *Good Food Guide* critic observed, the breakfast menu is already considerably longer than that offered by many small restaurants in the evening! A hearty English breakfast and the personal attention of the American pro-prietors are two of the key reasons why almost half the total number of visitors to Gidleigh Park come from the United States.

Probably the principle attraction of Gidleigh Park, though, apart from the outstanding beauty of its situation, is the extremely high standard of cuisine offered by chef Shaun Hill. Each evening a set-dinner of two cooked courses, followed by cheese, dessert and coffee, is offered for around £30 per person (including VAT). There is a clear preference for luxury ingredients, and each main dish is accompanied by an array of four or five lightly cooked vegetables whose presentation is a work of art. First courses are exquisite, and range from a Terrine of Duck Foie Gras, with Brioche Toast, to Calf's Brain on Brown Butter. One and a half ounces of Beluga Caviar, with a Potato Galette and Sour Cream, are also available for a supplementary charge. Fish and meat dishes include roasted Challans Duck Breast with Thyme and Garlic Sauce, Steamed Turbot with a Tamarind and Lemon Grass Sauce, and Calf's Fillet, Kidney and Sweetbread with Meaux Mustard and Shallot Sauces.

Whatever your choice, Gidleigh Park has easily one of the best wine lists of any Country House Hotel in England with over 400 bottles available, plus a 'bin end' list of 250 wines which you are advised to order by 5 p.m. because of the time it takes to search out a particular bottle from the cellars! The range of French wines is particularly strong (notably some of the better Alsace wines from the last couple of decades) and, understandably, there is a good choice of American wines as well.

Gidleigh Park has a total of fourteen bedrooms which, for a hotel of this calibre, vary quite considerably in size and price. The best rooms are the ten which have expansive views over the Teign Valley; the other four face the forest behind the house, but, having said this, all rooms are beautifully decorated, have *en suite* bathrooms, colour television and direct-dial telephones.

The most obvious nearby attraction is Dartmoor, the largest National Park in the south of England, which lies all around the hotel. Gidleigh Park has 40 acres of its own on the edge of Dartmoor and facilities on the estate, and the National Park, for walking and horse riding are superb. Dartmoor also happens to be one of the richest areas in Britain for viewing prehistoric settlements and stone circles. The only other leisure facility of note offered by the hotel is an all-weather tennis court, although there are two croquet lawns, and guests have been known to enjoy a swim in the north Teign River which runs through the grounds and is said to be one of the best-known cures for a hangover!

107

GLENCOT HOUSE

Glencot Lane, Wookey Hole, near Wells, Somerset BA5 1BH
Tel: 0749 77160

Nearest town Wells.
Directions From Wells follow signs for Wookey
Hole. On approaching the village look for a small
sign on your left saying Glencot House first left.
Follow this lane towards the hotel.
Open throughout the year.
Special breaks for two nights inclusive half-board
accommodation are available all year.
The hotel is not really suitable for the disabled; children
and dogs are welcome.
Price for dinner, with wine, bed and breakfast for
two – under £100.
Credit cards Access and Visa.
Overall mark out of ten 7

Glencot Manor is a charming late Victorian house which was
built to very high specifications by the famous artist and
architect Ernest George. The manor was commissioned by the
Hodgkinson family who were the nineteenth-century owners
of the famous Wookey Hole caves and nearby paper mill. The
style of the house is mock-Jacobean, and today the hotel
stands amid eighteen acres of private garden and woodland
close to the Wookey Hole caves.

This is not a large hotel and, having only been open since

the end of 1985, has yet to attract much recognition from the guides of the leading tourist, consumer and motoring organizations. Its reputation is slowly building up on the basis of friendly, informal service, enhanced by the fact that a lot of the original Victorian character of the house has survived. The public rooms and the bedrooms are well proportioned and comfortably furnished, with many featuring oak and walnut wall panelling.

The main public room is the elegant dining-room, whose half oak-panelled Victorian decor makes a charming backdrop for residents to enjoy their evening meal. Seating capacity is only 25 so, regretfully, non-residents are not accommodated. All food is home-cooked using fresh local produce. The style of cooking is traditional British and is overseen by proprietor Mrs Jenny Attia. It is hoped that a full-time chef will be employed in the not too distant future.

A selection of at least five or six dishes is available for both the starter and the main course. Typical starters include Egg Mayonnaise, Rollmop, Garlic Prawns and a home-made Soup. Main dishes always include at least a couple of fish options, perhaps Grilled Trout or Fried Dabs, but you might prefer instead Lamb Chops in Red Wine, Sirloin Steak (sautéed or grilled as you prefer) in a Rich Red Wine Sauce, or Chicken Escalope. All main dishes are served with a selection of local vegetables and either a jacket potato or generous side salad.

Sweets include an enormous helping of Sherry Trifle, home-made Fruit Pie, or a Meringue Glacé Flan. Cheese and biscuits are available as an alternative. The restaurant is licensed, but the range of wines is unremarkable, so residents are well advised to look no further than the excellent house white or red.

The hotel has fourteen bedrooms, all decorated in a style of informal country elegance: comfortable chairs and pleasing chintzes. Many rooms have private bathroom facilities, colour television, telephone and tea- and coffee-making facilities. All are accessible by a number of stairs, but there is one large bedroom with two double beds which is particularly popular with elderly visitors, or disabled persons with limited mobility away from a wheelchair. For that special romantic break, there is also a four-poster master suite available.

Glencot House has a number of leisure facilities available for residents. These include a jet stream pool, sauna, sun bed, snooker room, basic exercise equipment, and a table tennis room. A hairdresser and beautician work in the hotel five days a week. Fishing can be enjoyed on the private stretch of River Axe which runs through the hotel's estate, and the hotel is close to three major golf courses.

The estate surrounding the hotel is quite idyllic, not only because of the river running through it, but also because of features such as the waterfall and private footbridge which residents can appreciate during a relaxing pre-dinner or Sunday afternoon stroll. Other nearby attractions include Wells Cathedral, the Roman town of Bath, Glastonbury Abbey (where legend says King Arthur was once buried), the world-famous caves at Cheddar Gorge, and the popular coastal resort of Weston-super-Mare.

108

HATTON COURT

Upton Hill, Upton St Leonards, Gloucester GL4 8DE
Tel: 0452 617412

Nearest town Gloucester.
Directions The hotel is located three miles east of
Gloucester. From there, you should aim for the
B4073 signposted to Upton St Leonards and the
hotel is two miles along on the right.
Awards AA *** graded; Egon Ronay
recommended (75%).
Open throughout the year.
Special **mid-week** and **weekend breaks** are
available all year.
The hotel is unsuitable for the disabled; children are
welcome but dogs are not allowed.
Price for dinner, with wine, bed and breakfast for
two – £100–£150.
Credit cards Access, Visa, Amex and Diners
Club.
Overall mark out of ten 8

If there were an award for the 'newest' Country House Hotel
in Britain, it would be a reasonably safe bet that Hatton Court

would take it. Although the mansion house was originally built in the seventeenth century, details about the history of the building are completely unknown, even among local historians. The magnificent ivy-clad façade is an excellent example of the architecture of the period, but practically nothing inside, in terms of either decor or furnishings, survives from the three hundred years or so that Hatton Court was a private residence. This is a weak criticism, however, as you will soon discover once you have had the opportunity to experience the effects of a £2 million refurbishment programme that was completed in 1987. The public areas all have a distinctly 'modern' feel to them, but, nevertheless, are furnished extremely comfortably and to the very highest standards. A blazing log fire, with its antique polished surround, is the welcoming focal point of the spacious main lounge.

The room which saw most up-grading during the refurbishment programme was the old dining-room. The end result was Carrington's, a large, cheerful restaurant which can seat up to 84 in elegant style. Soft pinks and greens blend well with large crystal chandeliers, sweeping drapes and the combination of Wedgwood china and glassware which adorns the tables. It would be hard to imagine a more impressive setting in this part of England for dinner than Carrington's and, should you ever tire of the room's modern decor, then you can enjoy the wide panoramic views across the picturesque Severn Valley and distant Malvern Hills.

The style of cooking is modern French, although traditional English specialities have not been forgotten. There is also an extensive wine list available to complement your meal with some 230 bins on offer. An interesting feature of Carrington's restaurant is the wine-shop built into one corner of the dining-room. In the style of a Victorian street-shop, this delightful little 'shop' offers guests an all too rare opportunity to stock up on some really first-class wines which they may have enjoyed at their table over dinner.

All 53 bedrooms were completely refurbished in 1987 and, although the hotel states that they have been designed to combine the best available modern facilities with period charm, it would be fairer to indicate that the bedrooms are essentially luxurious modern rooms. Having said that, the standard of furnishings is exceptionally high, and no less than fifteen bedrooms include Jacuzzis as standard. Every room has a spacious private bathroom, remote control colour television (with free in-house video that changes daily), trouser press, direct-dial telephone and a host of other little extras. It is these little extras which really make the bedrooms at Hatton Court special, as the addition of a few magazines, complimentary sweets, cotton wool, good quality toiletries, a large bathrobe and so on, makes such a difference to a guest's impression of a hotel – yet costs so relatively little.

Most sport and leisure facilities are available within a short drive of the hotel, and at present there is an outdoor heated swimming pool. It is hoped by the time of publication that an indoor leisure centre will be in operation. This will feature a heated swimming pool, mini-gymnasium, Jacuzzi, sauna and solarium. There are a great many places to visit within a short drive of the hotel, including the old towns of Cheltenham and Bath, the castles of Sudeley and Berkeley, Birdland at Bourton-on-the-Water, Prinknash Abbey, Gloucester with its cathedral and new dockland development, and the natural beauty of the Wye Valley and Forest of Dean.

109

HOMEWOOD PARK

Hinton Charterhouse, Bath, Avon BA3 6BB
Tel: 022 122 3731

Nearest town Bath.
Directions From Bath, take the A36 Warminster/
Salisbury road and continue for just over five
miles. Turn left towards the two villages of
Sharpstone and Freshford, and you will see the
hotel at the end of the first turning on the left.
A member of the **Prestige Hotels** consortium.
Awards Egon Ronay Hotel of the Year 1987; AA
*** (red) graded and rosette; British Tourist
Authority commended; Michelin three (red)
turrets and red 'M'; 1986 *Good Hotel Guide* César
Award for 'classic country excellence'.
Open from 7th January until 23rd December.
Mid-week winter breaks are available from
November until the end of March.
The hotel is suitable for disabled visitors; children are
welcome but dogs are not allowed.
Price for dinner, with wine, bed and breakfast for
two – £100–£150.
Credit cards All major cards accepted.
Overall mark out of ten 9

Under six miles from the centre of Bath, Homewood Park has
built up its reputation by offering a much more informal type

of luxury accommodation than comparable hotels in the town of Bath proper. The cellars are the oldest part of the house, dating back several centuries, although the hotel as it now stands was built in stages between the mid-eighteenth and mid-nineteenth centuries. Essentially, though, Homewood Park is an appealing Victorian-style house which remained a private residence until present proprietors Stephen and Penny Ross opened it as a hotel at the end of 1980.

The front porch is one of the most interesting architectural points of the house as it is certainly older than the rest of the building. A ruined abbey is near the hotel and it is known that, for many years, Homewood Park was the abbot's house. It is not inconceivable that the porch was transferred from the crumbling abbey to the house by an enthusiastic Victorian owner.

The main staircase rises from the public entrance hall and, apart from the comfortable bar, the main public area is the lounge with its large fireplace, soft armchairs and good views across the rambling gardens – look out for the unique bronzes created by a local artist. There are a number of smaller private rooms available for business meetings, including two more secluded dining-rooms which are normally reserved for private functions, in addition to the main dining-room.

As the rest of the hotel, the dining-room is decorated in bright colours and has cut flowers everywhere, adding a special freshness to the whole room. Staff are predominantly young and enthusiastic to serve – although never inexperienced. The dining-room overlooks the gardens and serves a two- or three-course table d'hôte menu each evening. Starters include Salmon and Scallops wrapped in pastry and bathed in a Sauce of Sherry and Tarragon, and a unique speciality of chef Stephen Ross, Turbot marinated with Limes and served with a Salad of Fennel and Orange. Main dishes display the chef/proprietor's desire to find distinctive and unusual flavours by using fresh local ingredients to create delicate and interesting meals. Choices vary seasonally, but there is always fresh fish, according to the market, and you are likely to find Duckling Roasted in a Sauce of Lentils and Smoked Bacon;

Baby Guineafowl with Sauces of Shallot and Sherry Vinegar and Garlic Cream; and Stuffed Loin of Veal in pastry with a Sauce of French Mushrooms, Cream and Wine.

There are fifteen bedrooms at Homewood Park, all doubles and all individually styled and furnished. Each one is finished in a blend of soft colours – perhaps a pale yellow and pink with an apple-green carpet, or a soft honeysuckle-patterned wallpaper with a Victorian dressing table – and there are at least a couple of pieces of antique furniture in each room. Most of the beds are a luxurious six feet wide and all the bedrooms have spacious private bathrooms decorated with oak panelling (right down to the loo seats). In each bathroom you are likely to find at least one flourishing plant, and plenty of space to spread out your toiletries. All rooms have colour television, direct-dial telephone and radio.

The hotel offers facilities for tennis and croquet. Horse riding, golf, fishing and any number of beautiful walks in the surrounding Limpley Stoke Valley are available nearby. Tourist attractions within an easy drive include the towns of Bath, Avebury, Marlborough and Salisbury, the famous standing stones at Stonehenge, Ston Easton Park, Hunstrete House at Hunstrete, the Clifton suspension bridge, and the SS *Great Britain* in Bristol.

110

HUNSTRETE HOUSE

Hunstrete, Chelwood, near Bristol, Avon BS18 4NS
Tel: 07618 578

Nearest town Bath.
Directions From Bristol, follow the A37,
branching on to the A368 towards Chelwood
when you see the signs. Aim for Hunstrete village
and you will soon see the hotel sign.
A member of the **Relais et Châteaux** consortium.
Awards AA *** (red) graded.
Open throughout the year.
Winter breaks are available from November until
the end of March.
*The hotel is suitable for the disabled; children under
nine and dogs are not allowed.*
Price for dinner, with wine, bed and breakfast for
two – over £150.
Credit cards All major cards accepted (but *not* for
winter breaks).
Overall mark out of ten 9

Set against the backdrop of the Mendip Hills, Hunstrete estate
has a history that goes back several generations before the

Norman Conquest of England in 1066. For centuries a monastery stood on the estate offering hospitality and shelter to weary pilgrims making their way to or from the abbey at Glastonbury. The abbey was completed in 1184 and flourished in the couple of hundred years which followed.

Hunstrete House as it now stands dates from no earlier than the eighteenth century, and although much of its honey-coloured stonework has weathered to a stately grey, it has lost little of its Georgian charm. The tradition of hospitality was resurrected in 1978 when the present owners, Thea and John Dupays, carried out a considerable programme of refurbishment and renovation in order to convert the house into a Country House Hotel.

Hunstrete's public rooms reflect the owners' keen interest in collecting antiques. Every room has an assortment of interesting oil paintings, and both the library and the drawing-room have shelves laden with early pottery and fine porcelain. The library is a quiet, sunny room with a small but beautifully ornate white fireplace that contrasts well with the decorative frieze around the edges of the ceiling. The main bookcase is an interesting Georgian style, with a good selection of books that residents can enjoy during their stay.

The main public room is the Terrace dining-room. Its huge arched windows look out on to an Italianate, flower-filled courtyard: the ornate fountain one would associate more commonly with a bustling Italian square than an English Country House. The three-course table d'hôte menu changes every five or six weeks within each season. The proprietor takes pride in the extensive wine list which is by no means one of the longest in the country, but is certainly one of the most broad-based.

Head chef Robert Elsmore embraces the best modern British techniques, and a choice of about four hot or four cold hors d'oeuvres is available to start your meal each evening. Favourites include Quenelle of Chicken Mousseline, and a Salad of Cornish Mussels, served with a chilled Vermouth Sauce. Main dishes range from Medallions of Pork, panfried and served on a bed of Spinach Leaves and coated with an interesting Sauce made from Creamed Stilton. Other options usually feature Saddle of (Scottish) Venison cooked pink and coated with a Juniper and Gin Sauce, garnished with fresh Cranberries, and Red Mullet served on a Coulis of Vegetables moistened with Butter and Rosemary.

The hotel has 21 bedrooms, all individually decorated in a variety of colours. Each room is named after a wild bird which is native to the British Isles and includes a framed print of the bird on the wall. Seven of the rooms are in a converted stable block, and they do vary quite a bit in size: from the spacious Dove Room with its eighteenth-century four-poster, right down to three small singles. For extra seclusion, the hotel offers the quaint Swallow Cottage, which comprises a double bedroom, bathroom and sitting-room – perfect for a honeymoon. All rooms have private bathrooms, colour television, telephone and radio.

Hunstrete House has its own heated outdoor swimming pool, together with an all-weather tennis court and a croquet lawn during the milder summer months. Horse riding is available through riding stables in Hunstrete village; there is excellent trout fishing nearby, and there are a number of golf courses. For something completely different, hot-air ballooning can be arranged with prior notice from the hotel grounds.

Nearby attractions for the sightseer include the fine Roman remains and more recent Georgian architecture of Bath, Wells Cathedral, Stourhead Gardens, Longleat House and Safari Park, Berkeley and Sudeley Castles, Dryham Park, Lacock Abbey, Sir Peter Scott's Wildfowl Trust at Slimbridge, Cheddar Gorge, and the ancient abbey of Glastonbury where King Arthur is said to have been buried.

111

LAINSTON HOUSE

Sparsholt, Winchester, Hampshire SO21 2LT
Tel: 0962 63588

Nearest town Winchester.
Directions Travel south on the M3 following the signs for Winchester city. Leave the motorway at signs for Winchester city centre and follow the signs for Stockbridge A272. Turn left after two-thirds of a mile and you will see the hotel on your right.
A member of the **Prestige Hotels** consortium.
Awards AA *** graded and rosette for food; RAC *** graded; British Tourist Authority commended; Egon Ronay and Michelin recommended.
Open throughout the year.
Weekend breaks are available.
The hotel is ideally situated for the disabled with one or two specially adapted rooms and toilet facilities within easy access; children are welcome, as are dogs, but not in the public areas.
Price for dinner, with wine, bed and breakfast for two – over £150.
Credit cards Amex, Access, Diners, Visa.
Overall mark out of ten 8

Two miles north-west of the old cathedral city of Winchester, Lainston House stands in 63 acres of superb downland Hampshire countryside. The first recorded owner of Lainston estate is Simon de Winton, who died in 1316, although the present house dates from the William and Mary period at the end of the seventeenth century. For a single decade in the nineteenth century, the house was home to nearly a hundred lunatics, but thankfully this darker side to the history of Lainston House came to an end in 1853.

Probably the most colourful person associated with the House was Elizabeth Chudleigh, a flighty young girl of sixteen who first came to stay when the house was owned by John Merrill, a prominent local Whig (Liberal) politician. Elizabeth became maid of honour to the Princess of Wales and met, fell in love with and married the grandson of the Earl of Bristol in 1774. A child was born but died soon after, and before very much longer Elizabeth became the mistress of the Duke of Kingston, whom she bigamously married. After her trial for the crime of bigamy, she left Europe and set up a brandy factory in Imperial Russia where, it is said, she was kindly received by the mighty Empress Catherine the Great.

A large portrait of the wicked, but ultimately shrewd, Lady Elizabeth still hangs in the main entrance hall to the hotel. The public rooms are elegantly furnished, but none more so than the Cedar Room. This finely panelled bar doubles as a small library filled with leather-bound books, and a plaque on the wall notes the fact that an enormous cedar tree, which fell to the ground during a storm in January 1930, supplied enough wood to panel the entire room.

The main restaurant is made up of two dining-rooms, the smaller of which used to be the nursery when Lainston House was a private residence. The decor is eau-de-nil, restful on the eyes and complementing the lawns which sweep away from beneath the large windows. Up to 35 can be accommodated on one side and 25 on the other, and as the restaurant is popular with non-residents, advance booking is advised.

The style of food prepared by head chef Frederick Litty is traditional English Country House, using a great deal of local produce, although his German origins help add a noticeable continental touch to many dishes. A delightful candlelit à la carte and table d'hôte meal is available each evening. Starters range from Sautéed Scallops, tossed in a Lemon Dressing and served on a bed of mixed lettuce, to Dublin Bay Prawns on a bed of lettuce with Oyster Mushrooms and a Lemon Dressing.

Main dishes include a delicious Breast of Duck on a light Garlic Sauce, served with Apple and Celeriac Layers and a mixed Salad with a Truffle Dressing, and Fillet of Veal with a Cream and Armagnac Sauce served with Mange Touts, Sauté Potatoes and Wild Mushrooms. One recommended fish speciality, served usually as a main dish, is Roast Turbot on a bed of Wild Rice and presented with a delicate Saffron Sauce. A selection of popular wines is shown on the menu, according to what dishes are on offer.

Lainston House has 32 bedrooms, including a number of suites and the delightful Delft Room. Fourteen rooms are located in Chudleigh Court, a recently completed annexe which reflects the charm and elegance of the bedrooms in the main house. All rooms are individually designed and furnished, although the style of decor is modern throughout. Each one has *en suite* bathroom, colour television, private mini-bar, direct-dial telephone and a wall safe for that extra security.

Among the leisure facilities available for residents to enjoy are two all-weather tennis courts, a croquet lawn, clay pigeon shooting, and the possibilities for endless walks around the 63-acre estate. In addition, golf, fishing on the River Test, horse riding and indoor pursuits including squash, sauna and solarium can be easily arranged through the hotel's reception.

Nearby attractions are detailed in an eight-page booklet given to all guests on arrival and, as you might imagine, there are a large number of places to visit and sights to see in this part of southern England. Among the more famous are Breamore House; Beaulieu (including Lord Montagu's famous motor museum); Wilton House; the public gardens at Exbury and Heale House (note these are only open during the summer); Salisbury and Winchester Cathedrals; Marwell Zoo, and the town of Portsmouth with its superb naval attractions – HMS *Victory*, the *Mary Rose* ship and museum, and the Royal Navy submarine museum.

112

LITTLE THAKEHAM

Merrywood Lane, Storrington, West Sussex RH20 3HE
Tel: 09066 4416/7

Nearest town Storrington.
Directions From Storrington (48 miles from
London) follow the B2139 towards Thakeham.
After just over a mile turn right into Merrywood
Lane and the hotel is 400 yards on left.
A member of the **Pride of Britain** consortium.
Awards British Tourist Authority commended;
Egon Ronay and Michelin recommended.
Open throughout the year (except Christmas
period).
No **special breaks** or winter rates available.
There is one ground-floor bedroom suitable for the
disabled; children are allowed, but no dogs.
Price for dinner, with wine, bed and breakfast for
two – over £150.
Credit cards All major cards accepted.
Overall mark out of ten 7.5

The *Book of Modern Homes* described Little Thakeham thus:
'Amongst the less frequented roadways [and] views of the
countryside, which are unsurpassably charming . . . we may
meet with this charm of the "back-water" country, free from
busy traffic and the mad rush of motor-cars.' That description
was first written in 1909 and it holds true today. Little

Thakeham has a superb setting on the South Downs, with commanding views across six acres of orchard and private gardens, and yet remains within an hour's drive of London.

Little Thakeham is reckoned to be one of the finest examples of a Country House built by the renowned Edwardian architect Sir Edwin Lutyens. It dates from around the turn of the century, and although it is by no means one of the largest Country House Hotels in England, its public rooms have been designed and furnished to give a definite impression of space.

All the bedrooms and public rooms include at least one or two pieces of antique furniture, and the medieval-style Minstrel's Gallery is particularly attractive. One of the most striking features about the symmetrically designed rear of the house is the enormous five-sided bay window which protrudes from the centre of the building. A writing-table sits behind these huge windows offering commanding views across the gardens.

The restaurant seats 30 and is decorated in a charmingly period 'arts and crafts' style. The chairs are contemporary with the house as a whole, having been fashioned by Ambrose Heal in 1901. Guests eat with antique silver cutlery, and pink linen napkins and tablecloths set off the decor of the room nicely. Food is prepared in a blend of traditional English and modern French styles and presented as a five-course à la carte menu.

Starters range from Warm Duck and Citrus Salad, to Mushrooms stuffed with Crabmeat, and include more unusual dishes like Avocado with Stilton and Walnut Dressing, and Potted Chicken Livers with Green Peppercorns. Main courses include Fresh Salmon, grilled and served with Lime Butter, Roast Rack of Southdown Lamb with garden Mint Sauce, and Fillet of Hare with Beetroot and Orange. The wine list is extensive, with the emphasis on French wines and including many rarer French châteaux wines and some fine vintage ports.

Little Thakeham has ten bedrooms, all double- or twin-bedded, and a number have been carefully converted from old attics and nurseries. Each one comes with a private bathroom (all of which are bright and modern in design), remote-control colour television and direct-dial telephone. Rooms are of a good size, and are better described as 'small suites' as they all have a reasonable amount of space to let you stretch out and relax in front of the television, enjoy a drink, or just sit and read if you so choose.

Among the leisure facilities available for guests are a heated outdoor swimming pool, a grass tennis court, and a croquet lawn. In addition, Little Thakeham sits in six acres of magnificent gardens which were created by Gertrude Jekyll, one of the foremost garden planners of the nineteenth century. The hotel is within an hour's drive of the outskirts of London and all that the capital has to offer visitors to southern England. Other nearby attractions include Arundel Castle, ancestral home of the Duke of Norfolk, and the country houses of Petworth, Parham Park and Goodwood. For businessmen or visitors to Britain, Gatwick Airport is just 22 miles away.

113

LYTHE HILL

Petworth Road, Haslemere, Surrey GU27 3BQ
Tel: 0428 51251

Nearest town Haslemere.
Directions From Guildford, follow the A286
towards Haslemere. Head left along the B2131
when you see the road signposted and you will
soon reach the hotel (on your right).
Awards Details of up-to-date awards were not
available at the time of publication due to a
recently completed refurbishment programme.
Open throughout the year.
Weekend breaks are available all year round.
The hotel is not suitable for the disabled; children and
dogs are both welcome.
Price for dinner, with wine, bed and breakfast for
two – £100–£150.
Credit cards Access, Visa, Amex and Diners
Club.
Overall mark out of ten 7.5

Situated in one of the most naturally attractive and unspoilt
parts of southern England, the Lythe Hill hotel sits amid
fourteen acres of beautiful parkland and even has its own
private lake for guests to admire. The oldest part of the hotel
began life as a farmhouse in the late fourteenth century. Early

histories of buildings this age are always sketchy, but the estate was known to be in the possession of one Peter Quenell, a yeoman, in 1511 and it stayed in his family for several generations. Peter's son, Thomas, leased some of the land in 1570 to the first Viscount Montague of Cowdray, and the Imbham Ironworks were subsequently built on that ground. No traces remain of what must have been one of the busiest local industries in the late sixteenth century, other than the hammer-pond close by the hotel. Interestingly, Montague failed to produce his quota of arms for Queen Elizabeth I and was summoned before the Privy Council to explain himself. The Viscount's land soon reverted back to the family when Thomas Quenell's brother, Robert, took over the furnace in 1574.

The public rooms retain much of their Tudor charm. A 'new' wing, today's East Wing, was added in 1580 and its square-and-circle-patterned timbering presents a fascinating contrast to the late fourteenth-century part of the house. Seldom will you have the opportunity to see so finely preserved contrasts in English architectural style. Antique furniture has been used throughout the house, although modern comforts have not been forgotten. The main lounge has an assortment of large armchairs, and is dominated by a big open fire. The owner has a large collection of copper and pewter which is displayed in various public rooms.

Entente Cordiale is the name of Lythe Hill's popular main restaurant, although there is a smaller but more atmospheric restaurant, Auberge de France, which is open from Tuesday until Sunday in the oldest part of the hotel. Advance booking is strongly advised for both restaurants. The oak-panelled Auberge offers classic French cuisine and terrific views overlooking the gardens and lake. The Entente, on the other hand, offers more traditional English dishes, although subtle continental influences can be detected in the choice of herbs and sauces.

Starters in the main restaurant, in which most residents will dine, are on the whole tasty and original and, in one or two cases, unique to Chef de Cuisine Roger Clarke. They include a smooth Pâté of Guineafowl and Cream, blended together with real ale, garnished with Redcurrant Jelly and served with hot toast, and Deep Fried cubes of Limeswold Cheese in a light batter, garnished with fried parsley and a Gooseberry and Lime Sauce.

For your main course, the style of cooking is no less imaginative. Typical specialities range from a Prime Scottish Fillet of Steak panfried with a Purée of Pickled Walnuts, to Poached Rainbow Trout filled with a compote of Prawns and coated with a light Mustard and Dill Sauce. A popular (and very filling) dish for two persons is a whole Honey Roast Duckling served with a delicious Apricot Stuffing.

As a result of the refurbishment and renovating programme which was completed by the start of 1988, Lythe Hill now has 38 comfortable bedrooms. Six rooms are in the oldest part of the hotel, the Auberge de France. The standard of decor and furnishings in all rooms is high, although most are very modern in style with little or no concession to the age of the hotel. One of the older rooms has a magnificent wood-carved four-poster bed which dates from 1614. This is one of the oldest beds in regular use in any hotel in Britain, and the bedroom in which it is located is furnished in first-clast Tudor style, complete with wooden beams and wall-mounted candle-style lights similar to those which adorned the walls in the days before electric lighting. All 38 rooms, regardless of their age or history, have private bathroom facilities, colour television, and direct-dial telephone.

Within the hotel grounds, leisure facilities available for guests include a hard tennis court, a croquet lawn, and a French *boules* pitch. Golf, horse riding and squash can easily be arranged nearby. Local tourist attractions include Clandon Park near Guildford, Hatchlands (an eighteenth-century red-brick house, with sizeable park, that was decorated by Robert Adam in 1759 as his first commission), Petworth House, Parnham House near Pulborough, and the remains of a Norman fortress at Bramber, near Steyning in Sussex.

114

MAIDEN NEWTON HOUSE

Maiden Newton, near Dorchester, Dorset DT2 OAA
Tel: 0300 20336

Nearest town Dorchester.

Directions From Dorchester, take the A37 Yeovil road for four miles, then fork left along the A356 to Crewkerne. After a further four miles, fork right in the centre of Maiden Newton, at the village cross, and the hotel can be seen to the left of the war memorial.

Part of the **Wolsey Lodge** and **Heritage Circle** marketing consortia.

Awards RAC Highly Acclaimed; British Tourist Authority Design Award for Commended Hotels 1988; recommended by Ashley Courtenay, Michelin and Egon Ronay guides.

Open February until just after New Year.

Winter breaks from November until the end of March; also two-day half-board terms.

The hotel is not suitable for the disabled; children under twelve are not particularly welcome (except babies in cots); 'small, well-behaved' dogs are allowed.

Price for dinner, with wine, bed and breakfast for two – £100–£150.

Credit cards Access and Visa.

Overall mark out of ten 8.5

Maiden Newton House is one of those typical old English manor houses whose appeal to overseas and home visitors alike remains as strong now as it has ever been. It is therefore not difficult to appreciate why the village of Maiden Newton was immortalized by Thomas Hardy as 'Chalk Newton' in his classic *Tess of the d'Urbervilles*. Today Maiden Newton House stands in the beautiful valley of the River Frome and is easily accessible by all the main routes through Dorset.

The house was built of mellow stone in medieval style. It was originally built in the fifteenth century but was substantially altered in the early nineteenth century by the Hon. William Scott, younger son of the fourth Baron Polworth. Resident proprietors Bryan and Elizabeth Ferriss restored much of the ageing building before opening it as a hotel in Spring 1985 and, for both, it was the realization of a lifelong ambition to own and run a luxury Country House Hotel. The Ferrisses have deliberately set out to recreate the atmosphere and environment of a luxury private home rather than a hotel. There is undoubtedly no 'hotel' design scheme: the reception formalities are brief and all the public rooms are extremely well appointed. Fine porcelain, antique furniture, rich oil paintings and good books are all part of the decor which you find here, as, indeed, you would expect in a better private home. Guests are made to feel more like favoured friends than customers.

Dining arrangements at Maiden Newton are unusual, though not entirely unique. Dinner is served 'en famille' in the charming dining-room whose long, narrow windows allow the evening sun to pour through during the long summer months. All guests sit around the same large table with Bryan and Elizabeth, who act as host and hostess, rather like at a proper dinner party. The maximum number dining is twelve, and particular attention is given to seating arrangements depending on how well guests know each other, whether they are foreigners with limited English, and so on. Non-residents can occasionally be accommodated when the house is not full, but are advised to ring well in advance.

Elizabeth Ferriss describes her style of cuisine as 'imaginative dinner party cooking'. Menus vary according to what's in season, and portions are just the right size to allow room for a helping of local cheeses (there's usually a selection of six or seven from which to choose). Guests are advised in advance what is likely to be on the evening's menu, but a typical dinner would open with a Smoked Salmon Pâté, and be followed by a main dish such as Fillet of Pork with Coriander and Vermouth. Sweets and local cheeses follow in that order.

All the hotel's five bedrooms are individually furnished in typical Country House style. They are better described as small suites as each one is remarkably spacious and furnished with traditional antiques wherever possible. The finest room is the William Scott Suite, a first-class room with a large four-poster bed and magnificent views far across the river. This is the largest bedroom and features a private dressing-room. All the rooms have their own bathroom facilities and a colour television is available on request.

For fishing enthusiasts, Maiden Newton House offers some excellent private facilities for you to enjoy your sport while staying here. A three-quarters of a mile, double banker stretch of the River Frome is attached to the house and this is ideal for game fishing; rods and flies are available through the hotel reception. The hotel stands in 21 acres of parkland, and the informal gardens around the house include a croquet lawn during the milder months. Golf, tennis and horse riding can be arranged locally.

Among the many nearby attractions are Maiden Castle, the Dorset coast ten miles away, the historic houses at Athelhampton, Montacute, Parnham and Kingston Lacy, and the large public gardens at Abbotsbury, Minterne Magna and Clapton Court. In addition, the towns of Dorchester, Yeovil and Bournemouth are a short drive away.

115

MEADOW HOUSE

Sea Lane, Kilve, Somerset TA5 1EG
Tel: 027 874 546

Nearest town Williton.
Directions From the M5, take the Bridgwater exit (junction 23 from the north and 24 from the south). Follow the A39 towards Minehead and at Kilve village turn right just before the pub into Sea Lane. From here, the hotel is about half a mile down the road.
Awards W & A Wine List of the Year 1986/7.
Open throughout the year.
Three-day breaks available all year, except public holidays.
The hotel is not suitable for the disabled; children under nine and dogs are not allowed.
Price for dinner, with wine, bed and breakfast for two – £100.
Credit cards Access, Visa.
Overall mark out of ten 7.5

Perfect peace and quiet and the opportunity for the connoisseur to sample some exceptionally fine young and mature wines are two good reasons why you should visit Meadow

House. It is a lovely whitewashed old rectory, Georgian in style but essentially much older. Its early history is uncertain, but present owners David and Marion MacAuslan have worked hard to create a gem of a hotel which, naturally enough, specializes in offering 'quality rather than quantity'.

With a maximum of about ten residents at any one time, the hotel never feels busy; rather, it almost feels as though you have stepped back a few decades in time to enjoy one of those typical English Country House parties which, the Edwardian middle and upper classes would have us believe, weekends were made for. Apart from the restaurant, the main public room is the sunny drawing-room, although if you seek to get away from it all for an hour or so, the solitude of the study is the perfect place to pore over a good book, or to sit and catch up on letter writing. Both rooms have a log fire when the weather demands it.

The small restaurant has a typically Country House (as opposed to Country House *Hotel*) style decor, with fine oil paintings and carefully chosen antique furnishings. It is quiet and intimate with large French doors opening out on to the terrace which overlooks the garden. Dinner is occasionally served out of doors when the weather is exceptionally mild. Only twelve can be seated at any one time, and naturally preference is given to residents, but non-residents are welcome provided they give at least a couple of days' advance warning.

The style of cuisine is essentially quality home cooking, although the influences of Cordon Bleu and *nouvelle cuisine* are unmistakable. A four-course table d'hôte menu is available each evening: there is an alternative for both the sweet and the main dish but the starter and the light fish course are set. A typical menu would open with a Salmon, Sole and Watercress Terrine, or perhaps a Warm Salad of Sliced Duck Breast, Bacon, Walnuts and Chicory, and be followed by Crab in the style of Brehat (that is, mushrooms cooked in port, topped with Crab and Cheese, and grilled).

Main dishes include Breast of Pheasant with White Wine and Orange, Collops of Lamb with Onion and Mint Purée and

Redcurrant Gravy, or Stir Fried Fillet of Beef with Mango. The hotel has an exceptional wine list which is particularly strong on reasonably priced modern bottles. One keenly priced wine is the delicious Lebanese Château Musar 1978 which is a steal at under £10 a bottle.

Meadow House is one of the smallest Country House Hotels featured in this guide, with just five bedrooms. In the foreseeable future, it is likely that a nearby cottage will be converted into a self-contained suite, with bathroom, sitting-room and luxury double bedroom, but at present accommodation is restricted to the main house. Four of the five bedrooms are unusually large, and all are extremely well appointed with soft decor and antique furniture where possible. The four larger rooms have large bathrooms *en suite*. All five rooms have remote-control colour television, direct-dial telephone, and excellent views across the gardens, together with tea- and coffee-making facilities, a complimentary selection of continental biscuits, and bottled mineral water.

Meadow House markets itself with the claim to provide peace and perfect tranquillity in the heart of Somerset. It does offer limited leisure facilities in the form of a croquet lawn and billiards room, together with eight acres of very peaceful private grounds which include a small stream, a waterfall and a rocky beach about half a mile from the main hotel building.

Nearby attractions include the home of Somerset cider at Taunton, the natural beauty of the Quantock Hills, the towns of Bridgwater and Minehead, the city of Bristol with its many historic sights (including the restored SS *Great Britain*), the Clifton suspension bridge, and the south Wales coast.

116

NETHERFIELD PLACE

Battle, East Sussex TN33 9PP
Tel: 04246 4455

Nearest town Battle.

Directions The hotel is two miles north-west of Battle. From Battle, continue along the A2100 towards Netherfield and you will soon see the hotel signposted on the left-hand side.

Awards AA *** (red) graded.

Open all year except for three weeks over Christmas and New Year.

No **special breaks** are available.

The hotel is not really suitable for disabled guests unless they can manage shallow stairs to the first-floor bedrooms; children are welcome, but dogs are not accepted.

Price for dinner, with wine, bed and breakfast for two – £100–£150.

Credit cards Access, Visa, Amex and Diners Club.

Overall mark out of ten 8

In the heart of historic Sussex, Netherfield Place stands amid 30 acres of delightful gardens and parkland. It is just a few miles from the site of the Battle of Hastings, probably the most famous battle in world history, and certainly the most significant of English history. Netherfield Place is a relatively young building, having been built, in Georgian style, only in 1924. The house was originally owned by Sir Peter Reid, founder and owner of Reid Paper Mills.

Inside, the public rooms are bright and comfortable. The standard of decor and furnishing is high, and proprietors Michael and Helen Collier aim constantly to up-grade the hotel. A log fire usually burns in the main lounge (off which the cocktail bar can be found) and there really can be few more relaxing places in this part of southern England in which to sit back and relax with an aperitif, or after-dinner liqueur.

The restaurant at Netherfield Place is an attractive wood-panelled room, popular with residents and non-residents alike, and has a seating capacity of 40. Comfortable elbow chairs match the light-coloured panelling. The style of cooking is modern French, and Michael Collier takes charge personally in the kitchen to ensure his guests are served with the highest standards of cuisine possible.

Fresh fruit and vegetables are selected daily for the kitchens from the one-acre walled garden, and a number of more unusual herbs are included among this impressive display. Menu specialities, naturally, vary from season to season, but a typical selection of hors d'oeuvres is likely to include a smooth Chicken Liver Pâté, wrapped in Brioche pastry and accompanied by a Warm Butter and Herb Sauce, Mediterranean Prawns which can be served either hot or cold with Garlic Butter or Marie Rose Sauce depending on your preference, and a delicious 'surprise' House Salad composed of strips of Mango, Pineapple, Grapes, Apple and Toasted Almonds presented on a bed of wild lettuce accompanied with a fresh Yoghurt and Cherry Dressing.

The range of entrées is highly commendable and includes one or two more unusual choices such as fresh Quails, boned and filled with a light Chicken Mousse and served with a Port Wine and Grape Sauce, and a most original veal dish made up of thin slices of Veal rolled with Spinach on a bed of Tomato coated with Calvados and Pistachio Sauce. One fish dish which stands out as an alternative main course is Steamed Turbot filled with Crab and coated with a fresh Herb and Butter sauce. Whatever your preference, the hotel has an excellent wine list which includes nearly 300 bins.

There is a total of fourteen bedrooms including one particularly comfortable room, the Pomeroy, which features a large four-poster. The best room in the hotel is the Mandeville Suite, a bright, warm room decorated with a blend of soft colours. All rooms have private bathroom facilities, colour television (with Teletext), telephone and radio, and come complete with an assortment of welcoming little extras such as a bowl of fruit, fresh flowers and complimentary mineral water.

Netherfield Place has its own tennis courts, in addition to which there is a good range of popular sports, including squash, tennis and golf, available nearby. For the fishing enthusiast, trout fishing can be arranged at the Bewl Bridge Reservoir, and horse riding is possible along a wide selection of country lanes and National Trust footpaths.

Nearby tourist attractions include the town of Battle, where William the Conqueror defeated Harold at the Battle of Hastings in 1066; the castles of Bodiam, Hastings, Pevensey, Leeds, Chiddingstone and Rye; the former homes of Sir Winston Churchill at Chartwell and Rudyard Kipling at Batemans, and the magnificent public gardens at Sissinghurst.

117

NORTHCOTE MANOR

Burrington, near Umberleigh, North Devon EX37 9LZ
Tel: 0769 60501

Nearest town Umberleigh.
Directions Follow the A377 Barnstaple road
from Exeter for 30 miles. Just after the Portsmouth
Arms railway station, turn left immediately
opposite the Portsmouth Arms pub. From there,
proceed up the hill for one mile until you reach
the hotel.
A member of the **Best Western Hotels**
consortium.
Awards AA and RAC *** graded; British Tourist
Authority commended; English Tourist Board four
Crowns; Michelin recommended.
Open from mid-March until early November, and
also over the Christmas period.
Getaway breaks are available throughout the
season.
The hotel is unsuitable for disabled visitors; children
will be accommodated but are not encouraged; dogs are
allowed by prior arrangement.
Price for dinner, with wine, bed and breakfast for
two – under £100.
Credit cards Access, Visa, Amex and Diners
Club.
Overall mark out of ten 6.5

Northcote Manor is set in the seclusion of twelve acres of wide lawns and landscaped gardens within easy reach of main road and rail links to north Devon. The solid L-shaped old manor house overlooks the Taw Valley and dates back to 1716 when it was built by a local squire. It remained the home of the local squire for about 250 years, and when the last squire died in the early 1970s the entire estate was sold off. It remained a private residence for a few more years before falling into a state of dilapidation. A wealthy American converted Northcote Manor into a Country House Hotel and the present proprietors, Glenda and Peter Brown, took over the hotel in 1987.

They both aim to provide guests with comfort, peace and tranquillity in a homely atmosphere and, overall, they have succeeded in achieving this. The public rooms are decorated and furnished in a rather old-fashioned, as opposed to a particular period style, which means the end result is a very 1960s feel throughout the hotel. Northcote has, however, an extremely sociable atmosphere, and that really is what makes it so attractive to guests who come back year after year. It also represents exceptionally good value considering that three-star accommodation dinner, bed and breakfast for two can still be enjoyed at under £50 per person per night.

The style of cooking in the spacious restaurant is best described as typical Country House cuisine. A six-course table d'hôte menu is available each evening with a good range of traditional British and continental dishes on offer. One impressive feature is the very generous size of portions offered! The service is friendly and informal, and although the restaurant can seat up to 70, never more than 30 are accommodated at any one time. Non-residents can dine at Northcote Manor if they wish, but the restaurant caters primarily for residents and a number of regular local guests rather than a steady non-residential trade.

Starters range from House Pâté with Hot Toast, to Mushrooms Sautéed with Garlic Butter. Main dishes follow a homemade Soup of the Day, and come complete with an impressive selection of local vegetables. Although the choice varies from season to season, a typical selection might include

415

local Rainbow Trout grilled with Butter and served with Roasted Almonds, or a delicious Beef Stroganoff made from prime fillet of beef with lashings of Cream and Brandy.

Northcote Manor has eleven bedrooms, all doubles or twins, which come complete with private bathrooms, colour television, radio, telephone and tea- or coffee-making facilities. An added bonus is that all the beds have orthopaedic mattresses to ease your back as you sleep. The style of decor is comfortable and many of the bedrooms are furnished with antiques.

Most popular outdoor sports can be enjoyed nearby. There are eighteen-hole golf courses at Westward Ho and Saunton Sands, and locally at Chulmleigh Gliding. Horse riding and fishing are easily arranged, and there are beaches at Instow Sands, Westward Ho, Hartland Quay, Spekes Mill Mouth, and Saunton Sands.

Nearby attractions include the National Trust properties at Arlington Court, Castle Drogo, Killerton House and Lydford Gorge, together with the Alscott Farm Museum, the Maritime Museum in Appledor, and the city of Exeter.

118

PLUMBER MANOR

Sturminster Newton, Dorset DT10 2AF
Tel: 0258 72507

Nearest town Sturminster Newton.
Directions The hotel is located half-way between the towns of Sherborne and Blandford, just off the A357.
A member of the **Pride of Britain** consortium.
Awards AA Rosette.
Open from the third week in February until the end of January.
Bargain breaks are available during the months from April to October.
The hotel is suitable for the disabled; children under twelve and dogs are not allowed.
Price for dinner, with wine, bed and breakfast for two – under £100.
Credit cards Access and Visa.
Overall mark out of ten 8

At the end of a long, winding chestnut tree-lined driveway, just off the main A357 which connects Sherborne and Blandford, you will find Plumber Manor. The house has been home to the Prideaux-Brune family since the seventeenth century, but it has only been open as a Country House Hotel since 1972. Today it is still under the personal supervision of the family, and home to Brian and Richard Prideaux-Brune with his family.

A magnificent collection of family portraits lines the main gallery, which leads to the six bedrooms located in the main house. These really are fascinating to stand and admire for ten minutes or so before dinner, and give you a real sense of continuity and local history, all the more interesting once you have had the opportunity to meet one of the members of the family involved in the day-to-day running of the hotel now.

All the public rooms are elegantly furnished with family antiques and a rich period decor. Some of the accumulated family treasures are fascinating: the large stuffed and mounted Greenland falcon, for example, has to be one of the most intriguing ornaments in any British Country House Hotel! Fresh flowers are added to most rooms in the hotel and some of the displays are quite magnificent.

There are three dining-rooms at Plumber Manor, all of which are furnished in typical English Country House style, and the main one (which seats 40) is extremely popular with residents and non-residents alike. Advance booking by at least two weeks is strongly recommended. Brian Prideaux-Brune takes charge in the kitchen, and his style of cooking is an excellent combination of English and French.

Two table d'hôte menus are available each evening, with a difference of a few pounds between them because of one or two more expensive base ingredients (like smoked salmon) on one of them. On both menus there are at least four or five choices for the main courses. Starters include Melon with Port, Moules Marinières, and a delicious combination of Avocado with Melon, Prawns and Crab Marie Rose.

Main dishes feature Roast Rack of Lamb, Breast of Duckling, and Calf's Liver with Onion, Sage and White Wine. One particularly enjoyable dish for two or more persons is Beef Wellington, which is served with an exquisite Madeira Sauce. There is a nominal supplement of about a pound for this dish, and you will need to allow twenty-five minutes for it to be prepared, but it is, however, well worth the additional considerations.

Accommodation at Plumber Manor is divided between the main house, where there are six bedrooms facing south and west, and a converted natural-stone barn where another six double bedrooms were opened in August 1982. The barn rooms are particularly appealing and they all have window seats overlooking the stream and garden. All twelve bedrooms have private bathrooms, with no shortage of huge bath towels large enough to envelop most frames, colour television and telephone.

The only leisure facilities at Plumber Manor are a tennis court and croquet lawn, in keeping with a small comfortable hotel of this nature. Several golf courses, coarse fishing on the River Stour, horse riding and clay pigeon shooting are all available nearby. Other attractions in the surrounding area include the eighteenth-century model village of Milton Abbas, built by the Earl of Dorchester in 1770; Giant's Hill overlooking Cerne with its 1500-year-old chalk carved figure; the agricultural town of Sturminster Newton itself complete with its fine sixteenth-century bridge over the River Stour; the hilltop town of Shaftesbury where Alfred the Great founded a nunnery and placed his daughter there as Abbess, and the coastal towns of Lyme Regis and Abbotsbury.

119

ROCK HOUSE

Dunsford, near Exeter, Devon EX6 7EP
Tel: 0647 52514

Nearest town Exeter.
Directions From Exeter, follow the
Moretonhampstead road for six miles. Take the
first left turning *after* you see the Dunsford turn-
off. From there, follow the hotel signs as indicated.
A member of the **Wolsey Lodge** hotel
consortium.
Open throughout the year.
There are no **special breaks** or two-day half-
board rates available.
The hotel is not suitable for disabled visitors; children
under fourteen are not allowed; dogs are most welcome
(the owners have four, plus four cats!).
Price for dinner, with wine, bed and breakfast for
two – under £100.
Credit cards None accepted.
Overall mark out of ten 7.5

Rock House is a rather unusual hotel in many respects. For a
start, it is younger than many of the guests, having been built
only in 1934 as a traditionally styled Devon long house. It has
just three bedrooms and absolutely no staff (except on special

occasions like VIP weekends and Christmas) other than the enthusiastic proprietor Richard Hutt, who doubles as chef and herb gardener, and his mother, who is the hostess and also takes charge of the formal gardens.

Richard Hutt's grandmother and step-grandfather built the original house a few years before the Second World War, and it was designed and styled according to their explicit desires. It went out of family hands until 1972 when Richard's mother and step-father repurchased it and, after his step-father's death, Richard and his mother took the bold step of turning the former family house into the comfortable Country House Hotel and restaurant it is today. The end result is a wonderfully informal place where anonymous couples, VIPs and honeymooners alike can relax and enjoy the very best of traditional English hospitality. 'Informal' is a worryingly over-used description of so many British hotels which are anything but, yet the pace of life at Rock House is such that you do genuinely feel 'part of the family'.

The decor throughout the house is bright and homely, and antique family furniture crops up in every room. In addition, the large drawing-room has a comfortable suite and a set of armchairs perfect to sit back in with the Sunday papers, and let the rest of the world slip past. Large windows give sweeping views across the lawn and the rest of the garden.

Almost identical in size and design to the drawing-room is the dining-room, better known locally by the curious name 'Insults Restaurant'. Don't let that put you off, as insults are the last thing you are liable to be served with here. It is difficult to categorize Richard Hutt's style of cooking, although he terms it himself as 'cuisine naturelle'. It is influenced greatly by rare and fresh herbs, all of which are grown on his own herb farm within the hotel grounds. There are over 150 varieties, 90 percent of which are culinary, and because these include some of the rarest herbs in Britain you can expect some pretty unique and interesting flavours at dinner.

An interesting, and quite possibly unique, feature is that all aperitifs, wines and liqueurs which you have with your meal are complimentary. At the time of publication, dinner was £25 per person for residents and £30 for non-residents. The restaurant seats just fifteen people, so advance booking is essential if you wish to enjoy the unique blend of choices Richard prepares.

Everything depends on which herbs are in season, but typical openers include a speciality Rock House Salad, Seafood Cocktail and Chicken Liver Crouté. Fish courses range from Swordfish with Sorrel Sauce (highly recommended) to Trout with Mint. For your main dish you can reasonably expect anything from Loin of Lamb with a curious Sauce made from Marmalade and Rosemary, to a Magret of Duck with Lemon Balm.

With just three bedrooms, two doubles and one twin, Rock House qualifies as the smallest hotel in this guide. As you might expect, the three rooms vary considerably in terms of furnishings (although they all have a few choice antiques) and decor. They have private bathrooms and a colour television is available on request: in keeping with the tranquil nature of the place, they don't come as standard. To stay here is rather like staying in someone's home as a guest, which is precisely what is intended, and this could be spoiled all too easily by one or two guests just turning a television on for the sake of it, as so many hotel visitors do.

Rock House offers little in the way of leisure facilities, although for the brave (or foolhardy!) there is a freshwater (unheated) swimming pool. A different sort of croquet from normal is available since it is played around the apple trees in a style which verges on Crazy Golf. Golf, tennis, horse riding and most other popular sporting activities are available locally. The hotel is perfectly situated for touring the West Country, and obvious attractions include Dartmoor, Exeter (with its famous cathedral), Cornwall and Plymouth.

120

THE ROYAL CRESCENT

Royal Crescent, Bath, Avon BA1 2LS
Tel: 0225 319090

Nearest town Bath.
Directions The hotel is situated in the centre of
Bath, overlooking the Royal Victoria park.
A member of the **Prestige** and **Leading Hotels
of the World** consortia.
Awards AA **** (red) graded; RAC **** graded;
Michelin four red Pavilions; Egon Ronay 88%;
Egon Ronay Hotel of the Year 1980.
Open throughout the year.
Special breaks Winter breaks from 1st
November to mid-March; occasional special
weekends (e.g. antiques weekend).
*The hotel is not really suitable for disabled visitors;
children are accepted but dogs are not allowed.*
Price for dinner, with wine, bed and breakfast for
two – over £150.
Credit cards All major cards accepted.
Overall mark out of ten 9

You may wonder what this famous town hotel is doing in this guide, but it is, I feel, justified in its inclusion, as although the Royal Crescent is not a Country House Hotel in the strictest sense of the word, it offers every comfort and facility that the best Country Hotel should offer, and has the feel of one, with the added attraction of a most impressive town centre location.

The Royal Crescent is named after one of the greatest eighteenth-century crescents in Europe, in which it sits: 30 grand houses with identical façades stretch out in an enormous 500-foot curve that overlooks Bath's famous Royal Victoria Park. The crescent, and naturally the hotel exterior which is an integral part of this architectural masterpiece, was designed by John Wood the Younger between 1767 and 1775.

The art collection assembled by Lord Crathorne is now very much part of the decor of the public areas: one of the most striking is the large painting of Lady Waldegrave and her family by a student of Reynolds, which dominates the wide inner hallway. The standard of furnishings throughout the hotel is exceptionally high, and the main sitting-room is no exception, with its marvellous carved fireplace that is perfectly complemented by an enormous antique mirror hanging above it. As a critic said in *Previews* magazine, one could easily run out of superlatives to describe the public rooms 'of what is undoubtedly one of the finest hotels opened in Europe in the last decade'.

The main dining-room can seat up to 70 and is extremely popular with non-residents. Residents are therefore asked to confirm whether or not they require a restaurant reservation when they confirm their accommodation. The dining-room itself is sumptuous, and is dominated by two fine portraits by William Hoare of Bath, who was a founder member of the Royal Academy. The quality of food, prepared in new English style, is a perfect match.

Chef Michael Croft prepares an impressive, but never heavy, table d'hôte and à la carte menu each evening, using the very finest local produce, with a significant hint of continental influences in the sauces. Typical starters include Hot Chicken Liver Parfait with Collops of Lobster in a Shellfish Sauce, and Foie Gras Terrine with an Endive and Hazelnut Salad (there is a supplement for this dish). Your main courses can be selected from eight or nine choices on the table d'hôte alone, ranging from Fillet of Salmon topped with a Salmon Mousse and served on a Chive and Vermouth Sauce, to Roast Wild Pigeon in a Rich Red Wine Sauce and served with Glazed Turnips. There is a wonderfully detailed wine list to accompany the menu, with a range of red Burgundies that would delight even the most particular connoisseur, and which includes a number of excellent bins under £10 for diners who are less particular.

There are a total of 45 luxurious bedrooms at the Royal Crescent, seven of which are in the Pavilion in the gardens of the hotel. The size of the bedrooms can vary considerably, but the decor and quality of furnishing are always outstanding, combining the very best in modern luxury with an imaginative regard for Regency period style. There are thirteen suites, all completely individual and containing a host of extras such as luxurious bath robes, a display of fresh flowers and quality toiletries. The suites are named after famous men and women who have lived in Bath over the last couple of centuries: Sarah Siddons, Sir Percy Blakeney, John Wood the Younger and so on. Each room has private bathroom facilities, direct-dial telephone and a colour television with a video telling you a little about the history of the house and the services available for guests.

The Royal Crescent has a range of leisure facilities available for residents to enjoy, or which can be arranged nearby: there are, for example, one or two Jacuzzis for guests to relax in. There is a croquet lawn for the milder summer months and within easy reach you can enjoy golf, tennis, squash, shooting, the full facilities of a health club, and even hot-air ballooning.

Nearby attractions include the Theatre Royal, the eleventh-century Abbey, and the Roman Baths in the town of Bath itself. Slightly further afield you can visit the popular coastal resort of Weston-super-Mare; Longleat House and Safari Park;

the ancient standing stones at Stonehenge and Avebury, and the cathedral towns of Wells, Glastonbury and Salisbury. A range of chauffeur-driven tours are available to all these attractions: a typical four-hour tour will cost you around £80.

121

SOUTH LODGE

Brighton Road, Lower Beeding, Horsham,
West Sussex RH13 6PS
Tel: 040 376 711

Nearest town Horsham.
Directions From London, follow the M23
Brighton road which leads on to the A23. Take
Handcross turn-off and follow signs to Horsham on
the A279. At Lower Beeding, turn left on to the
A281 Cowfold road and the hotel is about 125
yards on the right-hand side.
A member of the **Prestige Hotels** consortium.
Awards AA *** (red) graded and rosette; Egon
Ronay recommended (78%).
Open throughout the year.
Weekend breaks are available.
The hotel has one ground-floor suite suitable for disabled
visitors; children and dogs are welcome.
Price for dinner, with wine, bed and breakfast for
two – over £150.
Credit cards Access, Visa, Amex and Diners Club.
Overall mark out of ten 8.5

Since opening at the beginning of the summer season of 1985,
South Lodge has quickly established itself as one of southern

England's most popular three-star Country House Hotels. It sits in 90 acres of spectacular gardens containing many dozens of rare plants and shrubs, and these really are a delightful enhancement to this stately Victorian Country House, particularly if you have the opportunity to visit in late spring or early summer.

South Lodge was originally built by the distinguished Victorian explorer and botanist Frederick Ducane Godmain in 1883. Most of the magnificent gardens which you still see today were designed and planned by him over a century ago. The house remained a private residence until the early 1980s when it was extensively renovated and refurbished to its present standards.

The public rooms are well proportioned and have lost little of their late Victorian beauty, despite considerable renovations shortly before South Lodge opened as a hotel. All the public areas have ornate plaster ceilings, and the lounge is a particularly fine room. It is completely wood panelled, and large Chinese carpets cover the polished wooden floor. Crystal chandeliers and antique chinaware adorn the shelves beside and above the carved fireplace and complete the wonderful period feel of this impressive room.

The dining-room is no exception to the spaciousness which is typical of all the public rooms at South Lodge, and it also enjoys good views across the South Downs. With rich oak panelling all around, crystal chandeliers, and a seating capacity of 40, this generously proportioned room is never too crowded, and residents and non-residents alike can enjoy a first-class meal in comfortable surroundings. Chef James Hayward prepares an imaginative combination of English- and French-style cuisine, and meals are served on wide wooden trays.

An à la carte and a set table d'hôte menu, which changes daily, are available each evening and, although selections vary considerably from season to season, many of the fruits, vegetables and finer herbs are grown in the large garden within the hotel grounds. Among the interesting specialities normally on offer are a Salad of Oyster Mushrooms dressed with

Raspberry Vinegar, and a main course option of Boned Quail filled with a Pistachio Stuffing.

South Lodge has 26 bedrooms, although a further fourteen are likely to be in use by the time of publication. The majority of rooms are large doubles enjoying magnificent views across the gardens and South Downs. All the rooms are individually styled and decorated in a fashion which manages to combine an ageless appeal with the best in modern furnishings. Each room has a private bathroom, many with polished marble fittings, and all rooms have colour television and direct-dial telephones.

Leisure facilities for residents include a hard tennis court, croquet lawns, clay pigeon shooting, trout fishing, and 90 acres of woodland, azalea, camellia and rhododendron gardens to be enjoyed. Other sporting activities, including golf, squash and horse riding, can be arranged locally by prior arrangement. Nearby attractions include Arundel Castle (stately home of the Duke of Norfolk), Chartwell (former home of Sir Winston Churchill), Glyndebourne, Hever Castle, Parnham Park Gardens, Leonardslee Gardens and racing at Goodwood.

122

STON EASTON PARK

Ston Easton, Bath, Avon BA4 4DF
Tel: 076 121 631

Nearest town Shepton Mallet.
Directions Ston Easton Park is situated just off
the main A37 from Bristol to Shepton Mallet. It is
six miles from Wells and eleven miles from both
Bath and Bristol.
Awards AA *** (red) graded and rosette; British
Tourist Authority commended; Egon Ronay
recommended; Michelin recommended; Egon
Ronay Hotel of the Year 1982.
Open throughout the year.
A special **Christmas and New Year programme**
is offered each year.
Children under twelve are not allowed, nor are dogs
allowed in public rooms or bedrooms, although free
kennelling is available.
Price for dinner, with wine, bed and breakfast for
two – over £150.
Credit cards All major cards accepted.
Overall mark out of ten 9.5

This outstanding old Georgian mansion first caught the public
imagination in 1982. The hotel opened to the public on 1st

June of that year and, remarkably, within a matter of months it was awarded the prestigious Egon Ronay Hotel of the Year Award, arguably the top honour which any British hotel can hope to achieve. Far from resting on their newly found laurels, proprietors Peter and Christine Smedley have sought to maintain, and if anything improve, the services and facilities on offer to guests since 1982.

A manor has stood on the site of the present hotel for centuries: indeed the estate was clearly recorded around the time of the Domesday Book, in the late eleventh century. In the eighteenth century, one John Hippisley-Coxe married Mary Northleigh of Peamore, a wealthy woman whose substantial means helped John begin building the manor as it now stands. Successive owners of Ston Easton distinguished themselves in social and political circles, and among the visitors to the house over the next couple of centuries were William Pitt the Younger, and Queen Mary – who insisted on arriving for afternoon tea one day during the last war, despite the fact that the interior of the house was covered in dust sheets.

The contents of the house were sold off at auction in 1956 and the future of Ston Easton looked bleak. Trees were felled on the estate, and a demolition order was signed in 1958 after lead had been stolen from the roof and much of the house vandalized. Thankfully it was saved, and successive owners since then (including a former Editor of *The Times*, Sir William Rees-Mogg) helped restore it to its present splendour.

The Palladian style and decoration of the house was restored in the late 1970s and early 1980s, supervised by Jean Monro, an acknowledged authority on eighteenth-century decoration, and today the hotel feels more like a stately home than 'just' a hotel. The first public room you enter is one of the more striking; with its coved ceiling and ornate plasterwork, the Entrance Hall truly is magnificent, and the eighteenth-century hanging lantern makes the perfect finishing touch. Other notable public rooms are the Saloon, with its main door flanked by Corinthian columns and its ceiling adorned with an elaborate ornamental plaster masterpiece; the delightful

431

Library with its mahogany bookcases, and the Print Room with its unique decoration of eighteenth-century engravings.

The main dining-room was originally the Old Parlour. It has a soft colour-scheme, with a surprisingly modern decor, and blends well with the rest of the house. The style of cuisine is a combination of modern English and French, with the best local produce used wherever possible. A four-course table d'hôte dinner is available each evening, and opening selections from the detailed range of options (which are more typical of an à la carte menu) include Marinated Salmon with Coriander and Chives, Smoked Haddock and Spinach Roulade with Quail Eggs and Caviar (no supplement for this exquisite dish), and Iced Ogden Melon filled with Lychees and Ginger.

Main courses include Fillet of Turbot with a light Dijon Mustard and Parsley Cream, Baked Sea Trout with an interesting Nettle and Sorrel Sauce, and panfried Calves' Liver with Oranges and Grand Marnier. At least one dish is included for vegetarian eaters and this might be something like Wholemeal Pasta with Local Mushrooms.

Ston Easton Park has a total of twenty luxury bedrooms, all of which are of a good size, and several have four-posters dating from the Chippendale and Hepplewhite periods. All the rooms have one or two pieces of antique furniture and a selection of framed prints. The one suite available has an open fire, a crystal chandelier and a comfortable seating area off the double bedroom. All rooms overlook the surrounding parkland and have private bathroom facilities, colour television and direct-dial telephone.

Nearby attractions include Dyrham Park; Castle Coombe; the Elizabethan mansion Corsham Court; the medieval village of Lacock which is now owned by the National Trust; the prehistoric monument at Avebury, and the Georgian house of Bowood.

123

TEIGNWORTHY

Frenchbeer, Chagford, Devon TQ13 8EX
Tel: 064 73 3355

Nearest town Chagford.
Directions The hotel is 2.5 miles south-west of
Chagford. From there, follow the signposts
towards Fernworthy and then Thornworthy. The
hotel is in the tiny hamlet of Frenchbeer.
Awards AA *** graded and rosette for food;
British Tourist Authority commended; Michelin
recommended.
Open throughout the year.
Winter breaks for stays of more than one night
from November to Easter.
*The hotel is not suitable for disabled visitors; children
under twelve, and dogs, not allowed.*
Price for dinner, with wine, bed and breakfast for
two – £100–£150.
Credit cards Access and Visa (though cheques
are preferred).
Overall mark out of ten 7.5

Standing over a thousand feet above sea level, right at the
edge of Dartmoor National Park, Teignworthy is one of Devon's best small Country House Hotels. Inspired by the style of

Lutyens, probably the greatest architect of his day, the house was built as a secluded private residence in the 1920s. It was constructed from local stone, and its distinctive Dartmoor granite exterior and steeply sloping Delabole slate roof make it look substantially older than its architecture suggests.

Inside, the house has been furnished in subtle modern comfort. A shallow staircase leads off the oak-panelled entrance hall up towards the six bedrooms that are located in the main house. The main public room is the bright sitting-room, with a wide open fire set in a large granite fireplace. The hotel is centrally heated throughout, but during the chillier autumn and winter months there can be few more relaxing locations in southern England where you throw off your boots after a long walk on the moor and sit back in front of a huge log fire. You will also find in the sitting-room a good selection of books and classical and jazz recordings which are perfect to help you pass a wet winter afternoon.

Guests are politely requested to 'take a little trouble with their appearance' at dinner, though jacket and ties are not absolutely insisted upon. John and Gillian Newell do, after all, like their guests to feel that they are staying with friends in the country. The dining-room contains just nine or ten tables which can seat up to 30 people, depending on the size of groups. Advance booking is recommended but not always essential for non-residents unless, of course, they choose to dine on a Saturday night or on a Bank Holiday, when you can reasonably expect the hotel to be busier.

The decor of the house and style of cooking are both straightforward, in keeping with the feel and period of the house itself. Food is best described as a blend of provincial French and *nouvelle cuisine*, and a keen aim of chef David Woolfall is that none of the dishes is 'overpowered' by rich sauces.

A three- or four-course table d'hôte menu is offered each evening and starters might include Marinated Raw Fillets of Mackerel and Slices of Sea Trout, served with Potato and Walnut Salad, or a light Scallop Terrine wrapped in Smoked Salmon and served with Spinach Sauce. A vegetarian main

434

course is always available, but non-vegetarian main courses range from local corn-fed Guineafowl studded with Oregano and Garlic, served in its own lightly Creamed Juices, to a delicious (if rather unusual) Escalope of Shark, quickly pan-fried with fresh Garden Herbs and Olive Oil.

There are nine bedrooms in all, six in the main hotel and a further three in a converted hayloft which also has a private sitting-room overlooking the courtyard. All the rooms have private bathrooms (the three in the hayloft have sunken baths), colour television and direct-dial telephone. Each one has a king- or queen-sized double bed, which can be divided if twin beds are preferred, and outstanding views across the nearby south Teign Valley and Dartmoor. There are the pleasing little touches of fresh flowers and a bowl of fruit to welcome guests on arrival in their bedroom.

The hotel has a grass tennis court, croquet lawn, sauna and sun bed which guests can enjoy during their stay here. It is situated in perfect walkers' countryside, right at the edge of the moor, and for non-walkers there is golf, fishing and horse riding available nearby. Other local attractions include the north and south Devon coasts, with their spectacular cliffs and long sandy beaches, and the cities of Plymouth and Exeter within an easy drive.

124

THORNBURY CASTLE

Thornbury, Bristol BS12 1HH
Tel: 0454 412647/418511

Nearest town Thornbury.
Directions When you reach the town of
Thornbury, continue downhill to the northern
edge where the Castle lies behind the very
prominent tower of the parish church.
A member of the **Pride of Britain** consortium.
Awards AA *** (red) graded and rosette; RAC ***
graded and Blue Ribbon; Egon Ronay and
Michelin recommended; former Egon Ronay Best
Restaurant in Britain Award-winner; 1984
Hideaway Report Country House of the Year
Award.
Open throughout the year, except for six days
over Christmas.
Winter breaks are available from October until
the end of March.
The hotel is not suitable for disabled visitors; children
under twelve, and dogs, are not allowed.
Price for dinner, with wine, bed and breakfast for
two – over £150.
Credit cards All major cards accepted.
Overall mark out of ten 9

With an enviable location in the valley of the River Severn, Thornbury Castle is one of the oldest surviving buildings in southern England still inhabited. Although traces of a manor house on the present site go back to pre-Norman times, the present building was built by Edward Stafford, the third Duke of Buckingham, who received a special licence from Henry VIII in 1510 to 'fortify, crenelate and embattle Thornbury Manor'. Sadly, Stafford did not live long to appreciate his fine new property, as his former master, the king, had him executed in May 1521 for having spoken certain 'treasonous words'.

The castle remained as a Royal territory for 33 years, arguably the most interesting period in its long history, and during this time Henry VIII himself stayed here for several days with his young queen, Ann Boleyn (who, coincidentally, was herself to die by the executioner's sword in 1536). Henry's daughter, Mary Tudor, lived at the Castle for some years, and once she became queen in 1553 returned it to the descendants of the Duke of Buckingham.

Today Thornbury Castle is still surrounded by its own private vineyard, just as it was in the sixteenth century, and visitors to its high walls can enjoy the same fine views across the Severn Valley which have appealed to at least two English monarchs, and generations of nobility, ever since. All the public areas of the hotel are furnished in magnificent splendour with antique furniture throughout. The main lounge has a number of old family portraits, and its wide (narrow-pane) oriel windows overlook the large walled garden.

The Castle has two dining-rooms, both decorated and furnished in traditional baronial style with solid oak-panelled walls, large open fires in ornate fireplaces, and heraldic shields all around. Although the hotel is constantly being refurbished, the character of the public rooms, and the dining-rooms in particular, has changed little down the centuries since the building was first constructed: the first Duke of Buckingham could easily have felt at home among the tapestries and high ceilings and, above all, with the fine cuisine prepared in new British style by chef Colin Hingston.

It is difficult to give more than a suggestion of what you might expect on the menu of a former Egon Ronay Restaurant of the Year, but whatever you choose you can be sure that it will have been prepared from the very best of local produce and that the presentation will be exquisite. Menus change weekly, with daily recommendations prepared on a separate sheet. Starters are likely to include Salmon marinated in White Wine and Orange Juice, and Californian Asparagus with Hollandaise Sauce. For your main dish, two recommended favourites are Veal Fillet Sauté, with assorted Mushrooms and Montilla, and Thornbury Castle's speciality Venison and Port Pie. One interesting fish choice, which is more usually served as a main course, is fresh Tay Salmon cooked in butter with Saffron and White Wine.

Thornbury Castle currently has fourteen luxury bedrooms, although one or two more may be added. All the bedrooms were carefully converted from the main apartments in the original castle. Each one is individually styled and furnished in a very traditional manner, with antique furniture and paintings, lavish drapes and fine fabrics. All the rooms have private bathrooms, colour television and direct-dial telephones.

Croquet is available at the Castle, and Thornbury Castle Shooting Club offers very good clay pigeon shooting facilities. Most popular indoor and outdoor leisure activities, including golf, tennis, horse riding, gliding and ballooning, can also be enjoyed locally.

Nearby attractions include the natural beauty of the West Country and, slightly further afield, the Wye Valley, south Wales, and the Cotswolds. Other attractions include Sir Peter Scott's famous Wildfowl Trust at Slimbridge, the Regency splendour and Roman remains in Bath, and countless towns and villages all around you including Bristol and Cheltenham.

CHANNEL ISLANDS

125

BELLA LUCE

Moulin Huet, St Martin's, Guernsey, Channel Islands
Tel: 0481 38764

Nearest town St Martin's.

Directions Hotel Bella Luce is situated two miles from both St Peter Port and Guernsey airport in Moulin Huet Bay. Marked no 26 on Guernsey Tourism's island map.

Awards AA *** graded; Ashley Courtenay recommended; Guernsey Tourism four Crowns.

Open throughout the year, except for three weeks in January and February when generally closed for redecoration.

No **special breaks**, but reduced winter rates are available from November until March.

The hotel is unsuitable for the disabled; children and dogs are both welcome.

Price for dinner, with wine, bed and breakfast for two – under £100.

Credit cards None accepted.

Overall mark out of ten 7.5

One of Guernsey's better hotels, Bella Luce has been carefully created from the shell of one of the Channel Island's oldest buildings, a twelfth-century Norman manor house. The original house dates from the time when the island – then known as 'Grenezey', which meant simply 'green isle' – was an integral part of Normandy; indeed, it was several centuries later before the Channel Islands became irrevocably British.

Bella Luce was extended considerably in the fourteenth century, and tastefully renovated and redecorated many times in the six centuries or so which followed down to the present day. The satisfying result is a peaceful haven, easily accessible to the rest of the island and even the UK mainland, which still retains something of its original medieval character.

All the public rooms are furnished in a traditional and comfortable style which has the effect of enhancing the period 'feel' of each room while, at the same time, never losing sight of the modern-day comfort upon which Hotel Bella Luce has built its reputation. The wide lounge is possibly the best example of a room which has achieved a near-perfect balance of comfortable modern furnishings and a traditional period structure, complete with beamed ceiling.

Much of the original stonework of the Norman mansion has been preserved and enhanced: on the main entrance wall, and overhead in arched fashion, in the two lounge bars which are the oldest part of the building. As with all Channel Islands hotels and bars, the wide selection of spirits, beers and liqueurs available is free of the fifteen per cent VAT guests are required to pay on the UK mainland.

Hotel Bella Luce has 31 bedrooms, including six family rooms and three more spacious family suites. Six bedrooms are in the impressive new extension. All rooms have private bathroom or shower facilities, colour television and the additional feature of intercom baby-listeners, making this hotel ideal for couples with young children who may appreciate the chance of enjoying themselves at a relaxing dinner in the restaurant, happy in the knowledge that their children are sleeping safely.

The main public room is the magnificent old oak-beamed dining-room which can seat up to 65 people. A huge dark wood carved fireplace dominates the far end of the restaurant,

442

and rich, warm colourings complement gleaming silver cutlery and polished glassware. A very extensive à la carte menu is available later in the evening for residents and non-residents alike, but the more modest four-course table d'hôte sitting is served earlier for those who require it. Both represent outstanding value – the quality of cuisine and standard of service on offer here would make this hotel considerably more expensive back on the mainland.

Both English and continental specialities are available: two highlights from the table d'hôte menu are Grilled Entrecôte Steak Garni and Roast Guineafowl cooked in a unique house style. The à la carte menu, however, is a real treat and runs to several pages of thick Gothic type on fine card. There are at least a dozen hot *and* a dozen cold starter options, including a most impressive Queensland Cocktail comprising Avocado mixed with Crab, Prawns, Mushrooms, Onions and Mayonnaise. Guernsey Scallops, served in a White Wine and Cheese Sauce, are an interesting alternative if you are keen to try a favourite island speciality.

If you feel you have room for a fish course, Dover Sole, Brill, Trout and Lobster are all available, cooked in a variety of fashions. Main dishes include a full page of steaks: at least sixteen varieties and styles of cooking, depending on your individual preference. Fillet steaks cooked with crushed peppercorns, whisky, paprika, brandy, cream, red wine and just about every conceivable variety of vegetables are available – although you may prefer the T-bone favourite, or one of the entrecôte specialities. If steak is not to your liking then there is a generous range of other options – from four varieties of duck to an assortment of lamb, pork and chicken dishes. Whatever you choose from over 100 options, making this one of the most extensive menus of any hotel featured in this guide, you will have the final dilemma of choosing from over two dozen salads and vegetables to accompany your main dish.

Leisure facilities at Hotel Bella Luce include an outdoor heated swimming pool, solarium, sauna, croquet and putting. Available nearby are facilities for squash, badminton, horse riding and sailing. Nearby attractions include the island capital St Peter Port, and the possibility of day trips to Jersey, the largest of the Channel Islands, and also to Herm, Sark and Alderney, the three smaller islands within the Bailiwick of Guernsey.

126

LA FREGATE

Les Cotils, St Peter Port, Guernsey, Channel Islands
Tel: 0481 24624

Nearest town St Peter Port.
Directions La Frégate is situated on a hillside overlooking St Peter Port, the main town on Guernsey. Awkward to find and the hotel suggests you phone for precise directions.
Awards AA *** graded and rosette for food; British Tourist Authority commended; Egon Ronay recommended.
Open throughout the year.
No **special breaks** or winter rates available.
The hotel is unsuitable for the disabled; children under fourteen, and dogs, are not allowed.
Price for dinner, with wine, bed and breakfast for two – under £100.
Credit cards Access, Visa, Amex and Diners Club.
Overall mark out of ten 7

Blessed with one of the best locations of any hotel on the Channel Islands, la Frégate is well hidden and, hence, extremely difficult to find. Guernsey Tourism provides an excellent and detailed map of the island which is available, free of charge, throughout the Channel Islands or by mail in advance from the tourist office or the hotel itself. La Frégate is clearly marked, but the hotel does recommend you phone them for precise directions. Once you do find the hotel it is impossible not to be struck by its magnificent location.

It is the location of this hotel which has prompted its inclusion in this guide. Though the cuisine is good and it is a comfortable hotel, it is not the Country House type of hotel that the Bella Luce is. It is, however, well worth a visit while on the island. Surrounded by its own terraced garden, it sits high on a hill overlooking St Peter Port's wide harbour. From here it is just five minutes' walk into the centre of this bustling little town. The hotel was originally built as a manor house in the eighteenth century when the beauty of the site was first recognized, and has lost little of its original character as it has evolved into a very comfortable modern hotel.

Fresh flowers are everywhere at la Frégate, including in most of the bedrooms, and these have the double effect of emphasizing the overall 'freshness' of the hotel and creating a lingering perfume which no amount of artificial freshener could ever achieve. The main lounge has a simple, dark fireplace, and the cocktail bar offers a roaring fire during the cooler winter months. The decor is simple and unelaborate – comfortable rather than luxurious – but the views from here are nowhere near as spectacular as those from the bar or dining-room.

The restaurant is a large, bright room furnished in modern style with contemporary furnishings. It was extended a few years ago to incorporate split-level seating; of all the rooms in the hotel, this one has the best views across the harbour. Air-conditioning and double glazing have been added for extra comfort, and up to 80 people can be seated at once. The menu is French-based, and extremely popular with residents and non-residents alike. Advance booking is always essential – by at least a week for weekend booking by non-residents during the summer months.

Almost exclusively fresh local produce is used in the preparation of all lunches and dinners, and Guernsey's mild climate means that, in season, there is an abundance of succulent fruits – strawberries, raspberries, melons, figs, peaches and grapes – available for the chef to turn into some quite memorable dishes. A four-course table d'hôte menu is available nightly: good value at around £12 per head, although a typical main course choice can be rather restricted, offering Grilled Entrecôte Steak, Fillet Steak, or Medallion of Pork. The more adventurous à la carte menu is particularly strong on fish, always one of the pleasures of dining in island hotels. Specialities include lobster, priced according to season and weight and cooked to your own preferred style. A favourite house dish is Suprême de Lotte à l'Andalouse: locally caught monkfish steaks cooked in butter with peppercorns, flamed with brandy, and served in a delicious orange juice and cream sauce. A well-balanced wine list is available.

There is a total of thirteen bedrooms, eleven of which enjoy outstanding views across the harbour. Six of those have private balconies, with huge sliding windows to allow you to really appreciate the hotel's superb location as much as possible. Such is the appeal of the panorama from the hotel that the management usually serves breakfast in the bedrooms to allow residents to enjoy the natural surroundings. Breakfast can also be taken in the dining-room, of course, but for most visitors the views are best enjoyed over an aperitif or an after-dinner coffee on the dark wood benches on the terraced lawns at the back and sides of the hotel.

All thirteen bedrooms are furnished to very high standards, complete with telephone and tea- and coffee-making facilities. Televisions are not provided as standard in all the rooms because the management, sensibly, has tried with considerable success to retain as much of the charm and tranquillity of the original house as possible. If you cannot live a night or two away from the box, portable televisions are available by prior arrangement at no extra charge, although surprisingly few take up the opportunity.

La Frégate has no formal entertainment, nor any special leisure facilities, because of its emphasis on relaxed comfort rather than organized luxury. Most sporting activities are available, however, at the nearby Beau Séjour Leisure Centre.

St Peter Port has most of the island's main tourist sights, and along with St Helier on Jersey is one of the Channel Islands' best shopping centres. The island as a whole can be explored easily by car or public transport, and day excursions are possible to Jersey and the smaller islands around Guernsey.

127

LA SABLONNERIE

La Sablonnerie Hotel, Sark, Channel Islands
Tel: 0481 83 2061

Nearest town St Peter Port.
Directions You must first travel by air or ferry to Guernsey. A regular boat service from White Rock pier in St Peter Port operates to Sark and tickets can be purchased on board or from the Isle of Sark Shipping Company at the pier. Alternatively, a hydrofoil service operates from St Malo to Sark, or occasionally from Jersey to the island. If you advise the hotel of your ferry time you will be picked up and driven the short journey to the hotel.
Awards Ashley Courtney and *Gourmet* magazine recommended.
Open from the 1st May until the end of September.
No **special breaks** available.
Children over the age of eight are welcome, but dogs are allowed only at the hotel's discretion.
Price for dinner, with wine, bed and breakfast for two – up to £100.
Credit cards Access, Visa and Amex.
Overall mark out of ten 8

La Sablonnerie is a modest little hotel located on Sark island, the smallest of the four main Channel Islands. The island itself lies just over seven miles away from Guernsey and about 22 miles west of the French coast. It is approximately 3.5 miles long by 1.5 miles wide, and offers a glimpse of what rural English life was like several decades ago; there are no traffic lights, no pedestrian crossings, very few roads and no cars to interrupt the tranquillity of your stay.

Sark is almost cut in two where la Coupée runs along the top of the ridge linking Big Sark and Little Sark. The Channel Islands were the only part of Great Britain occupied by Germany during the Second World War, and Sark did not escape the invasion. The single-track road which connects Big Sark and Little Sark — where the hotel is located — was constructed by German Prisoners of War in 1945, shortly after the island's liberation. The steep 200-foot drop on either side is an interesting sight as you cross this narrow ridge towards la Sablonnerie.

Wherever you go on this lovely island, you can be assured of relaxed tranquillity and a genuine feeling of 'getting-away-from-it-all'. This is obvious from the moment you reach Sark Harbour and, provided you have informed the hotel of when you plan to arrive (afternoons are preferred), then your first taste of the island's beauty will be from the horse and carriage which is sent to meet all guests. The drivers are well versed in their knowledge of the island's history and environment.

The hotel itself is, in fact, a discreetly modernized old Sark farmhouse. It is a credit to the present owners that they have succeeded in achieving the blend of farmhouse atmosphere with the comfort of a modern hotel. La Sablonnerie's first tenants had a rather grim past. Jean Nicolle was found guilty of sorcery at a Guernsey trial in 1620. For his sins, he was severely whipped and banned from the island for life. As a parting gesture, he had one of his ears cut off. The stern Guernsey judges were not so lenient seven years later when his wife, Rachel Alexandre, was found guilty of witchcraft — she was burned alive. An interesting reminder of the days when witchcraft was rife on the lonely Channel Islands can still be seen if you look closely at the hotel's original chimneys. The builders were careful to include the all-important overhanging ledges of flat stones as a precaution against tired witches landing on the roof and coming down into the house to rest!

La Sablonnerie does not pretend to offer itself as a hotel in the luxury bracket, but instead offers traditional Sark courtesy combined with the attraction of modern-day comforts. The atmosphere is relaxed and unhurried, and the public rooms are cosy and tastefully furnished. Duty-free bar prices are a pleasant plus. The hotel flanks a well-tended garden on two sides, and an appealing sun-lounge is the perfect spot to admire the garden on the occasional summer day when the weather is not kind enough to sit outside in the Tea Gardens, located just a few yards from the hotel.

The dining-room is small and intimate, and the old-fashioned decor enhances the 'olde worlde' feel of the rest of the hotel. Thirty-eight can be seated at any one time, of whom two-thirds are generally residents. This is one of the best eating-out spots on Sark, so advance booking for non-residents is recommended. Local produce is used throughout, with much of the fruit and vegetables grown in the hotel garden. Fresh local fish is a speciality, and a popular starter are Fresh Oysters served on a bed of Crushed Ice. Two recommended favourites from the small selection of main dishes are Scampi in a superb Pernod and Cream Sauce, and Lobster Thermidor which was still under £15 at the time of publication.

The hotel has a total of 21 rooms, including a beautiful Honeymoon Suite and a good selection of double, twin, single and family rooms. Only six have private bathroom facilities, while another six have private shower-rooms. If you book ahead you should be able to ensure private facilities.

Nearby attractions include countless lovely walks around the island, or boat trips arranged through the hotel reception to see the coastline at its best. The flora and fauna of the island of Sark are fascinating, and the island is a bird-watcher's paradise. This is particularly the case during early spring and autumn when large numbers of migrating birds use the island as a resting place. An old silver mine, which closed in 1845, is near the hotel and an interesting reminder of the island's nineteenth-century economy. Day excursions are possible to the larger Channel Islands of Guernsey and Jersey.

128

LONGUEVILLE MANOR

St Saviour, Jersey, Channel Islands
Tel: 0534 25501

Nearest town St Helier.

Directions Jersey can be reached by air or ferry from the UK mainland. From the airport, follow the B36, then A12, and finally A1 to St Helier. Near the harbour follow the sign indicating Tunnel and the East A17 to Georgetown. Then take the A3 (Longueville and Gorey road) for about half a mile and the hotel is signposted on your left.

A member of the **Relais et Châteaux** consortium.

Awards AA **** (red) and rosette for food; RAC **** graded, Egon Ronay recommended – with Star for food.

Open throughout the year.

Special winter breaks are available from November to March.

The hotel is unsuitable for disabled visitors; children under seven are not allowed.

Price for dinner, with wine, bed and breakfast for two – £100–£150.

Credit cards Access, Visa, Amex and Diners Club.

Overall mark out of ten 9

An enthusiastic American reporter described this tranquil manor house as 'a Queen with a French accent'. The hotel instinctively feels French, yet there is a touch of English charm which prevails in all the spacious public rooms, and in the quality of service which never quite lets you forget that you are still on British soil, despite Jersey's close proximity to the French coast.

There are few serious challengers to Longueville Manor's claim to be one of the best hotels on the Channel Islands. Certainly it is the only red star-graded AA hotel on any of the Channel Islands and, after the recent completion of their new half-million-pound West Wing, probably the most popular luxury hotel on Jersey.

The earliest recorded mention of Longueville Manor dates back to 1309 when it was recorded in the local Assize Poll as 'Lungevill'. The manor changed hands in 1367 when it was sold by Phillippe de Barentin to one Raoul Lemprière, and just prior to this date the Great Hall, which is now the hotel's dining-room, is believed to have been built. The original fourteenth-century arched entrance to the manor also remains, forming the hotel's main gateway today. Longueville's fortunes improved considerably after 1480 when the island's Bailiff, John Nichol, bought the manor and surrounding grounds. His great grandson also became Bailiff of Jersey and owned Longueville for many decades. Evidence of his family's long association with the house can still be seen by the coat of arms above the fireplace in the drawing-room.

The manor remained in private hands until 1948, when the present owner's parents bought the rather run-down old building and began the slow process of renovation. A year later, in July 1949, Longueville Manor finally opened its doors as a Country House Hotel with just thirteen bedrooms.

The hotel today has 31 doubles and two single bedrooms in addition to a couple of luxury suites, for which advance booking is essential during the peak summer season. All 35 rooms are individually decorated and styled, and have full private bathroom facilities together with colour television, in-house videos, and direct-dial telephone. The standard of furnishing and decor is very high and the rooms here are the best on Jersey. One bedroom still retains a touch of medieval charm with an authentic eighteenth-century four-poster bed, one of the oldest antique hotel beds in any British hotel. If you are planning that special romantic break then few bedrooms could offer a more idyllic atmosphere – but book early.

The centrepiece of the hotel and the undeniable highlight of a stay here is the time you spend in the magnificent dark wood-panelled dining-room which has lost little of its charm since it was built as the Great Hall six centuries ago. There is seating for up to 65 people in a relaxed atmosphere, and a couple of years ago a new Chef de Cuisine, Barry Forster, was recruited from London's Ritz Hotel to maintain the hotel's traditionally high standards of international cooking. A set menu is available every evening alongside an impressive à la carte choice. Half-board guests are allowed a reasonable deduction off the à la carte menu if that is their preference over the set menu on any particular evening.

Local seafood features prominently on both menus, as you might expect, and whatever your choice, presentation is exquisite. A sorbet precedes your main course, and is likely to be a variation like Spiced Tomato Sorbet, or Melon and Sauternes, rather than the standard orange or lemon dish. Main course specialities include Gratin of Dover Sole with Smoked Salmon and Fennel, and a delicious Roast Leg of Lamb filled with Garlic and Shallot Stuffing. A full wine list is available, but half a dozen suggested vintages are listed alongside the set menu on any given evening.

Nearby attractions include a wealth of sporting and leisure facilities. There are two excellent eighteen-hole golf courses in addition to two nine-hole courses. The hotel itself has a heated outdoor swimming pool, but the opportunities for sea-bathing and sunbathing are superb throughout the island. St Helier, the island's capital, has a wide range of shops offering the best of British and continental goods without the standard VAT (currently fifteen percent) which is normally added on the UK mainland. Another alternative is a boat trip round the island, or a day trip by ferry or hydrofoil to Guernsey, the next largest of the four main Channel Islands. Marine trips are generally available to Herm and Sark as well, particularly during the summer months.

129

OLD GOVERNMENT HOUSE

Ann's Place, St Peter Port, Guernsey, Channel Islands
Tel: 0481 24921

Nearest town St Peter Port.
Directions The hotel is in the centre of town near the harbour.
A **British Airways Associate** hotel.
Awards AA **** RAC graded; Guernsey Tourism 5 Crowns; Egon Ronay recommended.
Open throughout the year.
Special breaks Fully inclusive holidays available from March until October; Executive Winter Breaks from October to March; fully inclusive Christmas and New Year breaks available.
Unsuitable for disabled guests; children are welcome and all rooms are fitted with a baby listening service; small dogs are accepted but are not allowed in public areas.
Price for dinner, with wine, bed and breakfast for two – £100–£150.
Credit cards All major cards accepted.
Overall mark out of ten 7.5

One of the Channel Islands' smartest public buildings from an earlier era has been transformed into Guernsey's top luxury hotel. A more civilized base for any visit to Guernsey and the other Channel Islands would be difficult to find than this magnificent old house which was home to Guernsey's most senior public official for many years.

In 1796 the Guernsey government bought what was already a substantial private residence in order to provide a permanent Government House for the Bailiwick which, then, as now, included the smaller islands of Alderney, Herm and Sark. General Sir James Douglas was the last Governor to reside at Government House, and it ceased to be an official residence in 1842. It became a hotel in 1857 and over the next hundred years was slowly extended and up-graded to its present luxury standards. Precisely a century after it opened, in 1957, Her Majesty the Queen was guest of honour at a luncheon held in the hotel during an official visit to Guernsey. The meal, needless to say, was fit for a queen and the occasion is still remembered fondly by those who were on the island at the time.

Though not, strictly speaking, a Country House Hotel (it is located in the main town of Guernsey) O.G.H., as it is known, has all the qualities of one, and St Peter Port is hardly a built-up, smog-ridden urban development. If you want to be right out in the countryside, the Bella Luce (see p. 441) is decidedly more rustic, but few would find O.G.H. too busy.

A small library of books and brochures has been written about the hotel, and the most up-to-date history is given to all guests on their arrival. One of the older brochures, dating from the end of the last century, had some curious regulations governing use of the bathroom facilities: 'Each person is requested to take a slip from the tablet at the bathroom door to his bedroom at night, corresponding with the time at which the bath will be required. The slip is to be replaced in the tablet when leaving the bathroom in the morning . . . twenty minutes allowed per person. When an extra quantity of hot water is desired please inform the servant.' Thankfully the arrival of private bathroom facilities in all the bedrooms has considerably reduced the effort required to take a bath! The hotel today has a total of 73 bedrooms, including five suites, all furnished to very high standards and several with balcony and sea views.

The restaurant offers a mixture of both French and English cuisine with a choice of either table d'hôte or à la carte menus. Up to 200 people can be catered for at any one time, making this a popular choice for functions and more upmarket parties. It was completely redecorated a couple of years ago in ornate green and white, and the finishing touch of a variety of green leafy plants is pleasing. During the day, the panoramic views from this room are superb – far across to the smaller Channel Islands within the Bailiwick of Guernsey. At night, the tables are candlelit which makes a perfect setting for that special romantic meal.

Both menus are detailed and comprehensive. It is unlikely that you will be disappointed by the extensive choice which includes over twenty hot and cold starters and an appetizing variety of fish dishes. Six varieties of potato and two dozen vegetable and salad options accompany the superior à la carte dinner menu at very reasonable prices for non-residents – still under £20 per head at the time of publication. A rich variety of steaks is headed by an outstanding Grilled Chateaubriand Garni, fully garnished and served with Bordelaise Sauce, for two persons. As you might expect, there is a very good wine list available with a particularly strong field of French vintages to suit most palates.

Leisure facilities in the hotel are excellent. In addition to a heated swimming pool in the attractive garden, there is a solarium, a licensed (and soundproofed) discotheque, and a weekly dinner dance held on a Saturday night. Dancing is possible every night of the week (except Sundays) in the magnificent Centenary Bar, one of the most impressive public rooms, which was completely refurbished in 1957.

Nearby attractions include the Guernsey Aquarium, the Château des Marais, the prehistoric Dehus Dolmen, the Folk Museum, the Guernsey Museum and Art Gallery, all in St

Peter Port itself. Slightly further afield is the German Occupation Museum at Forest, the German Military Underground Hospital at St Andrew's, and a wide range of island tours and day trips to Jersey and the smaller islands of Alderney, Herm and Sark.

FURTHER READING

There are a few books on the market which look at the history of the country house in British society, which, if you are particularly interested in the subject, will be of relevance to you.

The English House by Hermann Muthesius. Published by Blackwell Scientific.

This is a superb academic work, detailing the social and historical development of the English house during the years 1860–1900. This was the period of Lutyens, Voysey and many other English greats, examples of whose work are contained in this guide. A detailed analysis of house interiors, including furniture, is included, and all the major architectural styles of this period are discussed.

A Country House Companion by Mark Girouard. Published by Century Hutchinson Ltd.

This book takes one inside the doors of the magnificent country houses of the English ruling classes and details the lives of many of the people who lived in this style. An anthology of anecdotes and reminiscences, taken from personal letters and diaries, provides a fascinating glimpse into the upstairs/downstairs existence in this era. The author is one of Britain's leading architectural historians and was Slade Professor of Art at Oxford University.

The Classical Country House in Scotland, 1600–1800 by James Macaulay. Published by Faber & Faber.

A superbly detailed history of the great houses of the Classical period, north of the border. Many famous houses and castles now open to the public (not as hotels but as national monuments) are graphically described in this work, and history, architecture, decoration and furnishings are all given equal importance. Dr Macaulay is senior lecturer in architectural history at the Mackintosh School of Architecture, Glasgow.

A History of Architecture by Spiro Kostof. Published by Oxford University Press.

This is a good definitive work for the enthusiast. It should be read more for architectural learning than for specific detail to our subject, as the book covers mankind's architecture from the prehistoric caves to present-day offerings, but it is a good reference book and its chapters on late eighteenth-century English houses and the Victorian Age are particularly enlightening.

Life in the English Country House by Mark Girouard. Published by Penguin Books.

A good book for the non-specialist which describes, as the title implies, how life proceeded in the great houses of England from medieval times to the mid-twentieth century. Beautifully illustrated and written, this is a well-priced taster which gives the reader a greater understanding of the points to look for in the house he visits. None of our hotels are listed, but many of the houses suggested as nearby visiting places are described in detail.

The English House through Seven Centuries by Olive Cook with Edwin Smith. Published by Penguin Books.

A beautifully illustrated record of English domestic architecture from Norman times to the present day. Excellent value in paperback and particularly strong on architectural analysis.

The National Trust Book of the English House. Published by Penguin Books.

Another illustrated volume tracing the evolution of the 'middle-class, middle-sized house', the likes of which are being converted to Country House Hotels today. A good introduction to the architectural history of this genre.

Fontana Paperbacks: Non-fiction

Fontana is a leading paperback publisher of non-fiction. Below are some recent titles.

- ☐ The Round the World Air Guide *Katie Wood & George McDonald* £9.95
- ☐ Europe by Train *Katie Wood & George McDonald* £4.95
- ☐ Hitch-Hiker's Guide to Europe *Ken Walsh* £3.95
- ☐ Eating Paris *Carl Gardner & Julie Sheppard* £2.95
- ☐ Staying Vegetarian *Lynne Alexander* £3.95
- ☐ Holiday Turkey *Katie Wood & George McDonald* £3.95
- ☐ Holiday Yugoslavia *Katie Wood & George McDonald* £3.95
- ☐ Holiday Portugal *Katie Wood & George McDonald* £3.95
- ☐ Holiday Greece *Katie Wood & George McDonald* £3.95
- ☐ Holiday Coastal Spain *Katie Wood & George McDonald* £3.95
- ☐ British Country Houses *Katie Wood* £5.95
- ☐ The Life and Death of St Kilda *Tom Steel* £5.95
- ☐ Back to Cape Horn *Rosie Swale* £3.95
- ☐ Fat Man on a Bicycle *Tom Vernon* £2.50

You can buy Fontana paperbacks at your local bookshop or newsagent. Or you can order them from Fontana Paperbacks, Cash Sales Department, Box 29, Douglas, Isle of Man. Please send a cheque, postal or money order (not currency) worth the purchase price plus 22p per book for postage (maximum postage required is £3).

NAME (Block letters) _____

ADDRESS _____

_____

_____

While every effort is made to keep prices low, it is sometimes necessary to increase them at short notice. Fontana Paperbacks reserve the right to show new retail prices on covers which may differ from those previously advertised in the text or elsewhere.